# BRIAN FRIEL

CASEBOOKS ON MODERN DRAMATISTS
VOLUME 20
GARLAND REFERENCE LIBRARY OF THE HUMANITIES
VOLUME 2018

# CASEBOOKS ON MODERN DRAMATISTS

KIMBALL KING, *General Editor*

# Brian Friel
## A Casebook

Edited by
William Kerwin

Garland Publishing, Inc.
New York and London
1997

Library of Congress Cataloging-in-Publication Data

Brian Friel : a casebook / edited by William Kerwin.
    p.    cm. — (Garland reference library of the humanities ; vol.
2018. Casebooks on modern dramatists ; vol. 20)
    Includes bibliographical references (p. ) and index.
    ISBN 0-8153-2478-2 (alk. paper)
    1. Friel, Brian—Criticism and interpretation.  2. Postmodernism
(Literature)—Ireland.  3. Ireland—In literature.    I. Kerwin, William.
II. Series: Garland reference library of the humanities ; vol. 2018.
III. Series: Garland reference library of the humanities. Casebooks on
modern dramatists ; vol. 20.
PR6056.R5Z6   1997
822'.914—DC20                                        96-36370
                                                          CIP

Printed on acid-free, 250-year-life paper
Manufactured in the United States of America

# CONTENTS

# GENERAL EDITOR'S NOTE

Brian Friel is, perhaps, the best-known living Irish playwright in the theatre world. *Philadelphia, Here I Come!* had highly successful runs in New York and London and is the work most closely identified with Friel in the public imagination. He is also an accomplished short story writer. Friel describes lonely, inhibited people trapped in a chilling, puritanical society, but his humorous dialogue and clever staging make his drama entertaining. There is an alarming darkness at the center of his work, however, which seems to be growing stronger. Not overly polemical, he is nonetheless sensitive to the divisiveness in modern society, and as a Northern Catholic writer, he has been deeply touched by recent political conflicts. Friel's innovative theatrical methods have given way to an increasing simplicity, but his characters continue to be authentic, recognizable, and compassionately drawn. His recent stage triumphs have included *The Aristocrats, Dancing at Lughnasa* and *Molly Sweeney*. Friel's important canon is closely analyzed in this wide-ranging collection of original critical assessments.

William Kerwin, who edited this volume, received his Ph.D. from the University of North Carolina, and now teaches at Florida International University. His dissertation, "Framing Healers: Social Medicine and English Renaissance Drama," reflected his combined interests in medicine and drama. An article on medical politics in the *Duchess of Malfi* is forthcoming in *English Literary Renaissance*. He contributed a chapter to Lillian Furst's collection of essays, *Women Healers in Literature*. He has read papers at the International Congress on Medieval Studies and at the Group for Early Modern Cultural Studies. At a graduate Irish Studies Conference, he analyzed Friel's *Faith Healer* and has lectured on other topics concerning Friel at the Southeast American Conference for Irish Studies.

Kimball King

# ACKNOWLEDGMENTS

I would like to thank the following publications for their kindness in allowing the republication of articles. Richard Kearney's "Language Play: Brian Friel and Ireland's Verbal Theatre" originally appeared in *Studies, An Irish Quarterly Review.* Declan Kiberd's "Brian Friel's *Faith Healer*" appeared in *Irish Writers and Society at Large*, Colin Smythe Limited. W. B. Worthen's "Homeless Words: Field Day and the Problem of Identity " appeared in *Modern Drama*.

# INTRODUCTION

## William Kerwin

In 1968, Brian Friel wrote an autobiographical sketch entitled "The Theatre of Hope and Despair." Almost thirty years later, responses to his work reflect both sides of that emotional split. The contributors to this volume find very different Friels before them: Friel as ironic or celebratory, caustic or hopeful. As much as any playwright in the Irish tradition, Friel evades categorization as either comic or tragic.

However, two questions do connect these essays: What features make Brian Friel the most significant Irish dramatist since the Irish Renaissance? And how does his work demonstrate the difficult epistemological and political challenges of the postmodern?

Friel's preeminence as a dramatic artist has been long apparent to audiences and scholars alike, but what constitutes his artistry and where it has most succeeded are very much matters of debate. His work has evolved continuously, creating several periods with dominant thematic and theatrical concerns. Having written more than twenty plays since 1958, Friel serves as a link between the anti-authoritarian romanticism of the 1960s to a more intellectualizing but still passionate interrogation of tradition in the 1990s. His most popular plays on the stage—*Philadelphia, Here I Come!* (1964), *Translations* (1980), and *Dancing at Lughnasa* (1990)—have spoken to audiences in Ireland, America and elsewhere in their evocative resonances of a lost innocence. At the same time, those plays have a hard edge of anti-sentimentality, an exposure of the destructiveness within the emotions they summon. This tougher gaze is especially apparent in Friel plays less celebrated by theater reviewers but now critical favorites—*The Freedom of the City* (1973), *Volunteers* (1975), *Faith Healer* (1979), *Aristocrats* (1979), and *Molly Sweeney* (1994). These plays draw much of their strength from a refusal to play along, from an adamant rebellion against cultural expectations. Friel's skepticism surely extends to a self-conscious examination of his own art: his plays do not merely employ language to create theater—they are about language and theater. As such, they are part of our cultural moment, the late-twentieth century concern with the embeddedness of language within politics.

It is the major goal of this collection to shed light on these two concerns. Most of the contributors are attempting to define Friel's distinctive contributions to literary tradition and his poststructuralism or postmodernism. Friel stages the effects of colonialism, gender formations, and the fracturing of the subject, highlighting his characters' fragile and historically conditioned definitions of identity. But even as a postmodernist Friel bucks, giving us no safe theoretical place on which to ride for long. His plays show people fighting back against their construction, attempting to transcend their linguistic and political places. At times, it is difficult to tell whether poststructuralism is friend or foe.

F.C. McGrath, in "Brian Friel and the Irish Art of Lying," explores Friel's place in the particular tradition of "Irish mendacity." Perhaps most memorably represented by Christy Mahon's testimonial to "the power of a lie," this lineage includes not only Synge but also Wilde, Joyce, and Yeats. McGrath examines Friel's career-long study of the fictions by which we choose to live. *Philadelphia, Here I Come!*, *The Freedom of the City*, and *Faith Healer* follow the leads of Friel's Irish predecessors; for example, in *Faith Healer*, with its series of contrasting monologues amongst which no objective authority can determine a true history, "Friel has, in a sense, recast *Playboy*." The essence of his recasting of that tradition is Friel's view of language, as fiction (or lying) creates both individual psyches and social contracts. McGrath discusses the social power of a lie in *Aristocrats, Translations, Making History,* and *The Communication Cord,* showing Friel's concern with history's dependence upon—and origin in—fictions. As McGrath writes, "In the world of his later plays no independently verifiable reality ever appears." But the fictional nature of personal and social orders leads to hope as well as skepticism; pointing to the influence upon Friel of George Steiner (including Steiner's memorable definition of the human being as "a mammal who can bear false witness"), McGrath emphasizes the creative and spiritually regenerative potential within fiction. Friel shows we must pay attention to language's createdness with what he calls "eternal linguistic vigilance"; when we treat language as a positivistic system (as do, for instance, many of the characters in *The Communication Cord*) we will certainly suffer.

Patrick Burke considers a very different element of Friel's work, the power of things outside of language, in "'As If Language No Longer Existed': Non-Verbal Theatricality in the Plays of Friel." Burke emphasizes Friel's strict organization of elements of setting such as stage design, lighting, costume, stage property and music. Arguing that these forms are only "seemingly functional," Burke reminds us that Friel's mastery of language—highlighted in the monologue-based plays *Faith Healer* and *Molly Sweeney*—should not prevent us from seeing his control of visual elements as well. For example, the setting of *Volunteers*, in its layered heights, gives us "an image of levels of human power." Again and again, one or two carefully staged non-verbal elements emphasize a play's major struggles, often embodying characters' attempts to get beyond the systems created by language.

Continuities with a literary past and the constructed nature of social order are the major concerns of Christopher Murray in "'Recording Tremors': Friel's *Dancing at Lughnasa* and the Uses of Tradition." Murray takes the adventurous step of employing T.S. Eliot's idea of a useable tradition to consider Friel's use of the Abbey Theatre, and in particular the peasant play. Arguing that the Field Day project was "an attempt to create another kind of Abbey Theatre," Murray shows how Friel reinvigorated (and reshaped) an interrupted tradition. *Dancing at Lughnasa* serves as a rich test-case for this argument, because it recasts a number of elements found in older Irish theatre. Friel's treatment of religion, memory and story-tellers all create a decentered version of earlier productions. Murray's argument that *Lughnasa* is distinctly postmodern draws strength from his comparison of that play with Tennessee Williams' *The Glass Menagerie*, which was being produced in Dublin (directed by Friel's daughter!) at the time of *Lughnasa's* opening at the Abbey. And Murray places his own essay in the context of a tradition—the phrase "recorded tremors" is D.E.S. Maxwell's, an image of Friel's ability to capture the feel of social change—and shows us a Friel who revitalizes Irish drama by reinventing it.

Claudia Harris reads Friel's plays as a meeting place of two forces: male writing and female experience. "The Engendered Space: Performing Friel's Women from Cass McGuire to Molly Sweeney" employs the concept of the male gaze to emphasize the particular roles Friel creates for his female characters. Harris argues that at some places Friel has created "open-ended women characters," whom female actresses can embody in liberating ways; at other times, Friel's women characters seem to follow the "angel/master" dichotomy imagined by Virginia Woolf. These latter characters, discussed in an extensive reading of the plays, create a pattern of women's roles that Harris finds disturbing. Her study seems poised on a dilemma: Friel's plays show, and perhaps contribute to, the construction of confining women's roles in Irish culture, but they also, though perhaps only occasionally, offer a stage for critiquing and transcending those roles.

Richard Kearney's "Language Play: Brian Friel and Ireland's Verbal Theatre," first published in 1983, has become a touchstone of Friel criticism. Kearney discusses the two theatrical traditions examined by McGrath and Burke—the verbal and the non-verbal—and outlines the resurgence of a "theatre of the senses" in contemporary Irish drama. Placing Friel in this context, Kearney examines the philosophy of language in his plays, especially in *Faith Healer*, *Translations*, and *The Communication Cord*. "Brian Friel's plays in the eighties have been increasingly concerned with the problems of language," he writes, creating "a theatre *about* language." Kearney traces the influence upon Friel of George Steiner and, through him, Heidegger. The Heideggerean aspiration to a life fully lived grounds Friel's "ontological approach" to language. Kearney writes: "Man's being-in-the-world becomes authentic when he ceases to abuse language as a strategic instrument for the manipulation of people and objects and responds to it instead as that which it truly is: the house of Being in which men may poetically dwell." This orientation to Friel's meditations upon language systems can be seen in *Translations* and *The Communication Cord*. The former play shows language unlocking Being, while the latter satirizes positivist models of language. The space between these two plays reflects the entire project of Field Day, "a new dialectical rapport between the timeless images of nature, and the transient facts of history."

Friel's attention to the systemic nature of language finds one outlet in comic characters, as Kathleen Ferris makes clear in "Brian Friel's Uses of Laughter." Friel's comedy is part of a "dark tradition" in Irish literature, best exemplified by Samuel Beckett. Friel shows the subversion of order by the powerless, even if that rebellion is only temporary, often by reversing the role of the stage Irishman, the comic character who gives an audience exactly what it expects. The patterns of seriousness in wit and caricaturing popular humor are enacted, for example, in *Volunteers*'s Keeney, whose humor pillories the social order that is about to destroy him. "A paean to the spirit of resistance," *Volunteers* has no illusions about resistance's ability to triumph. Ferris also discusses the parodic academics who voice rational theories about Irish culture but whose language is drearily lifeless, another type in the wide range of comic characters who play the roles of teacher, social critic, or object of satire.

Friel's relation to history is especially apparent in his involvement with the Field Day project. This company, formed in 1980, centered its activities on the relationship of language and politics, and W. B. Worthen, in "Homeless Words: Field Day and the Politics of Translation," considers the recent Irish fascination with translation and in particular with the story of Antigone. Translation has an inherently divided position in relation to an original—it is both homage and rebellion—and Worthen uses a post-colonial context to examine this "necessary betrayal" of received texts. Tom Paulin and Seamus Heaney have "translated" classical drama, Friel has produced versions of Chekhov and Turgenev, and Derek Mahon has adapted Molière and staged Fugard in an Irish setting. Friel's *Translations* not only adds to this cultural formation but stages much of its internal dynamics; always self-reflective, Friel has in effect created a meta-theater of Field Day's "translational politics." Worthen questions George Steiner's views on the power of translation to create continuity across time, instead emphasizing the ruptures revealed. Field Day's productions, notably Paulin's *The Riot Act,* Heaney's *Philoctetes*, and Friel's *Translations*, have been works of resistance in which translation has been "performing the difference between languages, cultures, agents, histories, mythologies."

*Translations* is also the site of Lauren Onkey's "The Woman as Nation in Brian Friel's *Translations*," which considers the tradition of representing Ireland as female, and Friel's relation to it. Dark Rosaleen, the women of the *aisling* poems, Queen Medbh, and Cathleen ni Houlihan are some of these women, representing the purity of Ireland, but coming from cultures where women were largely powerless. Using feminist readings of Indian colonial discourse, Onkey explores how gender takes particular form in relation to imperialism and nationalism. Given the male emphasis of Field Day's agenda (especially the *Field Day Anthology of Irish Writing*), how does Friel contribute to, or respond to, the symbolic representation of women?

Onkey argues that *Translations* enters "into the volatile symbolic and real history of women in Ireland." Although the women in the play, Sarah and Maire, have little institutional power, they are central characters because a struggle over the control of sexual life precipitates the play's closing violence. Other critics have emphasized the symbolic weight of Sarah, to the exclusion of Maire, but both stories are tragic because the women are read as symbolic of only public issues. In his portrayal of woman as "symbolic property," Onkey writes, Friel "re-reads and rewrites that hoary trope of woman as nation."

George O'Brien also writes about the processes that create cultural identity and political violence. "*Volunteers*: Codes of Power, Modes of Resistance" focuses on one play from the 1970s to examine Friel's portrayal of political victims as very specifically "casualties of language." The plays of the 70s gained Friel less acclaim than those of the 60s or 80s, but O'Brien argues that they are crucial to his development, and to his increasing incorporation of political issues into his art. *Volunteers* responded to the Wood Quay controversy of the mid-70s, when Dublin developers built an office block on the newly discovered site of a Viking settlement. Friel's play uses the artifacts in that site to suggest the indeterminate value of all cultural objects, and even of all individuals. The play *Hamlet*, the doomed "volunteers" (under sentence of death from their IRA colleagues), and the skeleton exhumed from his tomb share an inability to resist cultural appropriation or achieve a neutral meaning. The skeleton, like *Hamlet*, proves open to layered and opposing interpretations. Text, skeleton, and characters gain meaning through cultural struggles, a process in which the primary weapons are "imprisoning discourses." Nevertheless, the play valorizes resistance, even as it dramatizes its difficulties; here, as everywhere, Friel refuses an easy equation of power. The play celebrates the solidarity of the volunteers—they become "icons of community"—and the witty Keeney elicits an audience's support in "volunteering" to resist "identity-imposing forces." O'Brien argues finally that this evocative staging of the battle between power and resistance makes *Volunteers* "a central work in the Friel canon."

The 1979 play *Aristocrats* gives us a very different setting, the social privilege of a prestigious Ballybeg family. But like *Volunteers*, *Aristocrats* starts with an ironic title (a Friel staple: consider also *The Loves of Cass McGuire*, *The Freedom of the City*, and *The Gentle Island*). Garland Kimmer, in "'Like Walking Through Madame Tussaud's': The Catholic Ascendancy and Place in Brian Friel's *Aristocrats*," explores the ways Friel stages a Catholic ruling class's relations to Irish culture. Part of the irony is that it is just as often *English* culture that defines this odd social niche. The evolution of *Aristocrats* from the short story "Foundry House" emphasizes the O'Donnell family's dependence upon mythologies of place, stories that seek an alliance with the Anglo-Irish or the English. These myths shore up the O'Donnells' place in society but only by creating historical fantasies with great personal costs. The aristocracy proves as culturally shaped and as culturally resistant as volunteers.

1979 also saw the production of a very different Friel play, though one still fundamentally about the contradictory effects of narrative. Declan Kiberd writes of that work: "*Faith Healer* by Brian Friel may well be the finest play to come out of Ireland since J.M. Synge's *Playboy of the Western World.*" At the same time, Kiberd calls the play "one of the most derivative works of art to be produced in Ireland this century." Originality and tradition again dance together in a Friel play. Kiberd catalogues Friel's debts: to Faulkner, to the Deirdre legend, to Synge, and to Beckett. Faulkner is present in the play's structure—like the later *Molly Sweeney*, *Faith Healer* is composed of monologues providing different versions of history. Deirdre's story, staged by Synge, is eerily recast by Friel, distanced by the distorting lenses of the narrators. Beckett's relevance is his stark analysis of the artist's powers.

Frank Hardy, the title character, is both liar and artist, and that violently contradictory project becomes an emblem for staging plays and, ultimately, for living a heroic life. Kiberd compares Friel's use of the Deirdre legend to Joyce's of *Ulysses*. Frank Hardy, like Leopold Bloom, breaks free of what he imitates, even if he is not aware of it. Kiberd writes: "This may be Friel's and Joyce's underlying point—that heroism is more often unselfconscious of itself than not." But at the same time, Frank is cruel and tawdry. Friel always reins in either praise or blame, romanticism or satire, by staging its opposite, showing how forces such as creativity and destruction are mutually dependent. "Necessary fictions" both wound and heal. The mix creates here what Kiberd calls Friel's "most complex and under-rated play."

Clearly, *Faith Healer* stages questions about the artistic process, probing individual psychology. Friel is equally concerned with the public forces of history, and Claire Gleitman considers his approach to staging history as similar to the work of other playwrights in "Negotiating History, Negotiating Myth: Friel Among His Contemporaries." Tom Murphy and Frank McGuinness have staged history plays, and Gleitman focuses upon *Famine, Observe the Sons of Ulster Marching Towards the Somme, The Freedom of the City* and *Dancing at Lughnasa*. She argues that Murphy, McGuinness and Friel have created "a second Irish renaissance in dramatic literature," in part because of the shared ways in which they present historical episodes. "Their plays restage history and question its reliability," an attention to narrative bias that separates these post-modernists from the first Irish Renaissance playwrights. Demystifying and debunking, Friel "circumvents nostalgia by blending fondness with a trenchant critique." But this approach to history, if ironic, is surely not cynical: Friel shows that myths— "totalizing narratives"—have noxious effects, but that recognizing the ways we create them can help us live fuller lives.

Confinement and freedom, politics and the human spirit, suspicion and beauty—Friel sets all of these opposition in play. Friel's greatest achievement, the one which will be intriguing audiences and readers long into the future, may be his refusal to allow us to choose between these too easy alternatives, as he depicts language's dual potential to destroy or nourish. The different readings presented here of *Translations* and *Dancing at Lughnasa*, especially in regard to the presentation of women, are testaments to Friel's capacity to present both suffering and love, and demonstrate that the critical reception of Friel is becoming an arena for considerable debate. Hope and despair swirl throughout Friel's plays like the Mundy sisters at their wildest.

# CHRONOLOGY

| | |
|---|---|
| 1929 | Born on January 9, in Omagh, County Tyrone, Northern Ireland. |
| 1939 | Family moves to the city of Derry, Northern Ireland. |
| 1948 | Graduates from Maynooth College with B.A. |
| 1950 | Completes course at Saint Joseph's Teacher Training College, Belfast, Northern Ireland. |
| 1950-60 | Teaches in Derry, and writes fiction. Much of Friel's fiction appears in *The New Yorker*. |
| 1954 | Marries Anne Morrison. |
| 1958 | *A Sort of Freedom*, a radio play, is broadcast on BBC Northern Ireland Home Service. |
| 1959 | *The Francophile (A Doubtful Paradise)* premiers at Group Theatre, Belfast. |
| 1960 | Retires from teaching. |

| 1962 | *The Enemy Within* premiers at the Abbey Theatre, Dublin. English and American editions of *A Saucer of Larks*, a collection of stories. |
|------|-------------------------------------------------------|
| 1963 | *The Blind Mice* premiers at Eblana Theatre, Dublin. Friel studies dramaturgy with Tyrone Guthrie at the Guthrie Theater, Minneapolis. |
| 1964 | *Philadelphia, Here I Come!* premiers at the Dublin Theatre Festival--Friel's first major success. |
| 1966 | *Philadelphia, Here I Come!* is performed on Broadway; *The Loves of Cass McGuire* premiers on Broadway. English and American editions of *The Gold in the Sea*, a second collection of stories. |
| 1967 | *Lovers: Winners and Losers* premiers at the Gate Theatre, Dublin. |
| 1968 | *Crystal and Fox* premiers at the Gaiety Theatre, Dublin. |
| 1969 | *The Mundy Scheme* premiers at the Olympia Theatre, Dublin. |
| 1970 | *The Gentle Island* Premiers at the Olympia Theatre, Dublin. |
| 1972 | Elected member of the Irish Academy of Letters. |
| 1973 | *The Freedom of the City* premiers at the Abbey Theatre, Dublin. |
| 1975 | *Volunteers* premiers at the Abbey Theatre, Dublin. |
| 1977 | *Living Quarters* premiers at the Abbey Theatre, Dublin. |
| 1979 | Two Friel plays premier: *Aristocrats*, at the Abbey Theatre, Dublin, and *Faith Healer*, at Longacre Theatre, New York. The publication of *Selected Stories*. |

1980            The Field Day Theatre Company is founded, and presents as
                its first production Friel's *Translations*, at the Guildhall in
                Derry.

1981            Friel's translation of Chekhov's *Three Sisters* premiers at the
                Guildhall, Derry. *Translations* wins the Ewart-Biggs Peace
                Prize.

1982            *The Communication Cord* premiers at the Guildhall, Derry.
                Friel is elected a member of Aosdana, the National Treasury
                of Irish Artists.

1983            Awarded honorary D. Litt. by National University of Ireland.
                The publication of *The Diviner: The Best Stories of Brian Friel*.

1987            Friel's adaptation of Turgenev's *Fathers and Sons* premiers at
                the National Theatre, London. Friel is appointed to the Irish
                Senate.

1988            *Making History* premiers at the Guildhall, Derry.

1989            BBC Radio devotes a six-play season to Friel.

1990            *Dancing at Lughnasa* premiers at the Abbey Theatre, Dublin.

1992            *The London Vertigo* premiers at the Andrews Lane Theatre,
                Dublin, and *A Month in the Country* (another adaptation of
                Turgenev) premiers at the Gate Theatre, Dublin.

1993            *Wonderful Tennessee* premiers at the Abbey Theatre, Dublin.

1994            *Molly Sweeney* premiers at the Gate Theatre, Dublin.

# Brian Friel

# BRIAN FRIEL AND THE IRISH ART OF LYING

## F.C. McGrath

Brian Friel comes from a tradition of Irish writers who have elevated blarney to aesthetic and philosophical distinction. Synge and Joyce are Friel's most important predecessors in this tradition, but behind them we must also include Yeats and Wilde.

Wilde was one of the first since Berkeley to give an Irish character to the epistemology that eventually produced the linguistically sophisticated philosophies of thinkers like Heidegger, Derrida, and Foucault. Wilde had assimilated that epistemology from the ancestors of post-structuralism in German thought, including Kant, Schiller and Hegel, who were popular at Oxford when Wilde was an undergraduate. Wilde's essay "The Decay of Lying" in many ways sets the stage for the linguistic concerns of Yeats, Synge, Joyce, and Friel.[1] Here Wilde defends his famous thesis that life imitates art and not the reverse. Great art for Wilde anticipates life and molds its shape; it invents the archetypes by which we perceive nature and history. Consequently nature and history are human constructions, and what makes them credible is primarily a matter of style.

While Wilde's views fall within a tradition that can be traced from Vico through Foucault, for some reason it had special force in Ireland during the last decades of the nineteenth century and the first decades of the twentieth century. Yeats's theories of symbolism and the mask share Wilde's post-Romantic premise that consciousness creates its own reality, that, as he phrases it in "The Tower," "Death and life were not/Till man made up the whole" (107). Synge's plays *The*

*Well of the Saints* and *The Playboy of the Western World* also spring from this epistemological tradition. In *Playboy*, for instance, Christy Mahon transforms himself from timorous fugitive to ballad hero through the power of a lie. In the stories he tells of killing his father he creates an imaginative fiction of himself, what Yeats would have called his mask or anti-self, and then he makes that fiction his reality by becoming the hero of his own stories.

Joyce's stylistic experiments in *Ulysses* further develop this premise. In the "Scylla and Charybdis" episode, for example, Stephen Dedalus elaborates a wild theory of autobiographical aesthetics about Shakespeare that provides a powerful metaphorical model for neo-Hegelian, expressive theories of art, of which Joyce's *Portrait* and the first half of *Ulysses* are prime examples. Yet when asked if he believes his own theory Stephen readily says "No." Metaphors, in other words, communicate without requiring literal belief. In the second half of *Ulysses* Joyce pushes the theory of literature as lying even further. In these episodes various types of discourse forms themselves construct the realities inhabited by the characters. Nature is no longer created by the human mind but by language and discourse, which construct or re-present both mind and nature.

Friel inherits this distinguished tradition of Irish mendacity. Like Joyce and Synge before him, Friel acknowledges how the word becomes flesh through the power of a lie. At the level of individual perception and memory, for example, Friel dissolves the traditional distinction between fact and fiction. For Friel facts themselves are factitious. In an autobiographical essay Friel asks, "What is a fact in the context of autobiography?" He goes on to answer his own question: "A fact is something that happened to me or something I experienced. It can also be something I thought happened to me, something I thought I experienced. Or indeed an autobiographical fact can be pure fiction and no less true or reliable for that." He illustrates this point with a Wordsworthian spot of time he describes from his childhood. He remembers walking home one day with his father along a dirt road, after fishing in the rain. But then he realizes that some of the facts in his memory of that scene could not have been accurate. "The fact," he concludes, "is a fiction." He asks,

> Have I imagined the scene then? Or is it a composite of two or three different episodes? The point is—I don't think it matters. What matters is that for some reason . . . this vivid memory is there in the storehouse of the mind. For some reason the mind has shuffled the pieces of verifiable truth and composed a truth of its own. For to me it is a truth. And because I acknowledge its

peculiar veracity, it becomes a layer in my subsoil; it becomes part
of me; ultimately it becomes me ("Self-Portrait" 18).

Friel used this fishing trip memory with all the implications of its factual
inaccuracy in *Philadelphia, Here I Come!* (1964). For Friel then, as for Synge's
Christy Mahon, reality is something we construct out of our fictions of ourselves.
Or, in Wilde's terms, life imitates art.

Friel also has followed the lead of Joyce into distinctly post-modern modes of
perception and into developing literary forms appropriate to them. In *The Freedom
of the City* (1973), for example, Friel adapts techniques for the theater that are
similar to what Joyce developed in the "Cyclops" episode of *Ulysses*. Here Friel
gives us multiple perspectives on an incident of political violence through various
forms of public and private discourse; and no perspective coincides with another
and all of them distort the event with fatal consequences.

In his play *Faith Healer* (1979) Friel has, in a sense, recast Synge's *Playboy*.
*Faith Healer* characterizes individual memory as a verbal fiction of the past. In a
structure reminiscent of Faulkner's *The Sound and the Fury*,[2] three characters in
the course of four separate monologues remember their lives together as part of a
wandering faith healing mission in Wales. Their memories all differ on important
points about who did what and who wanted what. They each had constructed
images or fictions dictated by their own compelling needs. Frank Hardy, the faith
healer, says that in their memories "the whole corporeal world . . . had shed [its]
physical reality and had become mere imaginings." The characters themselves "had
ceased to be physical and existed only in spirit, only in the need [they] had for each
other" (*SP* 376).

In *Faith Healer* Friel gives us no account of events apart from those given by
the characters. The only truth available, in other words, is the truth of their
deepest needs as reflected in the versions of events they construct, their images of
the past. In this play Friel seems to be suggesting that once language takes hold of
something (and according to Heidegger, Derrida, and others, everything we
perceive has always already been taken hold of by language) that thing ceases to
exist in its own materiality, and it assumes the rarefied, gossamer materiality of
language as it enters the realm of human experience. This Hegelian view of
language was, by and large, the Romantic/Idealist ancestor of structuralism.

In *Aristocrats* (1979) an American scholar stays with a family in one of the old
Irish houses to study, he says, "Recurring cultural, political and social modes in the
upper strata of Roman Catholic society in rural Ireland since the act of Catholic
Emancipation" (*SP* 265). But his every effort to ascertain facts about the declining
family fortunes of his hosts is met with diverse memories of the past and

conflicting versions of the present. The only reality this scholar has available to him consists of the memories and images created for him by the individual family members. The whole play is imbued with an atmosphere of fantasy and illusion: items of furniture are named after great visitors to the house (G. K. Chesterton is a footstool he once fell off; O'Connell the Liberator is a chaise lounge that still bears the mark of his riding boot; Yeats is a cushion he once laid his head on for three successive nights waiting for the family ghosts to appear to him); on an overgrown lawn the family plays fantasy croquet games without mallets, balls, or wickets.

Friel's perceptions about language, autobiography, and individual memory also apply to his views of the larger social context. As Seamus Deane says, Friel exposes the "fictive nature of the social contract" by suggesting that "society itself is a fiction in which we all must persuade ourselves to live, always acknowledging that these selves are also fictions" ("Brian Friel" 9). For Friel, then, social contracts are grounded on fictions. The contract works when the fiction is mutually agreed upon, and it breaks down when there is no agreement. Most of Friel's writing, like *Faith Healer*, focusses on that lack of agreement in our social fictions. Perhaps this negative tendency has something to do with the fact that for centuries Ireland refused to accept its colonizer's fiction of itself.

For Friel, then, fictions are constitutive of the only realities we have. In the world of his later plays no independently verifiable reality ever appears; every reality is somebody's fiction, and his tragedies result from one fictitious construction of reality overpowering another. His plays, in other words, are very much like the "real" world, where people routinely bludgeon each other with their own fictive truths, whether in marital discord or in the discord in the Middle East. Married couples fight to establish their own versions of the truth or to defend their own self-images, just as Israel wants its version of a homeland to dominate the Palestinian version. In world politics establishing fictions, or to put it the way Friel, Synge, or Yeats might put it, asserting the right to become one's own fiction of oneself is a serious and often bloody business.

In Ireland competing social and political fictions were marked by a colonial structure. Articulating this structure very effectively, Seamus Deane says

> in divorcing power from eloquence, Friel is indicating a traditional feature of the Irish condition. The voice of power tells one kind of fiction—the lie. It has the purpose of preserving its own interests. The voice of powerlessness tells another kind of fiction—the illusion. It has the purpose of pretending that its own interests have been preserved ("Introduction" 18).

Friel's later views on language owe a good deal to George Steiner's book *After Babel: Aspects of Language and Translation*. Friel probably read *After Babel* around 1979 as part of his preparation for "translating" Chekhov's *Three Sisters*. *After Babel* provided Friel with a thorough and contemporary theory of translation, but Steiner's Heideggerian notions of translation extended far beyond translating between languages to investigate the fundamental nature of all language and communication. Steiner undoubtedly reinforced and solidified Friel's own sense of the fictive powers of language, which had been incipient in his early short stories of the late 1950s and early 60s.

One of the most fascinating sections of *After Babel* deals with the power of language to conceal and dissimulate. From Steiner's post-modern viewpoint we speak as much to conceal as to communicate (46). He says, "Only a small portion of human discourse is nakedly veracious or informative in any monovalent, unqualified sense." He explains how in many different ways discourse often "conceals far more than it confides," how communications always includes "what is *not* said in the saying, what is said only partially, allusively or with intent to screen" (229; Steiner's emphasis).

Steiner, however, pursues this issue far beyond the capacity of language to conceal. He sees the capacity of language to lie as fundamental to its function and power:

> The human capacity to utter falsehood, to lie, to negate what is the case, stands at the heart of speech and of the reciprocities between words and world. It may be that 'truth' is the more limited, the more special of the two conditions. We are a mammal who can bear false witness (214).

Even more emphatically, it is this capacity for untruth that has given the animal who speaks an evolutionary advantage. And that advantage is tied to a capacity to imagine that which is not the case. This power of language to "'unsay' the world, to image and speak it otherwise" (218), amounts to nothing less than our escape from time. Steiner says

> *Language is the main instrument of man's refusal to accept the world as it is.* Without that refusal, without the unceasing generation by the mind of 'counter-worlds'—a generation which cannot be divorced from the grammar of counter-factual and optative forms—we would turn forever on the treadmill of the present (217-18; Steiner's emphasis).

Far from being an abuse of language, this ability to "hypothesize and project thought and imagination into the 'ifness,' into the free conditionalities of the unknown . . . is the master nerve of human action" (217). In Steiner's analysis our capacity for lying is our passport to both past and future. It is commensurate with our capacities for remembering and construing and for dreaming and forecasting.

In plays Friel wrote after reading Steiner, he dealt much more confidently and explicitly with lying as fundamental to language. In *Translations*, for example, the characters of Hugh and Jimmy Jack are well attuned to the mendacious quality of language. Lt. Yolland remarks at one point that he has heard them "swapping stories about Apollo and Cuchulainn and Paris and Ferdia—as if they lived down the road" (*SP* 416). Jimmy Jack particularly escapes his present into an ancient classical past. This aging, unwashed, "Infant Prodigy" lives so thoroughly in the world of Greek heroes and gods that by the end of the play he has betrothed himself to Pallas Athene. The immediacy with which Jimmy Jack experiences the ancient classics of Greece or Rome is a product twice over of the capacity of language to construct a world out of words. First Homer did it and then Jimmy Jack projects himself into that Homeric world, or perhaps more accurately, Jimmy Jack appropriates Homer's world into his own.

One wonders if Friel's Jimmy Jack is not James Joyce displaced a century into his Gaelic past. They both have the same initials, both were child prodigies, and both bring Homer's gods and heroes to life in a contemporary present.

In the light of Steiner's analysis, Jimmy Jack's privatization of Homer is not an aberration of language but an exercise of its most ennobling power: "At every level," Steiner says, "from brute camouflage to poetic vision, the linguistic capacity to conceal, misinform, leave ambiguous, hypothesize, invent is indispensable to the equilibrium of human consciousness and to the development of man in society" (229). Furthermore, not only does mendacity distinguish us from the beasts on the evolutionary ladder, it also guarantees our survival:

> We secrete from within ourselves the grammar, the mythologies of
> hope, of fantasy, of self-deception without which we would have
> been arrested at some rung of primate behaviour or would, long
> since, have destroyed ourselves. It is our syntax, not the physiology
> of the body or the thermodynamics of the planetary system, which
> is full of tomorrows (227).

The character of Hugh in *Translations*, more than any other character in the play, becomes Friel's most articulate spokesman for Steiner's insights. He is much more consciously aware than Jimmy Jack of how the deceits of language are tools of survival, and he expresses that awareness pretty much in Steiner's own words: referring to Gaelic, Hugh says to Lt. Yolland, "Yes, it is a rich language, Lieutenant, full of the mythologies of fantasy and hope and self-deception—a syntax opulent with tomorrows. It is our response to mud cabins and a diet of potatoes; our only method of replying to . . . inevitabilities" (*SP* 418-19).

For both Steiner and Hugh the survival of the human spirit under chronically adverse conditions often depends on an inverse relation between capacity for linguistic elaboration and material well being. Virtually quoting Steiner, Hugh says to Yolland, "You'll find, sir, that certain cultures expend on their vocabularies and syntax acquisitive energies and ostentations entirely lacking in their material lives. I suppose you could call us a spiritual people" (*SP* 418; cf. Steiner 55).

In addition to the characters of Hugh and Jimmy Jack, in *Translations* Friel acknowledges the power of dissimulation in language through his metaphor of Lying Anna's Poteen. Hugh's favorite pub is Anna na mBreag's, whose name means "Anna of the lies" (*SP* 417). When Owen and Yolland rename all the locations in Baile Beag as they Anglicize it into Ballybeg, they are sustained and assisted in their project by Lying Anna's Poteen (*SP* 409-22). Anna's heady brew is a very appropriate metaphor, as Anna is an appropriate muse for all the deceptions, self-deceptions, concealments, and erosions that were involved in translating and transforming Gaelic Ireland into modern Anglicized Ireland.

History for both Steiner and Friel is also an act of creative lying. For Steiner history is a highly selective use of the past tense (29), with which historians literally *make* history (136), and the histories they make are not necessarily commensurable with each other (29). For Steiner ascertaining the meaning of history is no more assured than ascertaining the meaning of a literary text (136).[3] Friel's *Making History* (1988) dramatizes this insight by juxtaposing two historical versions of the Gaelic chieftain Hugh O'Neill. During the course of the play Archbishop Lombard composes his famous account of O'Neill as the last hero and defender of Gaelic Ireland, while the onstage action essentially dramatizes Sean O'Faolain's portrait of O'Neill as neither Irish hero nor traitor to the British crown, but as a profoundly ambivalent man torn between his allegiance on one hand to his native Ulster and on the other hand to England, where he had been reared and educated, whose culture he admired, and whose queen he had once loyally served.

*Translations* also demonstrates a keen awareness of the relations between fiction and history. In a key passage Hugh, the erudite hedge-school master about to become obsolete, says, "it is not the literal past, the 'facts' of history, that shape us, but images of the past embodied in language. . . . we must never cease renewing those images; because once we do, we fossilize" (*SP* 445). We can see more clearly what is at stake in Hugh's comment if we look at a statement Friel made in an interview in 1980, the year *Translations* was first produced.

> In some ways the inherited images of 1916, or 1690, control and rule our lives much more profoundly than the historical truth of what happened on those two occasions. The complication of that problem is how do we come to terms with it using an English language. For example, is our understanding of the Siege of Derry going to be determined by MacCauley's history of it, or is our understanding of Parnell going to be determined by Lyons's portrait of Parnell? This is a matter which will require a type of eternal linguistic vigilance ("Talking to Ourselves" 61).

Obviously for Friel history is not a matter of a disinterested, "objective" account. It matters to him who constructs Ireland's historical images and what are their allegiances, prejudices, and assumptions.

Friel further develops his thinking about language as lie in *The Communication Cord* (1982), written the year after *Translations*. In this play, as in *Translations* he structured some of Steiner's insights into its dramatic form. *The Communication Cord* is a wild farce of mistaken identities and fabricated images, all deliberately contrived to satisfy the immediate needs of each of the characters. One of the characters, Tim, is writing a thesis on discourse analysis based on the popular assumption that people converse by exchanging units of information that constitute a message according to an agreed code. The lies, charades, and wild fictions that follow completely refute this naive, positivist model of discourse. In the end Tim realizes he may have to rethink his thesis as he arrives at some of the same conclusions suggested by the plays of Pinter, conclusions such as "maybe the message doesn't matter at all" and "it's the occasion that matters" or "the reverberations that the occasion generates"; or perhaps what matters is "the desire to sustain the occasion," or "saying anything, anything at all, that keeps the occasion going." He even suspects, as Beckett and Heidegger have claimed, that "maybe even saying nothing . . . maybe silence is the perfect discourse" (85-86).

More than anything else *The Communication Cord* poses Steiner's suggestion that "possibly we have got hold of the wrong end of the stick altogether when ascribing to the development of speech a primarily informational, a straightfor- wardly communicative motive" (229). "It is not, perhaps," Steiner says, "'a theory of information' that will serve us best in trying to clarify the nature of language, but a 'theory of misinformation'" (218), which is precisely what Wilde and post- structuralists like Derrida have given us. For all its farcical nonsense, *The Commun- ication Cord* is just such a theory of misinformation in compact dramatic form.

Beyond his own plays, Friel's views on language inform the various projects of the Field Day Theatre Group, which he co-founded with actor Stephen Rea. Friel and his Field Day colleagues have focussed attention particularly on images and myths that have shaped Irish consciousness, especially those that have helped form the prejudices that divide the country today. In one of the Field Day pamphlets, for example, Declan Kiberd explores the uniquely posed thesis that "the English did not invade Ireland—rather, they seized a neighbouring island and invented the idea of Ireland. The notion "Ireland," he says, "is largely a fiction created by the rulers of England in response to specific needs at a precise moment in British history." Likewise, he claims that the "Irish notion of 'England' is a fiction created and inhabited by the Irish for their own pragmatic purposes" (*Ireland's Field Day* 83). One of Ireland's retaliations against England's myth of Ireland, Kiberd implies, was Oscar Wilde becoming "more English than the English" (*Ireland's Field Day* 86).

In demythologizing some of the traditional Irish images and myths, Friel and other Field Day writers hope to alter the cultural foundations that sustain many of the long-standing prejudices that inhibit cultural and political harmony. As they demythologize the old histories and myths they hope to supplant them, in a cautious and self-conscious manner, with new ones that are free from the colonial perspectives, those of both the colonizer and the colonized, that have encased Ireland's history for the past eight hundred years, free, that is, both from the old prejudices and myths handed down through the republican tradition and from the myths of official British history. And they expect to achieve their goals through the power of the lie.

# NOTES

1. Richard Ellmann discusses the influence of Wilde and of "The Decay of Lying" in particular in *Eminent Domain* (New York: Oxford University Press, 1967): 3-27.

2. Declan Kiberd was the first to point out this similarity in "Brian Friel's *Faith Healer,*" *Irish Writers and Society at Large,* ed. Masaru Sekine, Irish Literary Studies 22 (Gerrards Cross, Buckinghamshire: Colin Smythe, 1985; Totowa, NJ: Barnes and Noble, 1985): 106.

3. For a more detailed examination of Friel's and Steiner's views of history see my "Language, Myth, and History in the Later Plays of Brian Friel." *Contemporary Literature* 30.4 (1989): 534-45.

# WORKS CITED

Deane, Seamus. "Brian Friel." *Ireland Today* 978 (1981): 7-10.

Deane, Seamus. Introduction. *Selected Plays* by Brian Friel. Washington, D.C.: Catholic U of America P, 1986. 11-22.

Field Day Theatre Company. *Ireland's Field Day*. Notre Dame, IN: U of Notre Dame P, 1986.

Friel, Brian. *Anton Chekhov's Three Sisters: A Translation*. Dublin: Gallery Press, 1981.

Friel, Brian. *The Communication Cord* (1982). London: Faber, 1983.

Friel, Brian. *Making History* (1988). London: Faber, 1989.

Friel, Brian. *Selected Plays*. Washington: Catholic U of America P, 1986. (Includes *Philadelphia, Here I Come!*, *The Freedom of the City*, *Living Quarters*, *Aristocrats, Faith Healer,* and *Translations*.) Cited as *SP*.

Friel, Brian. "Self-Portrait." *Aquarius* 5 (1972): 17-22.

Friel, Brian. "Talking to Ourselves." With Paddy Agnew. *Magill* Dec. 1980: 59-61.

Joyce, James. *Ulysses*. New York: Random House, 1961.

Steiner, George. *After Babel: Aspects of Language and Translation*. New York: Oxford UP, 1975.

Synge, John M. *The Complete Plays*. New York: Random House, 1935.

Wilde, Oscar. "The Decay of Lying." *The Artist as Critic: Critical Writings of Oscar Wilde*. Ed. Richard Ellmann. New York: Random House, 1969. 290-320.

Yeats, William Butler. *Selected Poems and Three Plays*. Ed. M. L. Rosenthal. 3rd ed. New York: Macmillan, 1986.

# "AS IF LANGUAGE NO LONGER EXISTED": NON-VERBAL THEATRICALITY IN THE PLAYS OF FRIEL

## Patrick Burke

Since the late nineteen sixties the most important plays in the Irish theatre have come from two dramatists, Brian Friel and Thomas Murphy: plays such as *Philadelphia, Here I Come!*, *Aristocrats*, *Translations* and *Faith Healer* (Friel) or *The Gigli Concert*, *Conversations on a Homecoming* and *Bailegangaire* (Murphy) are already part of the canon of Irish drama. A notable feature of those plays is that, along with so much of the lesser work of both Friel and Murphy and the work of such lesser playwrights as Hugh Leonard, John B. Keane, Thomas Kilroy or Frank McGuinness, they are highly, even (as in *Faith Healer* or *Bailegangaire*) overpoweringly verbal. They place far less theatrical reliance, that is, on adventurous use of setting, lighting, stage space or the physical resources of the actors, though one must acknowledge the imaginative integration of music into *Philadelphia*, *Aristocrats* (both of which I refer to below), *Bailegangaire* or, preeminently, *The Gigli Concert*. That emphasis on the verbal is arguably central to Irish theatre which in its origins, under the impact of writers like Yeats and Synge, defined itself consciously as "The Irish *Literary* Theatre," with the poetic aspirations that such definition implied. And, with due acknowledgment of moves in the direction of less verbal and more imagistic theatre in the work of playwrights as early as Denis Johnston (1901-1984) and as recent as Thomas MacIntyre, that predominantly verbal focus may be seen to have underpinned the work of most of Ireland's considerable playwrights over a period of ninety years: one thinks, in addition to those already mentioned, of T.C. Murray, George Shiels, Paul Vincent Carroll, Brendan Behan.

Brian Friel has consistently lent support to the Yeatsian concern for the "ancient sovereignty" of words both in artistic practice and in his theoretical comments; "a play," he has observed, "exists essentially through its language."[1] His opposition to interference with the integrity of his play texts by directors or actors is well-known.[2] Moreover, directly or by implication, language is itself a theme in the work of Friel in plays otherwise as different as *Philadelphia, The Freedom of the City*, *Volunteers*, *Translations* and *The Communication Cord*.[3] For those very reasons some of the critical examination of Friel has tended to under-value the extent to which he is not merely aware of the significance of the non-verbal in drama[4] but, as this essay will attempt to suggest, consciously incorporates it as a structuring element in his plays.

I begin with some consideration of his use of stage setting, in face of the strongly stated view in a recent commentary that "Friel never really developed a sense of the possibilities of stage design as a way of expressing the imagery of his plays."[5] Such a view is challenged directly, to cite a number of obvious examples, by the adroitness with which Friel gives the schooltype clock—with its associations of insistent, man-made time and, in character terms, with the pathetic school-teacher Master Boyle—the strong, upstage centre position in *Philadelphia* (1964). Like it, the setting for *Translations* (1980) reflects the absence "of a woman's hand" (both S.B. O'Donnell, Gar's father, and Hugh Mor O'Donnell are widowers and have no daughters); as an image of desuetude, of possible collapse (the stairs lacks a bannister), it gives visible expression to the precariousness and vulnerability of the whole society of Baile Beag: we observe how *ascent* of the rickety stairs can lead nowhere (it is the location for Hugh's final, amnesiac speech, " *Urbs antiqua fuit*") and how *descent*, for much of the play, brings characters like Hugh and Manus into the midst of the new Anglicized order of reality imaged by the maps and cartographic books on the floor.

In similar, though more complex terms, the seemingly functional setting of *The Loves of Cass McGuire* (1966) supports that play's theme. We understand as the play advances that the "spacious, high-ceilinged room" present to our view "serves as the common-room in Eden House"—a home for the elderly— *and* "as the living room in the home of Harry McGuire," Cass's prosperous brother. This is more than spatial economy; it intimates powerfully that just as the bourgeois comfort of Harry's home may be threatened by the emotional depression and interpersonal vulnerability attaching to Eden House, the old folks' home is open in turn to the kind of comfort provided by Trilbe and Ingram and the assuaging set-piece "rhapsodies" they utter, and which Cass, from her pain, finally learns to join. Through the large upstage windows of the set, a "Cupid statue . . . frozen in an absurd and impossible contortion," images the ironies and paradoxes of human love in the play, while the windows themselves fulfill the function of a border zone between the actual, what Friel terms "the world of verifiable facts," and the other-worldly: it is through those windows that Trilbe beckons Cass to "join" her and Ingram at the very powerful conclusion of Act Two.

Friel's most skilled use of setting is in *Volunteers* (1975), where it illuminates thematic concerns of time and power. Because it is set in time present, on an archaeological "dig" which is to be the future site of a modern hotel, *Volunteers* compels intellectual address to the relatedness of past, present and future and, in particular, the recurrence of physical violence and manifold injustice. As Keeney, the leading character, observes: "What you see around you is encapsulated history, a tangible precis of the story of Irish man."

The spatial arrangement of that setting images lucidly and powerfully the complexities of human power in the play. The "volunteers"—a label both literal and paramilitary—work fifteen feet below the level of the public street, obscured by sheets of corrugated iron from the view of those as a consequence of whose derogated authority (judges, police, warders) they have been imprisoned: the punished and the punishers make no direct human contact. Within the visible setting the office of George, the civilian foreman of the "dig," is placed seven feet above the floor of the site, on stage right, functioning as a locus of power in the direct sense and also because contact with the outside world has to proceed through it. On stage left, across and down from the space on which the volunteers are working, is the cesspit. The totality of the setting thus offers, literally, an image of levels of human power, political and social: the men work close to an image of death, a skeleton, overlooked by George, and in proximity as it were, to the ultimate dumping ground, as Keeney bitterly reminds us in his final limerick:

> On an archaeological site
> Five diggers examined their plight
> But a kangaroo court
> Gave the final report . . .
> They were only a parcel of—

While lighting cues in the scripts of Friel's plays are unobtrusive and, literally, unspectacular, his sense of the symbolic potential of stage lighting is a sophisticated facet of such plays as *Philadelphia, Making History* (1988) and, in particular, *The Freedom of the City* (1973).

At the ending of *Philadelphia*, the lighting over the smaller stage area of Gar O'Donnell's bedroom is, if the script is strictly adhered to, more intense than that of the larger kitchen area which is "dimly lit," even though most of the action of the final sequence passes in the kitchen, including the broken-backed attempts by Gar and his father to communicate. This I take to mean that in the juxta-positioning of private and public spheres, of time-free and clock-dominated, of music and "noise" (Canon O'Byrne's term for the Mendelssohn Violin Concerto which Gar repeatedly listens to) and of the presiding influences, respectively, of Gar's dead mother and his father, it is the significance and power of the former which, in each instance, Friel's lighting serves to underline. That is why, in an otherwise pointless move, Private and Public "go into the bedroom" to voice the play's final lines on the purpose of Gar's imminent departure from home: he needs an alternative form of communication to that just, abortively, experienced.

Lighting is deployed to almost absurdist effect at the beginning of the final scene of *Making History*, set in Rome twenty years after the disastrous Battle of Kinsale, when the protagonist of the play, Hugh O'Neill, is "in his early sixties." Stage directions for the scene indicate that "the only light ... is a candle on a large desk," that O'Neill's "eyesight is beginning to trouble him" and that when he appears, "slightly drunk," "he is carrying a lighted taper." In a few moments "he bumps into a stool and knocks it over." These powerful cues to disorientation, to stumbling in the dark, to loss of focus (echoing possibly O'Casey's dramaturgy at the ending of *Juno and the Paycock*) are placed thematically against the pious confidence of the opening of Bishop Peter Lombard's proposed history of O'Neill's career, the book centrally placed on stage, which O'Neill myopically scans before he "lights the candles" on a small table. In this way lighting serves not simply to presage the expansion of that juxtapositioning into the play's conclusion but to illuminate the double meaning of "making history."

Friel's most skilled deployment of lighting is in *The Freedom of the City*, in particular during the opening sequence—the onstage darkness accentuated rather than relieved by the "cold blue" lighting over the apron on which the corpses of Lily, Skinner and Michael are lying, the nervous flashes from the press photographer's camera, the sudden intrusiveness of the spotlight on the judge sitting high, intimidatingly, upstage. Lighting bears on character: when the three protagonists re-enter the Lord Mayor's parlour of Derry's Guildhall in Act Two, their move from Brechtian to realistic theatre is indicated by having Lily, the mother-figure of the play, turn on the light. Conversely, at the play's ending, when they emerge to face what, in the Brechtian idiom, are at once the searchlights of the British soldiers outside the Guildhall and the spotlights of the theatre auditorium, it is the politically anarchic Skinner who switches the parlour light off. And just as the lighting at the start of the play, making for audience unease, tended to distance it from the action, the "battery of spotlights *beaming* on the faces of the three" as they look straight out at the end, about to be gunned down by the Army, inexorably compels audience implication in the political issues posed by a powerful play.

Though costuming in the work of Friel is, for the most part, functional, congruent with a character's role in a particular social *milieu*, it is occasionally used for slyly ironic effect as well. Thus, Senator Donovan's entrapment by an old-style cow chain in *The Communication Cord* (1982), while he is dressed in evening wear for a formal occasion, is an image at once of a certain type of modern "sophisticated" and sentimental myopia *vis-à-vis* the Irish past and the risk that such myopia will extend into or condone brutality.

In the well-known "love scene" in *Translations* (II.2) between the Irish girl, Maire, and the English soldier, Yolland, nothing in the text indicates other than that the latter is wearing his military uniform, the tunic of which would be red. The lovers' kiss is interrupted by Sarah who, as we are later reminded by Maire, is dressed in green. That contrast in colours, emblematic in the simplest way of the conflict between Ireland and England, is thus used not only to point up how threatened by negative forces is the burgeoning love relationship of Maire and Yolland, but also to anticipate the hostilities of Act Three, when, in the wake of Yolland's capture, those forces become overt on both sides—Captain Lancey versus the off-stage Donnelly twins.

Midway through the first act of *The Freedom of the City*, Skinner and Lily don the formal robes and head-gear of the Mayor of Derry and of other councillors. Skinner's quotation from *King Lear* as they do so—"Through tattered robes small vices do appear;/Robes and furred gowns hide all"—immediately points up the incongruity, so fundamental to this play, between socially assigned role and essential identity, an incongruity underlined by their subsequent song-and-dance routine in the course of which they mimic the statements and accents of "the Lord and Lady Mayor of Derry Colmcille." During this Lily has cast her shoes off, Skinner having earlier removed his shirt, wet from the water-cannon used by the army prior to the play's action. This highlights what they enact in their "borrowed robes" as parody; it also prompts the suspicion, relevant to the play as a whole, that, in a kind of Genetian idiom, the orthodox, conventional social processes for which the robes are deemed to be appropriate, are in themselves parodic rather than real, since the society of which they are ceremonially expressive is inherently unjust.

Friel has scarcely ever been given adequate credit for quietly effective deployment of stage properties in his plays, where they function often as a kind of dramatic shorthand. Examples would include the "broken implements," the creel and the "ancient gramophone" in *The Gentle Island* (1971) which intimate the backwardness, the impoverishment and restricted culture of the island, or the use in both *Translations* and *Making History* of documents, letters, books and maps to suggest "a paper landscape," a world of possibility defined by varying levels of abstraction from the existentially actual and, in both plays, injurious to it. Cass McGuire has frequent recourse to three props—drinks, cigarettes and make-up compact—which offer comforting distraction in times of distress: drinking is associated with concealment of her anxieties, make-up with protection against the temptation to escape into the dream world of Trilbe and Ingram, and smoking with her shifting relationship to the audience. We note, for example, how, at the ending of Act Two, when she is feeling most forsaken and is losing her hitherto gutsy grip on reality, all three props are used: *"(Pat) skips off. Cass, angry, sobbing, rushes into her room, takes the bottle from under the mattress and drinks . . .. Then she lights a cigarette and then makes up."*

In both *The Gentle Island* and *Translations* recurring use of the same stage property, a milk bucket, acts as an index of feminine feeling in relation to Sarah and Maire, respectively. When Sarah meets Shane for the first time, and shortly before Maire's first meeting with Yolland, each woman is carrying a bucket full of milk; there is a suggestion, that is, of a kind of *ubertas lactea* which is quickened by sexual attraction. By contrast, following, respectively, Shane's rejection of Sarah and the disappearance of Yolland, we hear references by Joe in *The Gentle Island* to a poor milk yield and are told by Maire herself in Act Three of *Translations* that her milk-can is empty; femininity has been hurt, traumatized.

In two of the plays stage properties are so cleverly used in the dramatic resolution as to image a whole vision of life. In *Crystal and Fox* (1968) the rickety wheel, part of the equipment in Fox's seedy roadshow, modulates at the end of the play towards troubling significance: Fox, having "ditched" all his friends and his wife, Crystal, stands—pointedly—at a crossroads and "viciously turns the rickety wheel." The aligning of one protagonist—who cries out "I don't know where I'm going or what will become of me"—with the Oedipal connotations of the crossroads as a critical place in destiny and the whirling randomness evoked by the spinning wheel, is splendidly theatrical and gives depth of focus to what are almost

Fox's concluding words—"the whole thing's fixed, my love, fixed-fixed-fixed."

The structure of *Dancing at Lughnasa* (1990) leads the audience to assume, until late in the play, that the view of life of the seven-year-old Michael on the activities of the other characters in the play is essentially as the adult Michael, the narrator, reports or speaks it—(Stage directions remind us that the young Michael speaks "in (the) ordinary narrator's voice" of the adult)—that is, contented and unthreatened. The indication that it might be otherwise, more truly reflective of the darker side of a child's psyche, comes from the kites on which Michael has been working for most of the play. At the ending, "*for the first time we all see the images. On each kite is painted a crude, cruel, grinning face, primitively drawn, garishly painted.*"

*Dancing at Lughnasa* is a convenient link to the next aspect of theatricality to be considered: gesture, movement and the use of space, since it contains the now legendary dance of the Mundy sisters in Act One. In its premiere production at the Abbey Theatre, Dublin, and subsequently in New York and London, that dance was generally lauded in terms of the energetically celebratory, an evaluation supported by the *joie de vivre* of the Chieftains' music which, anachronistically and counter to Friel's stage directions, accompanied it. Such an emphasis on celebration tended to ignore the text's emphasis on the ugly aspects of the dance— "*the sound is too loud; and the beat is too fast—and the almost recognizable dance is made grotesque . . . With this . . . parodic reel, there is a sense of order being consciously subverted, of the women consciously and crudely caricaturing themselves, indeed of near hysteria being induced . . .*" I contend, in other words, that the dance is as indicative of an unsatisfied hunger in these women to celebrate as it is a manifestation of such celebration.

Ambiguities even deeper and more sinister attend on the dance sequence in 1.2 of *The Gentle Island*. While Shane is dancing to Stephen Foster's "Oh Susannah" on the ancient gramophone, he is joined by the others, including Philly, Sarah's husband, who both denies and experiences homosexual interest in him and expresses that complex of emotion by punching him and shouting: "Dance, you bastard! Dance!" Referentially too, this play points up the eroding effects of island life on the passionate temperament of Sarah in as far as we note the contrast between her having worn out three pairs of shoes through dancing one summer in the Isle of Man and her use of "dancing" as a term of vilification before she herself tries to shoot Shane—"you dirty, dancing bastard!" And the ultimate sign of the destruction which the island wreaks on dance is Shane's shattered body.

Movement and gesture, in particular as they illuminate character, are very sensitively plotted in *Translations*—the boisterous physicality of Bridget and Doalty, the *joie de vivre* of Maire and Yolland after the dance, the drunken gait of Hugh, the stillness of Sarah, the limp of Manus. Act One highlights those movements—Doalty's dashing about prior to Hugh's first appearance, Maire's rising "uneasily but determinedly" to challenge Hugh on the learning of English, Owen's not-so-playful punching of Manus—and the tense atmosphere of Act Three endows them with self-conscious unease, which is reinforced by the *reported* movement of the now-hostile soldiers as, proceeding in wide line across the countryside, they level fences and ditches.

I have discussed in detail elsewhere[6] the importance of music and musical reference in the plays of Friel. These involve, in general terms, the pointed use of songs and song titles as commentary on the action of a specific play, introductory or background music, and music as significant elements in dramatic structure. Examples from the first category would be the ironically placed "It will not be long, love, till our wedding day" in *Philadelphia*; "A-hunting we will go," with its references to trapping a fox, in *Crystal and Fox*; Cole Porter's "Anything Goes" as background to a discussion of the morally and socially acceptable in *Dancing at Lughnasa*. While the second category is normally a function of directorial discretion, Friel is prescriptive in *Translations* in relation to the bridging of 2.1 and 2.2: the change in mood from the boisterousness and latent eroticism of the end of the former to the quietness and tenderness of the latter is managed in musical terms, by the gradual switch from the loud tune of an Irish reel to the gentler sounds of a single guitar.

In relation to the third category, I have already commented on the significance of the Mendelssohn Violin Concerto in *Philadelphia*. The other two plays in which music is central are *Aristocrats* and *Cass McGuire*.[7]

In the former, the offstage Claire, the youngest of the O'Donnell sisters and about to be married to a middle-aged man she does not love, spends much of the dramatic time playing Chopin. Some of the Chopin waltzes, sonatas and ballades she plays are evocative of family memories, in particular her childhood and that of her brother, Casimir. Her playing too is the vehicle of her protest against the "thwarting" of her musical talents by her autocratic father, whose death supplies the strong curtain to Act Two: at the onset of Act Three Claire is heard playing the Chopin Sonata No. 2 in B Minor but deliberately omitting the "Funeral March," the best-known part of it. Confirmation of that protest comes when Claire later appears: stage directions emphasize that, unlike the other characters, "she is not wearing mourning clothes."

Music is used also in *Aristocrats* to indicate the cultural space between the world of the O'Donnells at Ballybeg Hall and the humbler world of Ballybeg village of which Eamon, husband of the middle O'Donnell sister, Alice, is a native; the play suggests that part of his motivation in marrying was to become a part of the putative fineness of the Hall: he had previously proposed to Judith, the oldest sister. This is conveyed by his singing "So Deep is the Night" in Act Two, a popular ballroom song of the nineteen sixties, while the Chopin etude on which it is based, that in E Major, is playing on tape; both social worlds are thus adumbrated.

Music and musical form are central to *Cass McGuire*, which Friel has defined in an introductory note as "a concerto in which Cass McGuire is the soloist." The beautifully written "rhapsodies" of Trilbe, Ingram and, finally, after an unsteady beginning, of Cass herself, Friel recommends should be accompanied by the music of Wagner, in particular that of *Tristan and Isolde*. The latter, he also observed, "has parallels of sorts in Cass McGuire's story," an aspect of the play pointed up by the manner in which Cass's "rhapsody" is intercut by Ingram's reading of the Tristan story. Because, however, of the **pathos** attendant on our insight that Cass is a casualty of disappointment, lost love and, ultimately semi-senility, the parallel between her situation and that of Wagner's lovers is also made very ironic.

## CONCLUSION

The fact that such plays of Friel as *The Enemy Within* (1962), *The Mundy Scheme* (1969), *Living Quarters* (1977) or Friel's greatest work, *Faith Healer* (1979), have not been referred to above should not be taken to mean that one or more of the facets of theatricality discussed are not of significance in them. One need only think of the phones and dictaphones in *The Mundy Scheme*; the wicker chair and glass ornament, as well as the costuming, in *Living Quarters*; the props (dog basket, drinks, cigarettes), the song "The Way You Look Tonight" in *Faith Healer*, as well as that play's unique approach to setting. The relationship of *Faith Healer* to those and other aspects of theatricality (for example, lighting or gesture), as meaningful, proportionately, as in other more conventional plays of Friel, is a significant pointer to the playwright's success in overcoming the limitations of exclusively monologue form.

# NOTES

1. D.E.S. Maxwell, *Brian Friel* (Lewisburg: Bucknell University Press, 1973), 54.

2. See, for example, "Self Portrait," *Aquarius* 5 (1972), 17-22, p. 19, in which, having defined his "manuscript" as "an orchestral score," Friel requires of directors and actors that they "interpret that score exactly as it is written."

3. See Richard Kearney, "Language Play: Brian Friel and Ireland's Verbal Theatre," *Studies*, 72 (1983), 20-56, and in this volume.

4. See, for example, Paul Hadfield and Lynda Henderson, "Field Day—Magical Mystery Tour," *Theatre Ireland* 2 (January/May 1983), 65-66; and Joe Dowling, "Staging Friel," in *The Achievement of Brian Friel*, edited by Alan Peacock (Gerrards Cross: Colin Smythe Ltd., 1993), pp. 178-189.

5. Dowling, 187.

6. See Patrick Burke, "'Both Heard and Imagined': Music as Structuring Principle in the Plays of Brian Friel," in Donald Morse and Csilla Bertha (eds.), *A Small Nation's Contribution to the World: Essays on Anglo-Irish Literature and Language*. Debrecen, Hungary: Lajos Kossuth University, 1993.

7. In Friel's recent play, *Wonderful Tennessee*, which appeared too late for discussion here, music is well-nigh continuous throughout the play. See Brian Friel, *Wonderful Tennessee* (Gallery Press, 1993).

# "RECORDING TREMORS":
# FRIEL'S *DANCING AT LUGHNASA* AND THE
# USES OF TRADITION

## Christopher Murray

> *"A writer is the voice of his people"*
> —Brian Friel
> *"The Irish theatrical tradition . . . was once a very great*
> *theatrical tradition"*
> —Harold Pinter

"Tradition" is a construct of which we have rightly become suspicious in recent times. It is the conservative's *vade mecum*. In the area of literary criticism it has been used to create a narrow, exclusivist canon, as in Daniel Corkery's definition of Anglo-Irish literature or in F.R. Leavis's authoritarian account of the English novel under the title *The Great Tradition*. Nevertheless, let the postmodern theorists say what they will, it is unsatisfactory to discuss adequately those authors who invoke tradition, and whose work self-consciously is inserted within a debate on tradition, without historicizing both author and work. Thus far my apology for raising so distinguished and so experimental a playwright as Brian Friel in the context of what must seem like jaded and outworn ideas. I can only hope that what follows somehow justifies the context.

In one of his few pronouncements on Irish Drama, Friel insisted that Irish drama had no history prior to the opening night in May 1899 of the Irish Literary Theatre ("Plays Peasant" 305). With one impatient gesture, drama by Irish writers from Farquhar to Shaw is thus dismissed as exterior to a definition Friel could accept of Irish drama. It follows that Friel recognizes the tradition established by Yeats, Lady Gregory and Edward Martyn, incorporating the Abbey Theatre (founded 1904). Indeed, his first play of any note, *The Enemy Within* (1962) was presented at the Abbey. Whereas the internationally successful *Philadelphia, Here I Come!* (1964) was ostentatiously *not* an Abbey production, being given instead to the rival Gate Theatre, and whereas *The Mundy Scheme* (1969) was actually rejected by the Abbey (Smith "Two Playwrights" 223) the fact remains that Friel was always an Abbey playwright at heart. His return (to the new Abbey) with *The Freedom of the City* (1973) ushered in a period of intense activity during which four other new plays were staged there before 1980, when the Field Day project got under way. And Field Day, in its theatrical manifestation, was an attempt to create another kind of Abbey theatre.

The question is begged above: what is "an Abbey playwright"? The simple but unsatisfactory answer is the roll-call from Synge through O'Casey and Lennox Robinson to Paul Vincent Carroll, M.J. Molloy and John B. Keane. There both is and is not a reality to such a definition. It implies a mystification of what James W. Flannery calls the "idea" of the Abbey Theatre and it takes too little account of writers who went against the grain, such as George Fitzmaurice or Denis Johnston or Brendan Behan. It makes more sense to emphasize what an Abbey play was under Yeats's prescription. In "Advice to Playwrights" Yeats informed aspiring writers:

> A play to be acceptable for performance at the Abbey should contain some criticism of life, founded on the experience or personal observation of the writer, or some vision of life, of Irish life by preference, important from its beauty or from some excellence of style. . . (Gregory 100)

The subject-matter was to be Ireland, then, the attitude exploratory and analytical. The form, Yeats went on to insist, should be unified, coherent, neo-classical. Within a few years Yeats was complaining that the Abbey, with ambitions to create a theatre of "the heart," had succeeded only in creating a theatre of "the head" (*Explorations* 252-53). A style of realism had succeeded which killed the poetic spirit introduced by Synge, Lady Gregory, and Yeats himself. Mere reflections of social or political issues, however burning the issues, were not what Yeats wanted at the Abbey. Hence his welcome for and defense of the plays of O'Casey when these arrived in the early 1920s. *The Plough and the Stars* (1926), in particular, won his complete commitment because behind the circumstantial detail of material deprivation and behind the satire of romanticized patriotism lay a dream of a noble life, thwarted and destroyed. Yeats's rejection of *The Silver Tassie* (1929), however, revealed a certain narrowness in Yeats's idea of the Abbey tradition. Quite apart from its experimental qualities, the play aroused Yeats's ire because it dealt with the First World War, and was therefore extending the gaze outwards towards Europe and European concerns. O'Casey was not sticking to first-hand experience (Yeats, *Letters* 740-41). Here, perhaps, is the crux of the problem of tradition within the Irish theatre, and since it concerns Friel and his work it is necessary to pick at it a little further.

Yeats was highly conservative in his view of the Abbey repertory. In this regard he felt a strong obligation to be faithful to Synge, who firmly opposed the inclusion of foreign plays which did not, in some obvious way, impinge on the native drama. When in 1919 Lennox Robinson publicly debated the issue with Yeats of staging foreign plays at the Abbey, Yeats was adamant:

> I had all this out with Synge years ago. I was of your opinion, and
> he convinced me that I was wrong. He made his statement in
> writing, so important did he think it. He argued that the municipal
> theatre of Germany gave excellent performances of every kind of
> masterpiece, picked the whole world through, and that Germany
> herself remained sterile and produced no great creative school, and
> that such a school could only arise out of an absorbing interest in
> the country one lived in and perpetual attempts to put that interest
> on the stage. . . (Robinson (1942): 118)

In the 1930s Frank O'Connor found this traditionalism exasperating, since the Abbey was then in crisis and had to compete in a losing game against the cosmopolitan theatrical policy of the Gate theatre: "I don't think he understood that I admired the tradition as much as he did, but in the circumstances of the theatre I thought he was going the wrong way about saving it" (O'Connor 152). Yeats died in 1939, leaving the Abbey deep in crisis. Peter Kavanagh is caustic in his account of Yeats's "betrayal" by his successor as managing director, Ernest Blythe (Kavanagh 179-84). He concludes that the Abbey theatre died with Yeats: "It was his creation and he took it with him" (184).

Even if Kavanagh is right—and the history of the Abbey in the 1940s and 1950s makes dismal reading—the idea of a tradition did not necessarily die. It was prized loose, perhaps, and like one of Yeats's own phantasmagoria has wandered ever since in search of embodiment. It comes to rest, I would argue, in a particularly interesting way in the work of Friel. I have written elsewhere (Peacock, 69-90) about Friel and Yeats and would merely stress here the kinship in the matter of the elusive dream of a tradition both writers have pursued. Yeats could say, "It was the dream itself enchanted me" (*Collected Poems* 392). Friel, in interview, confesses to a "sense of rootlessness and impermanence" which "may well be the inheritance of being a member of the Northern minority. . . where you are certainly at home but in some sense exile is imposed on you. . . . In some kind of way I think Field Day has grown out of that sense of impermanence, of people who feel themselves native to a province or certainly to an island but in some way feel that a disinheritance is offered to them" (O'Toole 20). On the one hand there is an ambition to encapsulate experience along old Abbey lines:

> I would like to write a play that would capture the peculiar spiritual, and indeed material, flux that this country is in at the moment [1970]. This has got to be done, for me anyway, at a local, parochial level, and hopefully this will have meaning for other people in other countries. (Maxwell 109)

On the other hand, Friel believes "the days of the solid, well-made play are gone" (Friel, *Everyman* 21), and that the narrow focus of Abbey realism is too confining. Here he turns to T.S. Eliot for a wider notion of tradition and the individual talent. His aesthetic then fuses Yeats and Eliot.

Friel invokes Eliot when he makes the case that Irish drama is too rigidly mimetic:

> What I am suggesting is that in each of us the line between the Irish mind and the creative mind is much too fine. That there must be a far greater distinction between the Irishman who suffers and the artist's mind which creates. That the intensity of the emotion we all feel for our country. . . is not of itself the surest foundation for the best drama, as Eliot says, comes from "the intensity of the artistic process, the pressure, so to speak, under which the fusion takes place." ("Plays Peasant" 305)

Here Friel adapts Eliot's theory of impersonality as outlined in "Tradition and the

Individual Talent" (*Sacred Wood* 47-59). It is interesting that he silently transposes Eliot's comments on poetry into comments on drama. Presumably, he would agree also with Eliot's view that

> The essential is not, of course, that drama should be written in verse. . . . The essential is to get upon the stage this precise statement of life which is at the same time a point of view, a world—a world which the author's mind has subjected to a complete process of simplification. (*Sacred Wood* 68)

The Abbey tradition had to be subjected to the intense repossession of the artist's imagination.

What I am trying to establish through this rather laborious linking up of Friel with Yeats and Eliot is, in the end, rather simple. I am claiming a recognition by Friel of a number of things, as follows (i) the vital necessity of personal vision or point of view; (ii) a sense of place or nation; (iii) the need to find means, technically, of extending expression from the personal into the universal. In his lecture on Yeats at the Abbey in 1940 Eliot expressed most admiration for those plays where "the myth is not presented for its own sake, but as a vehicle for a situation of universal meaning" (Kermode 256). Yeats, he concluded, "was one of those few [poets] whose history is the history of their own time, who are a part of the consciousness of an age which cannot be understood without them" (257). Friel's concern is constantly to effect that transition between personal history or obsession and the broad experience of objective history. So, on the one hand, "The discourse is primarily and always with yourself" (Murphy TCD) while on the other, "You delve into a particular corner of yourself that's dark and uneasy, and you articulate the confusions and the unease of *that Particular Period*" (O'Toole 22, my emphasis). Moreover, "We are talking to ourselves as we must and if we are overheard in America, or England, so much the better" (Agnew 60).

It only needs to be added that Eliot reaches Friel modified by Sean O'Faolain. What is significant about O'Faolain's concept of tradition is that he Europeanizes it. In *The Bell*, which he founded in 1940 and where Friel's first short story was published in 1952 (Dantanus 17), O'Faolain constantly called for a wider intellectual framework for the understanding of Irish culture. In *The Irish* O'Faolain deplores the various forms of backwardness, introversion and repression which he observes in Irish life before the 1960s, and rejoices in the new signs of Ireland's emergence into the modern world. Friel quotes O'Faolain twice in "Plays Peasant." He was to use O'Faolain's *The Great O'Neill* (1942) as a primary source for *Making History* (1988), siding with the view that O'Neill "was the first step that his people made towards some sort of intellectual self-criticism as to their place and their responsibilities in the European system" (O'Faolain, 1942, 278). In all of Friel's plays the local is offset by the wider world as signified by Philadelphia, New York, London, Glasgow, Rome, and (in *Dancing at Lughnasa*) Uganda. His plays redefine the Irish tradition so that the tradition itself becomes a critique of the institutions held accountable for various kinds of impoverishment. Such writing, Norman Vance argues (260), acquires "ultimate significance and meaning" in the context of the wider, European world. Not just the European, it must be said, but the world at large.

*****

It is thus not surprising that *Dancing at Lughnasa*, in setting a "peasant" play, is a radical assault on traditional Irish modes of playwriting. That the content embodies personal material is openly acknowledged. Indeed, when *Lughnasa* was staged by the Abbey players in Glenties, County Donegal, for one night only, during a conference in Friel's honour, the autobiographical details were matters of common knowledge. The *Irish Times* reported (12 August 1991):

> Visitors and locals crammed into the hardly-adequate school hall to see the play in its original setting. Mr. Friel, who is in Glenties for the school [i.e. conference], based the play on his mother's family, the MacLoones. His mother and her sisters and brother lived just outside the village and, naturally, the neighbours and possibly the relatives, wanted to see "Lughansa" before it goes to Broadway in a couple of months.

The play, therefore, has its basis in Friel's family history. But even the man who conducted a tour of the landscape, a local retired physician, had to concede that not all of the characters in *Lughnasa* were "real":

> The doctor himself remembered Kate and Maggie. So the aunts were certainly real, names and all, but with Fr. Jack, Dr. McCloskey said, a certain poetic license had been taken. The real Fr. Barney was an ordinary priest, he said. (*Irish Times* 15 August 1991:9)

That Friel sets the play outside Ballybeg, the small town originally invented for the setting of *Philadelphia, Here I Come!*, is a reminder that Friel's world is fictional. The case of Fr. Jack, vital to the meaning of *Lughnasa* in ways to be discussed below, underlines the point. Michael, it need hardly be added, is not Brian Friel, whose parents were married and lived in Derry city where his father taught school.

*Lughnasa* subverts the peasant-play formula through avoidance of conventional plot. One of the main faults of Abbey realism in the 1950s was the insistent tying up of *denouements* with marriages and happy endings. The staple of plot was intrigue; the end brought joyous relief. Friel wants no truck with such out-moded structures. After all, as early as 1968 he had written that "the days of the solid, well-made play are gone" (*Everyman* 21). The author of *Faith Healer* was hardly likely to revert to the form popularized at the Abbey by Lennox Robinson's *The Whiteheaded Boy* (1916) and carried forward in the plays of George Shiels and his successors. Indeed, Friel's expertise in form, in the adjustment of story, mood, tone, and characters to the means of their deployment, makes each of his plays a new venture, unpredictable in its techniques. *Lughnasa* uses the framing device of a narrator, whose handling of the story constantly breaks the illusion which conventional plot (in realism) is there to foster.

On the technical level Friel's interruption of the narrative flow in *Lughnasa*, through Michael's announcements of the future histories of the characters, works as an alienation device, defying the audience's expectations of remaining within the time-structure of the play. Friel had used this kind of ironic interruption as early as *Winners* (1967); with *The Freedom of the City*, directed by the only Brechtian the Abbey has yet produced, Tomas Mac Anna, the device became even more ironic and alienating (Birker 153-58). *Living Quarters* succeeded in irritating Abbey audiences by its narrating director, Sir, who arranges and interrupts the characters seemingly at will but in accordance with the agreed "script" which prescribes the order of events. In *Living Quarters* it is the collective memory of the Butlers which creates the script; in *Lughnasa* it is Michael's memory alone. Perversely, Friel breaks with Synge, whose characters as story-tellers invariably are inserted into the action to reinforce rather than to break the dramatic illusion. (Compare the stage reaction to Christy's narrative in act 2 of *The Playboy*: "That's a grand story. . . . He tells it lovely": Synge 103.) Friel, on the contrary, can be said to be meeting the crisis in modern drama identified by Peter Szondi, by finding a dramatic form to express disclosures of interiority (Szondi 16).

There is also, on the level of content, the counter-action of such Abbey plays as the popular *Is the Priest at Home?* (1954), by Joseph Tomelty, in which a cosy communion between people and clergy is posited as a norm. Friel's purpose in *Lughnasa*, as elsewhere, is to locate the spiritual debility occasioned by false notions of what Victor Turner calls *communitas* (Turner 127-30). His play is, accordingly, a "criticism of life" in Yeats's terms, but in a refracted, postmodernist style. Accordingly, the plain resemblance in form to Williams's *The Glass Menagerie*

(1945) may be viewed as intentional. When *Lughnasa* premiered at the Abbey in April 1990, *The Glass Menagerie* was playing in the Peacock, the Abbey's annex, directed by Friel's daughter Judy. The Williams play serves in one way to extend the horizons of *Lughnasa* into an international context, in another way to reinforce (by intertextuality) certain themes, discussed below.

*Dancing at Lughnasa* is a play with an older narrator who also appears within the play. As memory play the resemblance of *Lughnasa* to *The Glass Menagerie* is striking. It also shares the time of setting, the year 1936, a peaceful time when the clouds of war were nevertheless gathering. Williams, looking back in 1944 to the days when he as a young man was struggling for independence within a difficult family (with no other man, also), refers to the socio-political background (265): "Adventure and change were imminent in this year. They were waiting around the corner for all these kids. Suspended in the mist over Berchtesgaden, caught in the folds of Chamberlain's umbrella—In Spain there was Guernica! But here there was only hot swing music and liquor. . . ." In Friel's play, set in rural County Donegal, hot swing music is certainly a possibility, courtesy of the new "god," the radio, and the Spanish Civil War features when Gerry Evans goes off with the International Brigade. Over the Mundys, too, as over the Wingfields in St. Louis, an ominous cloud hangs. As Kate, the eldest of the five sisters, puts it: "the whole thing is so fragile it can't be held together much longer. It's all about to collapse" (*Lughnasa* 35).

Friel thus balances his play at a point where some major shift or mutation is about to take place. In *Philadelphia* Gar's leaving for America was presented as a crisis with cultural as well as psychological implications: "an analysis of a kind of love: the love between a father and a son and between a son and his birthplace," as Friel himself has phrased it (Smith 222). That play is balanced on a knife-edge of uncertainty, and this destabilizing effect distinguishes Friel's drama from Tennessee Williams's. Friel concentrates on showing the fissures opened up by the collapse of a traditional support system (matriarchal and religious); Williams concentrates on dramatizing the cost of self-realization within a vulnerable family (matriarchal to a comic degree).

In Friel's plays change is usually ominous in ways not fully apparent and often left undefined. Thus *Translations* is pregnant with cultural and political revolution but ends as the symbolic clouds gather over the threatened community. *Aristocrats* (1979) is perhaps the only one of Friel's plays to embrace change. Here, too, things are about to break up. The Big House cannot be maintained after District Justice O'Donnell dies, even though the house symbolizes an outmoded cultural heritage. *Aristocrats* dramatizes the family's confrontation of historical change and its challenges. They (principally Judith) take the decision to strike out and create new lives in an uncertain future. This resolution is presented as at once lamentable and necessary, unlike the resolution of Gar O'Donnell to emigrate which is merely lamentable. In *Dancing at Lughnasa* imminent change is perceived tragically, in line with Friel's apprehension of a culture unable to supply the conditions for any kind of wholeness in living.

Friel's approach to this inevitable collapse is deceptive. Through the narrator Michael a golden time is presented, an interlude perceived by the boy as blissful. Friel's treatment of this romantic, Wordsworthian-style recollection may be illuminated by a comment in George Steiner's *In Bluebeard's Castle*:

> Most history seems to carry on its back vestiges of paradise. At some point in more or less remote times things were better, almost golden. A deep concordance lay between man and the natural setting. The myth of the Fall runs stronger than any particular religion. There is hardly a civilization, perhaps hardly an individual consciousness, that does not carry inwardly an answer to intimations of a sense of distant catastrophe. Somewhere a wrong turn was taken in that "dark and sacred wood," after which man has had to labor, socially, psychologically, against the natural grain of being. In current Western culture or "post" culture, that squandered utopia is intensely important. (Steiner 4)

Friel's art consists in his ability to focus on the individual's sense of such loss, such change, and provide it with massive spiritual implications.

One procedure employed is a series of binary arrangements whereby the posited reality (i.e. the representation) is undercut and destabilized. Thus in Michael's memory the radio and Uncle Jack are linked with the summer of 1936, and the unreliability of the radio's communication reflects upon Jack, whose every utterance is likely to break down in misnomers, aphasia or confusion. Maggie's singing is frequently called "parodic"; the central dancing scene is called "grotesque" (21) and, again, "parodic": "there is a sense of order being consciously subverted, of the women consciously and crudely caricaturing themselves" (22). It is as if masque, in the Jacobean sense, were overlaid by anti-masque, and a dissonance expressed. Other examples of this form of contradiction could be advanced, such as Gerry, very ill-at-ease and yet perpetually smiling (26), or the manner in which Maggie's memory of the dancing competition (20) is recalled when she and Kate observe Evans dancing with Chris (33): we bear in mind the sense of betrayal and injustice inherent in the earlier memory. Even the twin daughters of Bernie O'Donnell can be seen as subverting the image of fulfillment Bernie's presence in the narrative supplies: one is named Nora, the woman as loser in Synge's *The Shadow of the Glen*; the other is named Nina, the unhappy destroyer of Konstantin in Chekhov's *The Seagull.*

Another procedure is suggested by the ritualistic exchange of headgear between Jack and Gerry. Jack orders Gerry to "take three steps away from it - yes? - *a symbolic distancing of yourself from what you once possessed.* Good." (69, my emphasis) The latter phrase describes the narrator's own strategy. He must be both involved and detached, like Andy in the earlier one-act *Losers* (1967), except that here Michael is creator: he can turn all that happens into art. The play becomes a life-class, a demonstration of the process by which imagination and memory combine or conflict to transform so-called actuality into significant form. Thus Michael can make the play, his memory, deliberately self-conscious by the very opening line of the dialogue: "When are we going to get a decent mirror to see ourselves in?" (2). It is as if the Abbey tradition were being given a voice, demanding "decent" representation. Images suggest themselves of Christy Mahon in Synge's *Playboy* and the looking-glass "would twist a squint across an angel's brow" (Synge 95), and Stephen Dedalus's symbol of Irish art, "The cracked looking-glass of a servant" (Joyce 6). Friel's imbrication of such images gives a self-reflexiveness to the text which, in the end, unsettles: "we cannot be quite certain if it is happening" (71). Dislodged from realism, we experience a sense of loss which is ambivalent and complex.

The most important conflict in *Lughnasa*, however, is between two cultures, Christian and pagan. It has been long been Friel's criticism of Irish life that its forms and institutions fail to sustain the emotional life of the people. *Philadelphia, Here I Come!* is only partially and superficially a play about emigration, in the sense in which Abbey plays such as M.J. Molloy's *The Wood of the Whispering* (1953) and John B. Keane's *Hut 42* (1962) deal with this social problem. The issue in Friel's play strikes deeper, into the conditions which make it impossible for father and son to establish and maintain any emotional contact. The issue, in fact, corresponds to a universal situation, acutely felt as modern, whereby the individual consciousness is irretrievably cut off from others and thrown back on his or her own resources. It refers to the essential isolation of the individual, an evil in the sense that it involves suffering. Friel presents the issue amid a great deal of comedy in *Philadelphia*, but there comes a time when accusations have to be directed also. In the farcical scene where Gar's father and Canon O'Boyle are locked in combat (a game of checkers), Private Gar, unseen to them, suddenly switches from comic commentary to become "*Deadly serious.*" He levels his criticism straight at the priest, the man full of clichés and evasions:

because you could translate all this loneliness, this groping, this dreadful bloody buffoonery into Christian terms that will make life bearable for us all. And yet you don't say a word. Why, Canon? Why, arid Canon? Isn't this your job?—to translate? Why don't you speak, then? (*Selected* 88)

But Canon O'Boyle does not speak, much less intervene. Thus Friel accuses the clergy of failure to be healers, to divine and act upon divination. In *Freedom of the City* the tone is mocking rather than angry, as the parish priest shifts his position from his initial, solemn assurance that the three people shot by the British army "died for their beliefs" which should "stiffen our resolution," to the prudent supporter of the state apparatus who sees the three as involved with "evil elements" and as "victims" of a communist "conspiracy" (*Selected* 125, 156). In *Living Quarters* Fr. Tom Carty, close family friend to the Butlers and army chaplain, is an alcoholic, and totally incapable of helping Commandant Frank in his hour of need when he is about to kill himself:

> *FRANK*: Help. Chaplain.
> *TOM*: ( *Wakening*). Wha' - wha' - what's that?
> *FRANK*: Advice, counsel, help. Chaplain.
> *TOM*: What's the trouble, Frank?
> *FRANK*: I need help, Tom.
> *TOM*: Terrific, Frank - just terrific - terrific.
> *FRANK*: What does a man do, Tom?
> *TOM*: Yes, sir - yes, sir - just terrific.
> *FRANK*: What should a man do?
>          (TOM is asleep again . . . )
>          (*Selected*, 239)

And so Frank shoots himself.

In *Lughnasa* there are two priests. One, off-stage (like Synge's Fr. Reilly in *The Playboy*), is the arbiter of spiritual values in the community. He is emphatically *not* at home, nor can he be seen. At first Kate is merely puzzled by the priest's attitude to her as her employer/manager at the school:

> He said the numbers in the school are falling and that there may not be a job for me after the summer. But the numbers aren't falling, Maggie. Why is he telling lies? Why does he want rid of me? And why has he never come out to visit Father Jack? (35-36)

We infer that the parish priest, like the priest in *The Freedom of the City*, wishes to distance himself from the dangers of heterodoxy. He victimizes his employee, the schoolteacher Kate, and by extension the whole Mundy economy, because Fr. Jack is an apostate, a renegade in the eyes of the Catholic Church. Fr. Jack is a missionary priest returned to Ballybeg after twenty-five years in Uganda. Only gradually is his priestly function brought forward in contrast to the negative view of priesthood just encountered; even then, it is not a simple matter of the good shepherd as opposed to the corrupt priest, as in traditional literature (e.g. Chaucer's prologue to the *Canterbury Tales*) or in the plays of Paul Vincent Carroll. It is more subversive of traditional Irish attitudes than such a polarization suggests.

Fr. Jack gathers around him a rich and complex set of associations. He has lost touch with the English language and only gradually recovers control of it; thus he operates like a character from *Translations*, as one who has to learn codes all over again. In Friel, this disability is bound up with loss of identity: Sarah in *Translations* begins to speak by articulating her name. Fr. Jack has, in a word, lost his identity, and in that respect he is modern Ireland personified. The fact that he is dying reinforces the metaphor. Fr. Jack is the posited Faith Healer once again, come home to die. The community to which he returns cannot restore him; indeed it destroys him. "To find his own voice," Norman Vance has remarked, "to discover who he is, the Irish writer *and the Irishman* must understand and come to terms with past and present, predecessors and peers" (Vance 260, my emphasis).

Fr. Jack's dismissal from his duties arose from a complicity between the English district commissioner in Uganda and the church authorities. Jack describes how the commissioner knew Swahili but refused to speak it, exhibiting the imperialist arrogance so much a theme in *Translations* . The commissioner disapproved of Jack's going "native," called him "the Irish Outcast" (39), and complained to Jack's superiors. The church as collaborator in colonialist repression is thus clearly asserted. Back in Ireland Fr. Jack is even more of an Irish outcast, "lost,/Unhappy and at home," to borrow a line from Seamus Heaney which neatly describes the Frielian condition (Heaney 32). Jack has turned his back on Christian doctrine and ritual. Gradually he reveals the extent of his alienation, and in an interesting slip speaks of Uganda as "home" (68). The shock to his sisters, especially to Kate, is considerable, not least when Jack describes the polygamous system of which he is "completely in favour" (63). However, the support system Jack describes, the *communitas*, contrasts sharply with the precariousness of Chris's relationship with Evans, father of her son Michael. Likewise, when Jack self-consciously introduces into the text such words as *ceremony* and *ritual* the discourse invokes an absence in Irish society or culture. The significant part of the thanksgiving ceremony he describes is that "it grows naturally into a secular celebration; so that almost imperceptibly the religious ceremony ends and the community celebration takes over." Here Jack alters his pronouns from "they" to "we," indicating his own commitment to African ritual:

> We light fires round the periphery of the circle; and we paint our faces with coloured powders; and we sing local songs; and we drink palm wine. And then we dance—and dance—and dance—children, men, women, most of them lepers, many of them with misshapen limbs, with missing limbs—dancing, believe it or not, for days on end. (48)

At first sight this may seem like a crude piece of comparative anthropology, a contrast between the happy natives of Uganda and the unhappy natives of Donegal or between the cripples who can dance and the cripples who cannot, in two versions of post-colonial society. But the play is set in August, or *Lughnasa* in Irish: the name is derived from the Celtic god *Lugh*, a kind of Irish Mercury. An important source for the play is Maire Mac Neill's *The Festival of Lughnasa*, extracts from which were included as program notes for the premiere of the play at the Abbey (24 April 1990). The pagan rites of the festival, which survived into the early twentieth century, are summarized as follows:

> . . . a solemn cutting of the first of the corn of which an offering would be made to the deity by bringing it up to a high place and burying it; a meal of the new food and of bilberries of which everyone must partake; a sacrifice of a sacred bull, a feast of its flesh, with some ceremony involving its hide, and its replacement by a young bull; a ritual dance-play perhaps telling of a struggle for a goddess and a ritual fight; an installation of a head on top of the hill and a triumphing over it by an actor impersonating Lugh; another play representing the confinement by Lugh of the monster blight or famine; a three-day celebration presided over by the brilliant young god or his human representative. Finally, a ceremony indicating that the interregnum was over, and the chief god in his right place again. (Mac Neill 426)

It would be a fairly simple exercise to establish how many of these details Friel adapts and/or incorporates in his play (Evans on top of the sycamore tree attending to an aerial may be one of the more ironic touches); it is probably more important to notice how these rites are locally debased and rendered meaningless.

In particular, a residual rite of sacrifice for the festival is described as follows: "First they light a bonfire beside a spring well. Then they dance around it. Then they drive their cattle through the flames to banish the devil out of them" (16). It emerges that this year when the young people were "off their heads with drink," a boy got drunk, fell into the fire and got badly burned. And yet, in spite of the marginality and absurdity of the rites, the festival symbolizes a real need in the lives of the five sisters. As Agnes, perhaps the most sensitive of all the sisters, puts it when the subject of the annual dance at Lughnasa comes up: "I'm only thirty-five. I want to dance" (13), even though the autocratic Kate insists, "That's for young people with no duties and no responsibilities and nothing in their heads but pleasure" (13). Indeed, Kate refers to the participants in the cattle ritual as "savages" and deplores their "pagan practices" (17). The same vocabulary serves to describe the local people as to describe Fr. Jack's leper colony. Once we make the equation we can see the spiritual deprivation of this family whose culture can offer no support or sustenance. It knows only hardship and denial. Kate's problem is that she is too much the product of the system which denies her support. And yet she comes to see that each must make "his own distinctive spiritual search" (60).

The most extraordinary scene in the play, as anyone who has seen *Lughnasa* on stage can testify, is the spontaneous dance which erupts in Act One, as the five sisters join in a wild response to traditional Irish music on the radio. It is significant that the modern instrument here communicates traditional music (a well-known Irish reel) when at other times during the play (when Evans is about, for instance) it provides the more expected sounds of contemporary, American, popular music. The Irish music releases the buried life, the atavistic selves of five women slowly being by-passed by life: Bacchanalians in search of their Dionysus. Maggie, the most earthy of the sisters, is first described in the dance as wearing "a crude mask of happiness"; she then daubs her face with flour and patterns it "with an instant mask" (21). Peter Brook has said that the "traditional" mask is not a disguise but "an image of the essential nature" which actually un-masks:

> The traditional mask is an actual portrait, a soul portrait, a photograph of what you rarely see, only in truly evolved human beings: an outer casing that is a complete and sensitive reflection of the inner life. (Brook 218)

The non-naturalistic mask embodies "forces" (Brook 227). Maggie, in disguise, can reveal her true desires, her true self, in the dance, "a white-faced, frantic dervish" (21). There is a paradox in this process, Brook argues: the true mask, while hiding the self, also releases it. And so this dance supplies an image of Friel's dramaturgy, "a weave of complex steps" (22), which momentarily and as it were magically allows one to glimpse real yearnings behind the unreal mask of conventional living.

There is a contrast to be made between this wild Irish dance and the African dancing Fr. Jack describes, which signifies that "there is no distinction between the religious and the secular in their culture" (48). That distinction, that gap, lies at the heart of *Dancing at Lughnasa*, and may be said to be its major theme. Friel makes the point by introducing ballroom dancing as image of a competitive, unjust society (Bernie O'Donnell's experience, as related by Maggie), and an image also of loss of direction, evoking a culture where "Anything Goes" and people are "Dancing in the Dark."

*****

Richard Schechner, following Victor Turner, argues that the plot of drama moves from some breach to a crisis, re-dressive action, and reintegration (Schechner 168). In *Dancing at Lughnasa* the breach comes with Jack's return, which is related at various points to the spasmodic returns of Evans, equally a marginal or liminal figure whose challenge to convention (in fathering the narrator out of wedlock) parallels Jack's clerical heterodoxy. There is no single crisis in the play, however. Instead a confluence of disappointments and ominous developments creates a pattern for which no re-dressive action is available: Kate is as powerless to protect her job as Agnes and Rose are powerless to affect the industrial change which terminates their contract work. The crisis of Rose's absence acutely raises anxiety over her future, which her return, strangely transformed and tangentially affected by the Lughnasa festival (the blackberries, the "back hills") fails to dispel. Crisis is what Friel's play mainly enacts. Reintegration is possible only in the mind, in imagination, specifically in the collective mind of the audience as influenced by the narrator. The tableau formed at the end of the play deliberately recalls that at the beginning, with carefully stated differences: Rose is displaced and isolated, where Agnes was in the opening tableau, which highlights their common fate. In the final tableau, also, the costumes of Jack and Evans are soiled and shabby, in contrast to the "magnificent" and "spotless" dress specified for the opening scene. The ideal yields to the real, yet reintegration is not an option the play provides. On the contrary, it dramatizes disintegration.

Formally, the narrator insists on this failure. Even the kites do not get off the ground; the top will not spin; the black bicycle never arrives. Loss, death, and dissolution underlie the action, and Michael ensures that this knowledge is made part of our apprehension of his story. He forms a triangular relationship with Evans and Fr. Jack, being detached and involved at the same time. Evans, as drifter/trickster, recalls earlier portraits by Friel, e.g. Skinner in *The Freedom of the City*, Keeney in *Volunteers*, Eamon in *Aristocrats*, Owen in *Translations*. But where these all have an insight into the chaos around them, to which they respond clownishly, Evans has none, and in that impercipience he mirrors Fr. Jack, the saintly outsider. The ritual of exchange of headgear points up the emptiness of the heads as much as the kinship of the two misfits. Michael himself does not analyze the situation; Friel leaves this exercise to us.

"When my time came to go away, in the selfish way of young men I was happy to escape," Michael informs us as he returns to his Tom Wingfield role (71). But the ending he provides is completely different from that of *The Glass Menagerie*. When Michael looks back to 1936, "everything is *simultaneously* actual and illusory" (71, my emphasis). This is Friel's way of making space for the imagination amongst the ruins of time-dominated experience. Friel's notion of memory is that it falsifies and yet composes "a truth of its own" ("Self-Portrait" 18). We see the ambivalence in Gar's memory in *Philadelphia* of a happy day spent with his father; his father insists that the memory is false. For Gar it is a truth. In "Plays Peasant" (305) Friel refers to "that subjective truth—the artist's truth." This is what Michael privileges in *Lughnasa*. He, and not Fr. Jack after all, is the real Faith Healer. He transforms what we have already seen into a new kind of consolation; yes, he has Frielian tricks in his pocket, things up his Frielian sleeve. In the course of a single sentence he relates dancing to three of the key words in the play, *ritual*, *ceremony*, *sacred*. Dancing, in his final verbalization of its unverbal power, becomes the means "to be in touch with some otherness" (71). This is the central motive of Friel's drama: he works to put *us* in touch with that otherness.

D.E.S. Maxwell concluded his early book on Friel with the claim that *The Freedom of the City* was "recording tremors of a social mutation" (Maxwell 106). The claim is equally true of Friel's subsequent work, including *Translations* and *Dancing at Lughnasa*. It is a truism to say that Ireland has undergone and is still undergoing vast social changes since 1936. In responding to those changes Friel as artist transmutes them into tragic images, not into occasions for nostalgia.

It is not possible, therefore, to agree with Richard Pine (3) when he writes of Friel's general preoccupation with "a continual belief in the restoration of a way of living and thinking which was beneficent and provident but which now has turned tragic and punitive." That way nostalgia lies. Friel is not into "restoration" of a laudable past, nor is he saying that the past has "now" turned tragic: it was always so. Loss is his enduring theme. His fellow-playwright Thomas Kilroy (140) speaks of *Translations* as "the most comprehensive enshrouding of peasant Ireland in the modern Irish theatre," but at the same time "truly a 'victory' over the material, as Yeats would have it." But Kilroy points out that the kind of authenticity of vision Friel is in quest of can be interpreted (and thereby deflected) as nostalgia:

> Within the metropolitan centres there is always a nostalgia for cultures which are untouched, untainted by the ennui, the busyness, the crowdedness of the centre. . . In our century this has taken the form of a persisting interest in the primitive, the provincial, the remote even while the main expressions of the centre would appear to be a rejection of the values offered by the periphery. . . (Kilroy 140-41)

In his revision of the Abbey peasant play Friel expertly records its tremors, and finds in its inadequacies images for the all-too-real crises of spirit confronting the people of Ireland today.

## WORKS CITED

Agnew, Paddy. "'Talking to Ourselves': Brian Friel Talks to Paddy Agnew." *Magill: Ireland's Current Affairs Monthly Magazine* 4.3 (Dec. 1980): 59-61.

Birker, Klaus. "The Relationship between the Stage and the Audience in Brian Friel's *The Freedom of the City.*" *The Irish Writer and the City.* Ed. Maurice Harmon. Irish Literary Studies 18. Gerrards Cross: Colin Smythe; Totowa, NJ: Barnes and Noble, 1984.

Brook, Peter. *The Shifting Point: Forty Years of Theatrical Exploration 1946-1987.* London: Methuen, 1988.

Corkery, Daniel. *Synge and Anglo-Irish Literature.* Dublin and Cork: Cork University Press; London: Longmans, Green, 1931; repr. Cork: Mercier Press, 1966.

Dantanus, Ulf. *Brian Friel: The Growth of an Irish Dramatist.* Gothenburg Studies in English 59. Goteborg: Acta Universitatis Gothoburgensis, 1985.

Eliot, T.S. "Tradition and the Individual Talent." *The Sacred Wood.* London: Methuen, 1920. Repr. *Selected Prose of T.S. Eliot.* Ed. Frank Kermode.

Flannery, James W. *W.B. Yeats and the Idea of a Theatre: The Early Abbey Theatre in Theory and Practice.* New Haven and London: Yale University Press, 1976. Repr. 1989.

Friel, Brian. "The Theatre of Hope and Despair. *Everyman: An Annual Religio-Cultural Review* 1.1 (1968): 17-22.

————. *Lovers* [ *Winners* and *Losers*]. London: Faber and Faber, 1969.

————. *The Mundy Scheme: A Play in Three Acts*. New York: Samuel French. 1970.

————. "Self-Portrait." *Aquarius formerly Everyman: An Annual Religio-Cultural Review* 5 (1972): 17-22.

————. "Plays Peasant and Unpeasant." *Times Literary Supplement* 17 March 1972: 305-306.

————. *The Enemy Within: A Play in Three Acts*. The Irish Play Series No. 7. Newark, Del.: Proscenium Press, 1975.

————. Anton Chekhov's *Three Sisters: A Translation*. Dublin: Gallery Press, 1981.

———— *Selected Plays*. With introduction by Seamus Deane. London and Boston: Faber and Faber, 1984.

————. *Fathers and Sons: After the Novel by Ivan Turgenev*. London and Boston: Faber and Faber 1987.

————. *Making History*. London and Boston: Faber and Faber, 1988.

————. *Dancing at Lughnasa*. London and Boston: Faber and Faber, 1990.

Gregory, Lady Augusta. *Our Irish Theatre: A Chapter of Autobiography by Lady Gregory*. New York and London: Putnam, 1913. Rev. ed. Gerrards Cross: Colin Smythe, 1972.

Heaney, Seamus. *New and Selected Poems 1966-1987*. London and Boston: Faber and Faber. 1990.

Joyce, James. *Ulysses*. [1922] London: Bodley Head, 1960.

Kavanagh, Peter. *The Story of the Abbey Theatre*. New York: Devin-Adair, 1950. Repr. Orono, ME: University of Maine at Orono, 1984.

Keane, John B. *Hut 42*. Irish Play Series No. 2. Dixon. Cal.: Proscenium Press, 1968.

Kermode, Frank (ed.). *Selected Prose of T.S. Eliot*. London: Faber and Faber, 1975.

Kilroy, Thomas. "A Generation of Playwrights." *Irish University Review* 22. 1 (1992): 135-41.

Leavis, F.R. *The Great Tradition: George Eliot, Henry James, Joseph Conrad*. London: Chatto and Windus, 1948.

Mac Neill, Maire. *The Festival of Lughnasa*. Oxford: Oxford University Press, 1962.

Maxwell, D.E.S. *Brian Friel*. Lewisburg: Bucknell University Press, 1973.

Molloy, M.J. *The Wood of the Whispering: A Comedy in Three Acts*. Dublin: Progress House, 1961.

Murphy, Daniel (ed.). "Artists on Education: Brian Friel." Unpublished tape. Trinity College, Dublin. MS 10/69/3/9.

O'Casey, Sean. *The Plough and the Stars. Collected Plays Volume 1.* London: Macmillan, 1949.

O'Connor, Frank. *My Father's Son.* London: Macmillan, 1968.

O'Faolain, Sean. *The Great O'Neill.* London: Longmans, Green, 1942. Repr. Cork: Mercier Press, 1970.

———. *The Irish.* Harmondsworth: Pelican, 1947. Revised edn., Penguin, 1980.

O'Toole, Fintan. "The Man from God Knows Where: An Interview with Brian Friel." *In Dublin* 28 October 1982: 20-23.

Peacock, Alan (ed.). *The Achievement of Brian Friel.* Ulster Editions and Monographs: 4. Gerrards Cross: Colin Smythe, 1992.

Pine, Richard. *Brian Friel and Ireland's Drama.* London and New York: Routledge, 1990.

Robinson, Lennox. *The Whiteheaded Boy: A Comedy in Three Acts.* London: Putnam, 1921.

———. *Curtain Up: An Autobiography.* London: Michael Joseph. 1942.

Schechner, Richard. *Performance Theory: Revised and Expanded Edition.* New York and London: Routledge, 1988.

Steiner, George. *In Bluebeard's Castle: Some Notes towards the Redefinition of Culture.* New Haven: Yale University Press, 1971.

Synge, J.M. *Collected Works Volume IV: Plays Book 11.* Ed. Ann Saddlemyer. London: Oxford University Press, 1968.

Szondi, Peter. *Theory of the Modern Drama: A Critical Edition.* Ed. and trans. Michael Hays. Cambridge: Polity Press, 1987.

Tomelty, Joseph. *Is the Priest at Home?* Belfast: H.R. Carter, 1954.

Turner, Victor W. *The Ritual Process: Structure and Anti-Structure.* London: Routledge and Kegan Paul, 1969.

Vance, Norman. *Irish Literature: A Social History. Tradition, Identity and Difference.* Oxford: Blackwell, 1990.

Williams, Tennessee. *The Glass Menagerie* [1945]. In *Sweet Bird of Youth. A Streetcar Named Desire, The Glass Menagerie.* Ed. E. Martin Browne. Harmondsworth: Penguin, in assoc. with Martin Secker & Warburg, 1962.

Yeats, W.B. *The Collected Poems of W.B. Yeats.* 2nd edition. London: Macmillan, 1950.

———. *The Letters of W.B. Yeats.* Ed. Allan Wade. London: Hart-Davis, 1954.

———. *Explorations. Selected by Mrs. W.B. Yeats.* London: Macmillan, 1962.

# THE ENGENDERED SPACE:
# PERFORMING FRIEL'S WOMEN FROM
# CASS MCGUIRE TO MOLLY SWEENEY

## Claudia W. Harris

Moments of pure theatre are rare, those condensed moments which only dramatic action can convey—moments which require a stage, demand a performance, stun an audience, and which fully realize the promise of the theatrical genre. The desire for a visible realization of such visionary moments is probably what drives writers to the dramatic form in the first place. And no matter how rare, this possibility of creating pure theatre motivates the participation of the director and actors, as well. Brian Friel is one playwright who has given the stage several such distilled moments. An instance of pure theatre occurs during Act I of *Dancing at Lughnasa* (1990); Friel's stage directions describe in detail what should happen after Chris switches on the wireless:

> The music, at first scarcely audible, is Irish dance music—"The Mason's Apron," played by a ceili band.[1] Very fast; very heavy beat; a raucous sound. At first we are aware of the beat only. Then as the volume increases slowly, we hear the melody. For about ten seconds—until the sound has established itself—the women continue with their tasks. Then Maggie turns round. Her head is cocked to the beat, to the music. She is breathing deeply, rapidly.

Now her features become animated by a look of defiance, of aggression; a crude mask of happiness. For a few seconds she stands still, listening, absorbing the rhythm, surveying her sisters with her defiant grimace. Now she spreads her fingers (which are covered with flour), pushes her hair back from her face, pulls her hands down her cheeks and patterns her face with an instant mask. At the same time she opens her mouth and emits a wild raucous "Yaaaah!—and immediately begins to dance, arms, legs, hair, long bootlaces flying. And as she dances she lilts—sings—shouts and calls, "Come on and join me! Come on! Come on!" For about ten seconds she dances alone—a white-faced, frantic dervish. Her sisters watch her. (21)[2]

Friel then directs how each of Maggie's four sisters is to join in until all five are singing, shouting, twirling, and leaping around the kitchen. Even Kate whose movement is a more controlled Irish dance—arms close to her side, feet flying with intricate steps—even schoolmarm Kate is transfigured like the rest.

A pure theatrical moment encapsulates a play, exposing both the theme and the emotion fundamental to the writing. It is *not* simply a dramatic moment or meaningful change in the action; any good play will have several of these. To work as pure theatre, the heightened moment is the very *raison d'être* underlying the writing of the play itself.[3] But nonetheless, pure theatre is achieved finally in the performance not in the writing; it happens on the stage not on the page. No mere description of the theatrical moment can substitute for the experience of pure theatre itself. Moments such as these are very nearly indestructible; regardless of the limits of the production, the Mundy sisters' dance has the power to mesmerize.

This Irish dance with all its pagan undercurrents captures the essence of *Dancing at Lughnasa*—the characters, the theme, the emotion. A particularly apt example of pure theatre, these five rapturous minutes ignite the stage. The actors explode out of the roles to which they have been consigned and become fully embodied women dancing out their passionate yearnings. But it is at best a momentary rebellion; when the music stops abruptly, they are left raw and exposed and unsatisfied. Friel never allows his characters or his audience to reprise those moments of near orgasmic pleasure. It is Friel's view of the Mundy sisters, after all, which finally holds sway; as the writer he has engendered both them and the space within which the action occurs.

In giving full realization to the dance, the actors make use of the gap in the text created by Friel's attempt as a mature writer to reconcile his childhood witness of the radio's voodoo possessing those sensible women and transforming them into screeching strangers with his current adult acceptance yet continued male incomprehension of the womanhood expressed in the event. The actors need not only the freedom of an actual space on the stage, but also the imaginative license to exploit the brief removal of the unconscious patriarchal filter that normally colors their lives. Friel reproduces the distinctly *male* perception that society has of the women and that the women to a large extent have of themselves. Yet, by reproducing this inexplicable childhood event, he makes available an opportunity for its subversion. The actors themselves may not understand what they embody, but, as women, their unique, individual interpretation of the characters at that moment rings of an authenticity that everyone—actors, audience and Friel—can recognize. They bring their own sensibilities to Friel's open-ended portrait of the Mundy sisters, collaborating with the playwright to give flesh to such unrestrained but unfulfilled passion.

The play succeeds despite complaints that the narrative structure of *Dancing at Lughnasa* is static, and that Michael, the protoFriel, violates storytelling convention by disclosing the end at the beginning. This Act I scene in particular works despite criticism that the idea of paganism bubbling just below the surface in repressed, rural Ireland is unpersuasive. Moments such as this draw the audience into the writer's imaginative space along with the actors as participants in the performance. Every new Friel play and each subsequent production of an old Friel play will be judged against these exuberant, exhilarating moments in Act I. I believe it is these brief moments of daring that transcend language which captured the imagination of Friel's critics and earned him the Tony Award. Critics writing about the Dublin, London, and New York productions all focus on the passionate theatricality of this particular, pivotal scene.

This "extraordinary burst of ecstasy . . . is a brilliant and moving image that expresses Friel's point that there are emotions that lie far beyond words" (*Guardian*, 17 October 1990). The dance of the "transformed" women is "theatre magic—perhaps real magic if there is such a thing" (*Sunday Independent*, 29 April 1990). "At such times there is no doubting we are in the thrall of as masterly a dramatist as the theatre possesses" (*The Times*, 16 October 1990). The bacchanal fills "the house with all the frenzied passions of the lives they haven't led. It's an explosive moment that has us hungering for more " (*The New York Times*, 3 November 1991). This moment is described as a "glorious frenzied five minutes " (*Sunday Press*, 29 April 1990); as the sisters being "possessed by atavistic impulse and the stage sings, then blazes" (*Observer*, 6 May 1990); as a way "to exorcise the build-up of their disappointment and frustration or give temporary flight to their fantasies" (*Daily Mail*, 16 October 1990); as "a wild, parodic reel round the kitchen" (*Independent*, 17 October 1990); as "first an eerie and then a wild ecstatic dance" (*Spectator*, 20 October 1990); as the music seizing "the sisters in its spell, until even Kate's pious resistance cracks and, with a cry from the guts, she outdances her sisters" (*Independent on Sunday*, 21 October 1990); as "the women become whirling dervishes in surplices" (*Sunday Correspondent*, 21 October 1990); as releasing "a torrent of pent up emotional and sexual feeling" (*What's On*, 24 October 1990); as "a ferocious dance of pent-up sensuality" (*Listener*, 25 October 1990); as transforming the sisters "into wild women, whirling like dervishes to release their pent-up emotion" (*City Lights*, 25 October 1990); or as an astonishing "burst of pagan frolic" (*Atlanta Journal*, 31 May 1992). Even the largely unfavorable *New Yorker* review says that the scene adds "up to the idea that a little bit of pagan abandon in our Christian lives might not be a bad thing" (4 November 1991, 95-97).

Regardless of the language used to describe it, however, very few reviewers fail to mention this Act I dance. In fact, nothing else in the production merits such universal mention, not even the poppy-dotted golden field of barley covering nearly one-third of the stage. For these male reviewers (*City Lights'* Lyn Gardner is the only female exception), these shrieking, reeling women cast a spell. The emphasis in the reviews is clearly on the *wildness*, the *ferocity*, the *sexuality*, the *freedom* of the sisters as they dance. Those glorious five minutes become a release from pent-up emotion, an exorcism; the women become dervishes, whirling into ecstasy, demonstrating a frenzied atavism or paganism. Throughout these descriptions of how these dancing women fill the stage is the recognition that they also seize power in some fundamental, largely incomprehensible, almost fearful way.

Friel adds to his description of the sisters' uninhibited, joyous dancing: "With this too loud music, this pounding beat, this shouting—calling—singing, this parodic reel, there is a sense of order being consciously subverted, of the women consciously and crudely caricaturing themselves, indeed of near-hysteria being induced" (22). Friel concentrates here on the grotesque aspects of the dance— loud, crude, pounding, parodic, caricature, near hysteria. His reasonable male viewpoint intact, Friel seems to be standing back, coolly analyzing this emotional and physical outburst. But this description which emphasizes the freakish nature of the action does not describe what actually takes place on the stage, what leaves the audience hungering throughout the play for another transcendent moment that never comes. The performance, not Friel's words, captures the overflowing of female pleasure, the orgasmic quality of the dance, the utter rejection of male control, the realization of the Mundy sisters as full-bodied women. During rehearsals, the director Patrick Mason told me, Friel kept emphasizing the word *defiance*. But according to Friel's written directions, the sisters are supposed to look embarrassed when the radio shuts off abruptly; they are supposed to "look slightly ashamed and slightly defiant" (22) and avoid each other's eyes. But instead, defiance holds sway; very little shame is in evidence. Winded, they move restlessly around the room like runners after a race; they voice their irritation that the dance is over because the overheated radio is "a goddamn, bloody useless set" which keeps stopping much too soon (22); and, as if to emphasize the near orgasmic pleasure, Maggie, with a wicked twinkle, has a cigarette: "Wonderful Wild Woodbine. Next best thing to a wonderful, wild man" (23).

In this scene, and in the structure of the play as a whole, Friel has unwittingly, no doubt, created a multi-layered expression of the *male gaze*. Michael the narrator, now a young man, is remembering himself at seven watch his mother and his aunts "suddenly catching hands and dancing a spontaneous step-dance and laughing—screaming!—like excited schoolgirls" (2). So the play demonstrates two layers of male interpretation of the female. And behind this, of course, is a third layer as the mature Friel watches himself in the writing remember these women during the summer of 1936, aware "of things changing too quickly" (2) before his eyes. Friel struggles to capture dramatically the brief time before life changed utterly for them all at the end of that summer, a summer which was magic for him, in part, because he "had witnessed Marconi's voodoo derange those kind, sensible women and transform them into shrieking strangers" (2).

But the male filter doesn't stop here with the three-ages of Friel. The performance of the play invites the male gaze of the audience and, in particular, of the reviewer. Con Houlihan's idiosyncratic assessment epitomizes the male gaze: "I have long suspected that it takes men to understand women; Mr. Friel's insight bears me out" (*Evening Press*, 25 April 1990). Not only should Friel's view of these five women enrich us, but, according to Houlihan, Friel's may be the only angle which could offer any understanding of the sisters. Houlihan privileges the male gaze; his statement implies that "Friel's insight"—and, by extension, male insight alone—offers understanding of women.

The male gaze, a term common to film criticism, seems a particularly appropriate concept to apply to *Dancing at Lughnasa*. The argument is that "films construct male subjects gazing at female objects on three levels: characters within the film, the camera's 'eye,' and spectators looking at the film" (Austin: 81). In the theatre, the camera's eye, admittedly, is less controlled and fine-tuned than in film; the "eye" would be analogous to how the play is presented. Ordinarily, these three categories of male "looking"—characters, "eye," and audience—are fairly easy to translate into stage practice, especially where male writers and directors are involved, but with this play the transition is a little more complicated. As I've discussed, Friel has cast Michael in the roles of both on-looker and representative of the writer at different stages of Friel's understanding of the action. So the seven-year-old Michael is a character within the play hiding behind the bush watching his mother and his aunts, but the narrator Michael is also the camera's lens, the filter through which to view the action. Michael as narrator—a distanced, detached "eye"—becomes a spokesman for the writer by setting up shot after shot, moving the camera placement, changing the focus, verbally interpreting the scene.

The eye of the camera in a stage production would normally be controlled by the director and, by extension, of course, the writer. The director usually calls the shots because he represents the views not only of the writer but also of the production team and of the actors as well. The director, in consultation with the writer and the designer, decides how the play will be presented. In *Dancing at Lughnasa*, however, the writer's views take precedence because they are represented on stage by the character Michael. Despite the difficulty of separating discretely the first two categories of male subjects looking at female objects, of separating Michael as a character within the play from Michael/Friel as the camera's eye, the gaze is nonetheless overwhelmingly male: the writer Brian Friel, the director Patrick Mason, the designer Joe Vanek. Of course, the ongoing debate about the impossibility of there being such a thing as a *female gaze* since women also filter views of themselves through a male lens could render the maleness of the production team inconsequential. It would follow that the spectator's gaze is also male despite the gender make-up of the audience. Although the focus in terms of the male gaze might be similar, this third category of looking by the spectator is somewhat different for theatre as opposed to film: theatre audiences work harder; their role is hot participant as opposed to cool observer; an audience's participation can appreciably change any given performance of a play.

In a discussion of "woman as image" and "man as the bearer of the look," Laura Mulvey, in what has become a definitive early work on the subject, explains that the protagonist is nearly always a male whose proactive role is "forwarding the story, making things happen" (Mulvey: 367). Michael, the protagonist, does just that; he makes the story unfold in the particular way Friel, the writer, conceives. Mulvey discusses how women become objectified on two levels: "as erotic objects for the characters within the screen story, and as erotic objects for the spectator within the auditorium" (*Ibid.*). The objectified woman, according to Mulvey, is then either demeaned, punished, redeemed, or worshipped. Certainly for the young Michael and for the slightly older Michael and perhaps still for the more mature Friel, these staid Glenties women become almost frighteningly erotic in their uncontrollable dancing. Friel, after all, emphasizes the grotesque nature of the dance, and these passionate women are demeaned by his description. Although audience reaction to the dancing women might be more varied, the erotic nature of the dance, as evidenced by the reviews, is indisputable and is also, in part, inexplicable.

The dance, however, is what frees the actors to develop fuller portraits of these women, which briefly makes them subjects rather than objects. Through the dance, the characters become sexual beings and thus more understandable rather than less so, which is another aspect of the erotic. During that five minutes, the actors raise audience awareness; both men and women observing the dance connect with the humanity of the Mundy sisters. Underlying that implicit understanding and tacit acceptance is the appreciation that all humans are passionate beings, deep beneath the hard shell of rationality. Friel's style as a writer is to open up actual space to his actors and director, but he also creates imaginative space or gaps in the text for his collaborators to fill and, by so doing, he devises ways for his women to escape objectification and assert the existence of distinct identities.[4] Paradoxically, then, Friel seems to *save* his women from limitation while at the same time honestly exposing their limited circumstances. He may demean them but he also redeems them.

Friel has created many memorable women characters during the past thirty years, but few are more finely drawn than the Mundy sisters in *Dancing at Lughnasa*. Seeing the play caused me to wonder initially if this play then indicated a greater understanding or even a new freedom of expression on Friel's part. Does this play significantly question the validity of the widely held view that to have fully developed women characters portrayed on stage requires producing plays written and directed by women? Sandra Gilbert and Susan Gubar maintain in *The Madwoman in the Attic* that "a literary text is not only speech quite literally embodied, but also power mysteriously made manifest, made flesh" (Gilbert: 6). A masculine metaphor such as this one of the *author as father* creates blocks for women writers who must first redefine the act of writing before they can create their own work. Gilbert and Gubar explore the implications for women who see themselves left out of this process of engendering: "For if the author/father is owner of his text and his reader's attention, he is also, of course, owner/possessor of the subjects of his text, that is to say of those figures, scenes, and events—those brain children—he has both incarnated in black and white and 'bound' in cloth or leather" (Gilbert: 7) or, in the case of theatre, those figures he has placed on the stage.

The inherent power of the theatrical experience makes this engendering role of the playwright an extremely potent one. A persuasive performance can convince women not only of what they are but also of what they are not. And a powerful cumulative effect of the male gaze is the fact that women characters are nearly exclusively created by men. Because of the limited number of women playwrights, approximately fifteen percent, and an even smaller number of plays by women produced, about seven percent[5] (Wandor: 104), fostering a female gaze or treating women as subject rather than object and focusing on issues vital to women all seem an uphill battle. Certainly, some organizations do try to redress this imbalance; the Royal Court, consistent with its politically-correct stance, instituted a policy that forty-two percent of the plays produced at the theatre would be written by women after a survey disclosed that forty-two percent of its audience was female. A recent audience survey in Ireland revealed that women comprise far more than fifty percent of the theatre audience throughout the island; nonetheless, no similar, straightforward effort is being made to address that audience. Although these percentages certainly reinforce the need for the ongoing project of encouraging women playwrights, the limited number of women writing for the stage also seems to render unattainable, at present, the goal of producing enough new plays by women to act as a necessary corrective to the overwhelmingly male interpretation of the female.

Questions which Brendan Kennelly asks in the introduction to a new anthology *Ireland's Women* are questions every male writer must sincerely ask himself: "Can a man really imagine what it is to be a woman? . . . Does the man define the woman he is trying to imagine into being? Or does the imagined woman define the limitations of the imagining man?" (Donovan: xxii). Kennelly's questions clarify the responsibility the man/writer has as "bearer of the look," as the one who directs the gaze at the woman as "image" and, in so doing, turns her into a work of art. I would ask, however, additional questions: Does the very existence then of that man-imagined woman further define the limitations of all women? Does that heightened, artistic representation of woman by man somehow become an obstacle to be overcome by flesh and blood women? And finally, how can Friel as a man avoid stereotyping women while working within the theatrical genre which by its very form invites the male gaze? The obvious response to this final question is, of course, that Friel does not work alone; every woman character is co-created by a woman actor. So although no man, not even Friel, can really imagine what it is to be a woman, he can develop open-ended women characters, ones which leave room for interpretation. Actors want to play Friel's women because he makes room for them to bring their own understanding as women to the roles; as his collaborators, they can work to avoid stereotypical portrayals. Actors are artists in their own right.

Virginia Woolf argues in "Professions for Women" that, to be free to create, women must kill "The Angel in the House." Naming this phantom figure after the heroine of a poem by Coventry Patmore, Woolf describes her as "intensely sympathetic . . . immensely charming . . . utterly unselfish. She excelled in the

50    CLAUDIA W. HARRIS

difficult arts of family life. She sacrificed herself daily. If there was chicken, she took the leg; if there was a draught she sat in it—in short she was so constituted that she never had a mind or a wish of her own, but preferred to sympathize always with the minds and wishes of others. Above all—I need not say it—she was pure" (236). Woolf believes that a woman artist must have a mind of her own and express the truth about all aspects of life, and yet that relentless angel denies freedom and openness to women and dictates, instead, charm, subterfuge, and downright lies. So Woolf has no choice but to eradicate this phantom: "Whenever I felt the shadow of her wing or the radiance of her halo upon my page, I took up the inkpot and flung it at her. She died hard" (237).

Gilbert and Gubar extend Woolf's metaphor: "Women must kill the aesthetic ideal through which they themselves have been 'killed' into art. And similarly, all women writers must kill the angel's necessary opposite and double, the 'monster' in the house, whose Medusa-face also kills female creativity" (Gilbert: 17). Since any woman knows she cannot consistently be the "good" woman, her fear of therefore being perceived as the "bad" woman restricts her ability to write about the full range of her experience. The woman writer, however, is not the originator of this either/or thinking. I would argue that every male writer must kill his instinct to stereotype women in terms of either extreme, to define women as either angels or monsters. Every artist, male or female, must react against this historical tendency to see women in terms of these binary opposites, a tendency, by the way, that is especially pronounced in Ireland. Nonetheless, "for the female artist the essential process of self-definition is complicated by all those patriarchal definitions that intervene between herself and herself. . . . The woman writer [or actor] acknowledges with pain, confusion, and anger that what she sees in the mirror is usually a male construct, the 'pure gold baby' of male brains, a glittering and wholly artificial child" (Gilbert: 17-18). Like Woolf's phantom angel, this painful, artificial reflection is a byproduct of a relentless male gaze. Women artists not only have difficulty honestly relating their experience, they also distrust the authenticity of their creations.

For a woman actor to collaborate on any sort of equal footing with a writer of Friel's stature would be very nearly impossible; no matter how open to that actor's interpretation a male writer or a male director might be, the imbalance would still be there. And Patrick Mason is known as a director who works well with actors on new scripts. However, I suspect with *Dancing at Lughnasa* the numbers plus the situation created more of a balance which, in turn, produced believable characterizations of the Mundy sisters. Here five fine actors are required by a superb script to feel like sisters; during rehearsals, natural differences in personality and approach develop along story lines; the Mundy sisters become flesh. A supportive, confrontive, exclusive community of women has evolved. Even the setting—the country kitchen—signals that men are on the periphery; Uncle Jack may shuffle through but he never sits. These unattached women confront the stereotypes; and, in the end, slow Rose escapes the label *angel* just as stern Kate escapes the designation *monster*.

I do not believe I am in any way exaggerating the difficulties a woman encounters when attempting to fill a role written by a man; her willingness to try to do so is directly dependent, in the case of Friel, upon the quality of the writing, coupled, of course, with the sparseness of roles written by women. This acting to male direction, however, is not at all unusual for women, on or off stage; the male filter is so pervasive it is largely unquestioned. Theodora Jankowski presents the case strongly in *Women in Power in the Early Modern Drama* that male bias underlies gender distinctions: "Male control of the definition of 'woman' is not located solely in the critical practices used to question or demean images of women that appear in literature, it is located in the literature itself—as that literature participates in the creation of gender and gender stereotypes—and in the language that is its medium. Thus, if we accept the inevitable notion that our sex/gender system is socially constructed, then we must accept the corollary notion that literature, criticism, and language are also socially constructed and contaminated with the same sexist biases as the sex/gender construct" (Jankowski: 3). Women lack their own voice. The pervasiveness of the male bias is such that women struggle to criticize rationally the objectification concomitant with the male gaze which emotionally they know to be repressive.

Whether women can have perceptions of themselves divorced from ideas about what they should be in any given society is doubtful. The social construction of *woman* is a state issue, especially in Ireland where the ideological view of the appropriate woman's role is embedded in both church and constitution. Sandra Bem argues persuasively that the present research to pin down biological differences between men and women is misguided. Of course, there are differences, but biological differences become meaningful only within the social context. Calling the world women must negotiate *androcentric*, Bem explains that the problem is not simply that women "are different from men, whether biologically or in some other way. The problem for women—and what limits their chances for equality—is that they are different from men in a social world that disguises what are really just male standards or norms as gender-neutral principles. In other words, the difficulties women face stem from the fact that they are different from men in an 'androcentric' or male-centered world, one in which almost all policies and practices are so completely organized around male experience that they fit men better than they do women—and hence automatically transform any and all male/female differences into female disadvantages" (Bem: B1). So the ability to become pregnant can become a disadvantage for women when male-bias dictates social policy about health care, housing, and employment. In *Dancing at Lughnasa*, Michael, Chris's "love child," paradoxically brings the sisters both great pleasure and abiding shame.

Bem also cautions against research that enshrines female difference stereotypically, such as the popular belief that women are primarily concerned with human relationships and men with dominance. Differences such as these are not universal or natural but are categories shaped socially through unequal power relationships. Such efforts lead to what Bem calls *gender polarization* which "not only dictates mutually exclusive scripts for males and females—scripts that constrain everything from modes of dress and social roles to ways of expressing emotion and experiencing sexual desire. It also defines any person or behavior that deviates from these scripts as problematic—unnatural, immoral, biologically anomalous, or psychologically pathological" (Bem: B3). The Mundy sisters who momentarily but gloriously break through the constraints of their cultural script are, nonetheless, dangerous, inexplicable aberrations; they are monsters in an androcentric, male-centered world. Friel and the critics emphasize the sisters' witchlike wildness.

If gender is in itself a social construct, as Jankowski argues, then Simone de Beauvoir's 1949 statement in *The Second Sex* is all the more true within that particular context: "One is not born, but, rather, becomes a woman" (de Beauvoir: 295). The female child is an apprentice, gradually learning both the boundaries of her gender role and the adequate performance of it. As Judith Butler demonstrates, the way one becomes a woman is through observing and performing the gender role *woman*: "The act that one does, the act that one performs, is, in a sense, an act that has been going on before one arrived on the scene. Hence, gender is an act which has been rehearsed, much as a script survives the particular actors who make use of it, but which requires individual actors in order to be actualized and reproduced as reality once again. The complex components that go into an act must be distinguished in order to understand the kind of acting in concert and acting in accord which acting one's gender invariably is" (Butler: 277).

Acting one's gender then, off stage or on, is a largely unconscious, socialized act; deconstructing the gender role as I'm doing here, however, creates discomfort. The artistic representations of women, the behavior of known women, and the expectations of one's culture are all aspects of the social construct; what is deemed appropriate gender behavior is learned and then repeated, much like acting out a particular role every night on the stage. The *engendering* role of a writer then has a far-reaching effect. Friel has not only aesthetically reconstructed the Mundy sisters from selected memories of his mother and his aunts but he has also, without knowing it, socially constructed them as women within the ideological biases of his culture. The Mundy sisters are not simply Friel's artistic representation of women characters on the stage; their repeated performance teaches the gender role *woman*. Like life performances, stage performances teach the gender role both to the women who then tailor their own behavior, consciously or unconsciously, to fall within the supposed appropriate limits of the expressed role and to the men who reinforce those gender aspects deemed acceptable.

The performances of Friel's other plays teach, as well. And the education comes not only through the repeated performance of those women characters who fulfill gender expectations but also through what happens to Friel's women who are somewhat outside the gender norm of the culture. Their failures give a punishing message to women about the consequences of deviating. Identifying what might be learned about being a *woman* from a few of Friel's women over the years then could indicate what cumulative effect Friel's engendering might have had for actors and audiences, and specifically, what gender message Friel is giving to Irish women and men. A discussion of the women characters of such a prolific, influential writer as Friel yields a composite picture of the particularly Irish gender role *woman*.

Cass ( *The Loves of Cass McGuire*, 1966) is a wonderfully brash, resilient, and difficult old woman: "Oh, sure, sure, go back and show them how patient you all were with the terrible woman that appeared out of the blue after fifty-two years!— how her momma doesn't reconnize [sic] her, and how her brother is embarrassed by her" (15). The irony of Friel's title is inescapable, especially to this sad, unloved woman. Cass's brother Harry puts her, against her will, into an old-folks home, maintaining her there, ironically, by using her own money, a total of $7,419, the sum of what she had sent from America to support the family in Ireland. Harry saved the money over the years, saying he didn't want her to end up dependent on anyone. The other characters do not understand how Cass feels when she learns that the money she scraped together weekly for fifty-two years was never needed: Cass, almost whispering—"None of it . . . never bought nothing? . . . The kids' birthdays . . . and the doc's bills . . . and Father Tom's education . . . ?" (41). Thwarted desires and a wasted life. The play ends with Cass slipping into fantasy, a way of restructuring reality which other elderly residents of the home teach her to use. So her loud, coarse, ugly passion is controlled finally; this aggressive woman is made manageable in the end when she becomes docile in the rest home and learns to tell her own story palatably for the other residents. She ceases to be a monster and becomes an angel. In her pretense, she is visited regularly by an attentive brother Harry, and she becomes that loved auntie central to her family which she always wanted to be.

Mag (*Winners*, first act of *Lovers*, 1967) is irrepressible and pregnant. She is going to marry her baby's father, Joe, in three weeks. In the meantime, they are studying for their Leaving Certificates on a hill near their homes in Ballymore. Mag irritates Joe by talking incessantly: "Joe, we'll be happy, Joe, won't we? It's such a beautiful morning. So still. I think this is the most important moment in my life. And I think (she laughs with embarrassment), I think sometimes that happiness, real happiness, was never discovered until we discovered it. Isn't that silly? And I want to share it with everyone—everywhere." His response—"Stupid" (22). He accuses her of trapping him into marrying him. The day of planning and arguing and studying ends when they borrow a boat, not aware of its poor condition, take it out onto the lake, and drown. Winners then are apparently the young who don't live long enough to become disappointed with life or love.

Hanna (*Losers*, second act of *Lovers*, 1967) is caught between her passion for Andy and her invalid **mother** in the upstairs bedroom. So that her mother will think there is plenty of chatting going on when they court, Hanna makes Andy recite poetry, even though the only poem he knows is Gray's "Elegy Written in a Country Churchyard." Hanna throws in a word from time to time while Andy declaims the best he can: "And, by God, we'd hammer away at it until we'd stop for breath or for a sup of tea or something; or else we'd get carried away and forget the aul' woman altogether—and then the bloody bell would go and the session would be destroyed" (56). Friel's stage directions show Hanna to be in charge: "Very suddenly, almost violently, Hanna flings herself on him so that he falls back, and she buries her face in his neck and kisses and caresses him with astonishing passion. He is momentarily at a loss. But this has happened before, many times, and he knows that this is his cue to begin his poem" (57). After they marry, it is the brief moments of talking not the silences that cause the mother to ring her furious bell. Hanna develops an uncharacteristic, withering coldness towards Andy, and they go upstairs unwillingly but resignedly every night to recite the rosary kneeling at the mother's bedside. Losers then are seemingly those who live to regret their passions and to become disillusioned with life and love.

Crystal (*Crystal and the Fox*, 1968), unlike many of Friel's women, is unfailingly supportive; however, she is also dependent, fearful, witless, and doting. She is one half of a vanishing Irish theatrical institution—an itinerant group of players. But her husband Fox has an odd compulsion to return to the days when he traveled on his own, a compulsion Crystal is aware of even if she doesn't understand it:

Just when things were beginning to go well for the show . . . you got restless. That's what happened. My Fox got restless. Out go the Fritter twins. Out goes Billy Hercules. And I was frightened, 'cos I thought: he's going to wreck it all, break it all up. . . . And then you began to skip the places that were good in the past. And when we could have done four nights, you left after two. And then you poisoned Pedro's dog . . . You did, my love. I know you did. And I never understood why you did those things. . . . I was terrified that you were going to shake me off too. And I really didn't give a damn about any of them, God forgive me, not even Pedro, not as long as you didn't turn on me. That's all I cared about. And now we're back at the start my love; just as we began together. Fox and Crystal. To hell with everything else. (136-137)

By her own admission, Crystal accepts unquestioningly whatever Fox does, terrified that he might also reject her. But, although Fox is quick to claim that Crystal "is my constant enchantment" (63), he finally drives her away, as well, with the lie that he has turned their son over to the police. Only then does Crystal seem to be aware of right and wrong. Needing independence foremost, a man must test the limits; he must guard against the cloying woman; he must reject even constancy like Crystal's.

Mrs. Ryan ( *The Mundy Scheme*, 1969) is one of Friel's most unappealing women characters; she is shrewd, stern, and silly—all at the same time. F. X. Ryan, the Taoiseach, has this strange, symbiotic relationship with his mother whom Friel describes as "very old, very tiny, and lean as a whippet. To describe her as pixilated would be charitable: she was always a virago and now she is doting as well. Her son and herself have a peculiar relationship. When other people are present, he addresses her as crudely and insultingly as his vocabulary allows. She ignores this and treats him like a child. When they are alone together, his dependence on her is obvious and total" (180-181). Ryan calls his mother a stupid bitch, a bloody cow, a weasel, a bag; he tells her to go to hell, that he'll strangle her, that he'll kill her. It is all too over the top to be funny. Apparently, women will take any type of abuse and, nonetheless, will give unflinching adoration. Mrs. Ryan tells her son at the end of the play, "I was looking at you on TV. You were like . . . like a High King. . . . I was so proud of you. And the country's so proud of you . . . . If you do an odd bold thing, Frankie, it's for the good of the country" (314-315). And this in response to a plan to turn the west of Ireland into an auxiliary cemetery for New York and Paris and to his underhanded scheme to buy up the land in question and then sell it to the government at an inflated price. Mothers then, supposedly, have difficulty discriminating between right and wrong if their own children are involved. Seeking her approval as always, Ryan speaks the final words in the play: "Coming, Mammy" (316).

Sarah (*The Gentle Island*, 1971) wants to leave Inishkeen with the rest of the emigrating inhabitants, but her father-in-law, Manus Sweeney, her brother-in-law, Joe, and her husband, Philly, refuse to join the mass exodus from the barren island. Sarah pleads, "Philly, I don't want to stay here. I want to go with them; not with my father and mother, but with all of them and with you, all of us together. I'll go out of my head with loneliness, I know I will" (24). Philly, who is out every night fishing, promises to leave at the end of the summer after he has raised them a stake catching salmon; Sarah is convinced, however, that he won't leave the sea or his disabled father. As if in answer to her promise, Sarah becomes increasingly more difficult until she is raging. Into this closed community come Peter and Shane, a gay couple from Dublin, back-packing through the West of Ireland. Sarah is delighted with the wise-cracking Shane and tells him she wants to lie with him; Shane refuses her kindly. But later after Shane has gone out on the boat with Philly, Sarah tells Manus that she saw Philly stripped naked in the boathouse "with that Dublin tramp, Shane. . . . doing for the tramp what he couldn't do for me. . . . If you're the great king of Inishkeen, you'll kill them both" (61).

To Joe's horror, Manus sits with his gun by his side waiting for Shane and listening as Sarah goads him: "Mind—if you haven't the stomach, I have!" (63). When Shane comes for milk for breakfast, Manus holds the gun on him despite his protests: "I wouldn't have her. That's what's eating her. . . . Look at her for Christ's sake! She's insane!" (67). Manus hesitates even though Sarah orders him to "Shooooot!" In a frenzy, Sarah shouts, "Give it to me! I'll kill the tramp" (68); grabbing the gun, she fires on the fleeing Shane. "He falls on his face. Sarah stares at him. All passion is gone. Her mouth is open. Her whole body limp. The gun drops from her hands. Very softly she begins to lament—an almost animal noise" (68). So loneliness and rejection and sexual frustration have reduced Sarah to a rabid animal, a monster. After taking Shane and Peter to the hospital in Ballybeg the next morning, Joe leaves the island for Glasgow. Manus and Sarah enter a pact to hide the night's events from Philly, and Friel has, yet again, let irony name the play.

Helen, Miriam, and Tina (*Living Quarters*, 1977)[6] are the daughters of Commandant Frank Butler of the Irish Army, a greying, life-long military man in his early fifties. He has just returned from a U.N. tour as the "Hero of Hari" (27), and Tina and Miriam spend much of Act I getting his clothes ready for his recognition dinner. Miriam has left her own children this evening to serve her father: "The years may have passed but we're still Daddy's little beavers!" (26-27).

Helen is divorced and back from London for the celebration and is meeting, for the first time, her father's new wife Anna, who is barely twenty, younger than either Helen or Miriam. Curiously, none of the daughters attend the reception. Frank proudly takes only Anna: "There was no joy—the joy had gone. And that's what Anna did—she restored joy to me—she animated me again. If I'm a hero today—whatever that silly word means—it is because of her" (34). But Anna, in his absence, has had an affair with his son and chooses this triumphant night following the celebration to tell him: "We were lovers, Ben and I! And everybody in the camp knows! Everybody in Ballybeg knows! Everybody except the Butlers!" (84). After the revelation sinks in, Frank makes what he calls a formal protest about the unfairness of the particularly wounding manner in which his happiness has been snatched away and then leaves the family gathering, goes into the next room, and shoots himself.

Tina survives as a waitress in an all-night diner in London; Miriam has her husband and children; Anna goes to California and works for a large insurance company; but Helen, despite her "style and apparent self assurance" (6), is one of Friel's many women who does not survive emotionally; she breaks down: "I didn't survive the test. And I've cracked up three times since" (45). Much like a troubled mind repeats the thoughts that most disturb, *Living Quarters* is a replaying of that fateful day, "endlessly raking over those dead episodes that can't be left at peace" (9). Helen realizes that on the day of her father's death "many different conclusions would have been possible if certain things had been said or done or left unsaid and undone" (45), and it is that realization which forever destroys her contentment. And so in imagination, Helen, along with the others, "out of some deep psychic necessity" (9), reconvenes here periodically to reconstruct, to look for some tiny buried detail, to avert, at last, the "trap waiting to spring" (9). But, like many women, Helen also replays endlessly the details of her failed marriage and her outwardly disciplined but empty life; she is caught in a joyless existence from which she has no skill or will to escape.

Judith, Alice, and Claire (*Aristocrats*, 1979), daughters of the retired District Justice O'Donnell, have gathered, along with other family members, at Ballybeg Hall to celebrate Claire's wedding to a totally unsuitable man nearly twice her age, a greengrocer who drives a "great white lorry with an enormous plastic banana on top of the cab" (27). The crumbling Catholic bighouse, the marriages with "peasants," the sick, driven sisters, the dying father—all signify a decaying aristocracy. And the visiting American academic is fortuitously present to document the decline, although he must sort through, in the process, the apocryphal stories, wrong clues, and resentment at his intrusion. Judith has been obediently taking care of her sick father, her manic-depressive sister, Claire, and the dilapidated house. Seven years ago Judith put her out-of-wedlock child in an orphanage rather than disgrace the family; the child's father was a Dutch journalist whom she met while participating in the Battle of the Bogside.

Their father, Justice O'Donnell, dies suddenly of a stroke at the end of Act II when he hears his absent daughter Anna's voice on a Christmas tape; **Anna** has been a nun since she was seventeen and now works in Africa. Freed at last, Judith decides to close the bighouse, take her child out of the orphanage, and get a job. The alcoholic Alice decides to take Uncle George back to London with her for company. And since the wedding was put off to make room for the funeral, Claire has yet to decide whether or not she's going to marry her greengrocer and move into his house with him, his four children, and his sister **Ellen**: "She said to me that she'll carry on as usual—doing the cooking and the housework. So I'll have nothing to do. A life of leisure. Maybe take the children for walks—she suggested that. . . . He's buying a piano so that I can teach the children to play. Maybe one of them will become a concert pianist?" (38), Claire's earlier ambition in life thwarted by her demanding father. The action is punctuated by Claire's capable, classical piano repertoire and by the father's demented demands and accusations crackling over the intercom. In the end, Judith cannot win. She chooses to nurture her son rather than her siblings; she even forgoes the man she loves because he does not want the child. Still, by closing the house and dismissing the issue of whether or not Claire can survive without her help, Judith changes herself from an angel into a monster. The survivors, the strong-willed, the competent women apparently lack compassion.

**Grace** (*Faith Healer*, 1979) is Friel's most compelling, fragile woman character. Her monologue is magnificent in its vulnerability and honesty. Quietly, barely moving in her chair, Grace tells the story of her life with the difficult, abusive Frank Hardy, Faith Healer, of her attempts to leave him, of her stillborn baby, of her tentative hold on existence now that Frank's shocking death weighs on her. Even though she finally succumbs to suicide, her courage resonates: "I can almost measure my progress by the number of hours I sleep and the amount I drink and the number of cigarettes I smoke . . . . But I *am* making progress. And I suppose what I really mean by that is that there are certain restricted memories that I can invite now, that I can open myself fully to, like a patient going back to solids. . . . I had the baby in the back of the van and there was no nurse or doctor . . . and there was no clergyman at the graveside—Frank just said a few prayers that he made up. . . And he never talked about it afterwards . . . and because he didn't, neither did I. . . . God, he was such a twisted man! With such a talent for hurting. One of his mean tricks was to humiliate me by always changing my surname . . . and I was his mistress—always that—that was the one constant . . . knowing so well that that would wound me and it always did; it shouldn't have; I should have become used to it; but it always did."

"Faith healer—faith healing—I never understood it—never. I tried to. . . . But I couldn't even begin to apprehend it—this gift, this craft, this talent, this art, this magic—whatever it was he possessed, that defined him. . . . I wish you could have seen him. It wasn't that he was a handsome man. He wasn't really. But when he came out before those people and moved among them and touched them— even though he was often half-drunk—he had a special . . . magnificence. And I'd sit there and watch him and I'd often find myself saying to myself, 'Oh you lucky woman.' Oh, yes, oh indeed yes. . . . O my God I'm in such a mess—I'm really in such a mess—how I want that door to open—how I want that man to come across that floor and put his white hands on my face and still this tumult inside me—O my God I'm one of his fictions too but I need him to sustain me in that existence—O my God I don't know if I can go on without his sustenance" (21, 22, 24-25, 29, 31, 34). Movingly, Grace cries out the pain of her love for this twisted man. Women are seemingly fascinated with, defined by, and tied to their abusers.

Máire ( *Translations*, 1980), hardworking and levelheaded, is considering emigrating to America: "There's ten below me to be raised and no man in the house" (20). For that reason, she needs to learn English, a language her hedge school master Hugh refuses to teach even though she quotes Daniel O'Connell as saying that "the old language is a barrier to modern progress" (25). Máire wants Manus, Hugh's son, to apply as master of the new national school: "You talk to me about getting married—with neither a roof over your head nor a sod of ground under your foot. I suggest you go for the new school; but no—'My father's in for that'" (29). Contrary to her practical nature, however, Máire falls in love with Lieutenant Yolland, a young British soldier assigned to rename the country for the ordinance survey maps. During this process of translation, Yolland falls in love both with Ireland and with Máire; he disappears mysteriously toward the end of the play, an innocent casualty of the troubles. But the blameless Manus is also a casualty; just after he secures a teaching job, making it possible for him to marry Máire, Manus goes on the run, believing he will be accused of jealously hurting Yolland.

When Máire comes to the school seeking word of Yolland, Hugh offers to teach her English. The job at the new local school has gone to a schoolmaster from Cork, and the grateful Máire may now be Hugh's only student. In her distraction over Yolland, work is all that drives Máire: "I think I'll go home now. The wee ones have to be washed and put in bed and that black calf has to be fed . . . My hands are that rough; they're still blistered from the hay. I'm ashamed of them. I hope to God there's no hay to be saved in Brooklyn" (60). Máire is one of many Friel characters who struggle against Woolf's phantom angel. In the end, her sensible competence nets her little but the likelihood that she will emigrate. Motivated, pragmatic, industrious—women are responsible for the home and the children and for inspiring the men, as well.

Kate, Maggie, Agnes, Rose, and Chris (*Dancing at Lughnasa*, 1990) are the Mundy sisters of Ballybeg. As the eldest at forty and the only wage-earner, schoolteacher Kate is the recognized head of the family. Maggie keeps the house and makes the meals, but also, in that kitchen, she joyously leads the dancing to the radio. Passionate joker that she is, Maggie wants to name the wireless "Lugh after the old Celtic God of the Harvest" (1). Agnes and Rose earn pocket money knitting gloves; Agnes wants to use the five pounds she has saved to take them all to the harvest dance: "I don't care how young they are, how drunk and dirty and sweaty they are. I want to dance . . . I'm only thirty-five. I want to dance" (13). But Kate decides arbitrarily that they won't be going: "No, no, no! We're going nowhere! . . . Look at yourselves, will you! Just look at yourselves! Dancing at our time of day? That's for young people with no duties and no responsibilities and nothing in their heads but pleasure. . . . Do you want the whole countryside to be laughing at us?—women of our years?—mature women, *dancing*? What's come over you all? And this is Father Jack's home—we must never forget that—ever" (13). Rose is simple but, nonetheless, is being pursued by Danny Bradley, a married man with three small children who calls her his Rosebud. And Chris, the youngest, has had Michael out of wedlock, a child loved by all the sisters. Michael's father Gerry, a married Welshman, comes back twice that magic summer of 1936 and dances with Chris in the garden while the sister watch from the window. As Kate sees Chris smile and hears her laugh, she is beside herself, but Agnes, who also loves Gerry, calls Kate "a damned righteous bitch!" (34).

Everything changes at the end of that summer. Agnes and Rose go off to London but die there years later destitute; Maggie takes on their tasks, pretending nothing had changed; Chris spends the rest of her life hating her work in the knitting factory; and Kate begins to tutor because she isn't invited back to the school in the autumn. The whole family had lost status when their brother, Father Jack, was sent home after twenty-five years in Uganda ministering to a leper colony. No longer the revered leper priest, Father Jack never says Mass again but talks incessantly about strange African practices which Kate refers to as "his own distinctive spiritual search" (60). When he dies suddenly a year later, Maggie and Chris mourn him sorely but Kate is inconsolable. Michael, remembering that summer, thinks of it "as dancing. . . . Dancing as if the very heart of life and all its hopes might be found in those assuaging notes and those hushed rhythms and in those silent and hypnotic movements. Dancing as if language no longer existed because words were no longer necessary . . . " (71). Women are incontrovertibly controlled by the fortunes of the men in their lives. No matter how they might try to dance, women cannot escape their crushing responsibilities—the drudgery, the poverty, the disappointment.

Angela, Berna, and Trish ( *Wonderful Tennessee*, 1993) participate, along with their husbands, in a Godot-like wait on a deserted pier in Donegal for Carlin, the boatman, to take them to Oilean Draoichta—"Island of Otherness; Island of Mystery" (17). Terry has taken out an option to buy the island and brings his close friends to see it on his birthday. Like Godot, the boatman never comes, and these waiting pilgrims tell stories and sing the night away and then leave the next morning when their minibus collects them. The play focuses on what does not happen. Wonderful Tennessee is a place in the song that is never reached, and on that long night in Donegal, despite all the mysterious talk, Demeter's Eleusinian Mysteries are not fathomed either. Although the play seems disconnected, the group on the pier is related in convoluted ways. Trish is Terry's sister; Angela and Berna are sisters; Terry and Berna are married but he is in love with her sister Angela; Terry supports Angela, her husband Frank, and her children while Frank writes a book about clocks.

Berna, another of Friel's unstable women, pleads with Terry when they first arrive, "Take me home, Terry—please. . . . Have you any idea how desperately unhappy I am? . . . I don't think I can carry on" (5). Terry's response is to argue that her doctor says she is getting better and to ask her if she took her pills that morning. At the end of Act I, Berna gets everyone's attention by jumping off the high back of the pier into the black water. Trish's husband George is dying of throat cancer and plays his piano accordion throughout the night, accompanying and sometimes directing the singing. Trish nurtures everyone on the pier, but especially George. Angela comforts Berna, tries to avoid intimate talk with Terry, and sings and dances along the pier to George's music. Waiting becomes an empty gesture; modern life has stripped ceremony of its former relevance; rituals no longer resonate. Despite the nonstop music, the characterizations of the women do not sing; all three women seem tense, lack-luster, and strangely without mystery. None are proactive. Women, seemingly, have so little control over their lives that they invent meaningless games to pass the time.

Molly *(Molly Sweeney*, 1994) may be blind but she is comfortable in her blindness; she has come to accept her father's early judgment: "I promise you, my darling, you aren't missing a lot; not a lot at all. Trust me" (15). She walks vigorously with head held high, she rides her bike on the beach, and she swims: "I really did believe I got more pleasure, more delight, from swimming than sighted people can ever get. Just offering yourself to the experience—every pore open and eager for that world of pure sensation. . . . if they only knew how full, how total my pleasure was, I used to tell myself that they must, they really must envy me" (24). Molly is thirty-nine and working as a massage therapist in a health club when Frank becomes fascinated with her blindness. Frank, a man of enthusiasms, forever seeking out the exotic, sees Molly as a project. Before he takes her out for the first time, he spends the entire week in the library researching blindness: "You are going to ask this blind lady out for an evening. What would be the ideal entertainment. . . . The week in the library pays off. Know the answer instantly. Dancing. Take her dancing. With her disability the perfect, the absolutely perfect relaxation. . . . I am your eyes, your ears, your location, your sense of space. Trust me. Dancing. Obvious" (36).

After they had been married two years, Frank takes Molly to Mr. Rice, a formerly renowned ophthalmologist who now has a drinking problem and has settled for a Regional Hospital in Donegal. Through his research, on the strength of the information in the thick folder he has accumulated, Frank urges Mr. Rice to operate. Yes, it is possible for Molly to regain partial sight if he removes the cataracts; everyone, even Molly, asks—What has she to lose? And for an instant, Mr. Rice thinks: "The chance of a lifetime, the one-in-a-thousand opportunity that can rescue a career—no, no, transform a career—dare I say it, restore a reputation?" (18). And Frank lingers a little longer on the idea of success: "A new life! A new life for both of us! *Miracle of Molly Sweeney. Gift of sight restored to middle-aged woman. 'I've been given a new world,' says Mrs. Sweeney. Unemployed husband cries openly.* And why not? Oh my God . . . Sight" (26). At a party the night before the operation, Molly allows herself, uncharacteristically, to at least think about her anger: "None of this is my choosing. Then why is this happening to me? I am being used. Of course I trust Frank. Of course I trust Mr. Rice. But how can they know what they are taking away from me? How do they know what they are offering me?" (31). Then until Frank makes her stop, Molly dances alone frenetically around the apartment, skillfully, despite her blindness, avoiding every obstacle but frightening her guests.

The successive operations on each eye are a limited success; however, the patient does not survive. Seeing is not understanding. With only partial sight, Molly is unable to connect the confusing, fuzzy images she sees with her tangible, sensuous understanding of the world. Terrified, she begins to distrust her senses. In the end, Molly is totally sightless and housed in the same psychiatric hospital, where her mother died, where, according to Mr. Rice's estimation, Molly "was trying to compose another life that was neither sighted nor unsighted, somewhere she hoped was beyond disappointment; somewhere, she hoped, without expectation" (59). Or as Molly describes her blindsight: "My borderline country is where I live now. I'm at home there. Well . . . at ease there. It certainly doesn't worry me anymore that what I think I see may be fantasy or indeed what I take to be imagined may very well be real" (67). Molly has become agnostic. Freud first applied this term to conditions like hers—"seeing but not knowing, not recognising, what it is they see" (22). That use of the term *agnostic*, however, could apply as well to Frank and Mr. Rice as to Molly. Neither recognizing nor valuing Molly's experience of the world, both Frank and Mr. Rice interpret her difference as disadvantage. But more than that, they attempt to turn her supposed disadvantage to their own advantage. And having failed, they both move on to other enthusiasms and other posts. Trusting the men in her life, as so many women do, Molly relinquishes her pleasure, her independence, her unique mastery of her surroundings. She trusts and ceases to exist.

This chronological discussion of many of Friel's women characters is not meant to be exhaustive. I have chosen to name in particular these twenty-seven characters and outline their stories because gender is a significant aspect of the thirteen plays in which they appear. The gender focus of the discussion excludes, of necessity, important plays like *The Enemy Within* (1962), Friel's first success, and *Volunteers* (1975), neither of which has women characters. A remarkable woman character like Mabel in *Making History* (1988) is also an historical figure which requires then a special treatment in response to known facts. Mabel, therefore, is omitted along with characters Friel translated from other sources because I am examining women characters Friel engendered; this discussion focuses exclusively on those women Friel created by means of his particular vision of women. One of Friel's best known plays *Philadelphia, Here I Come!* (1964) is not included because the play is so clearly about Gar, the protagonist; nor is his political play *Freedom of the City* (1973) included because the gender of the characters is, for most part, insignificant.

A final caveat. Any discussion which focuses narrowly on a single topic, such as this one does on gender, runs the risk of being reductionistic. For instance, Friel's plays concern larger theoretical subjects than simply the stories and the characters portrayed. Along with being women, many of these characters, such as Molly Sweeney, are also metaphors for the abstract ideas Friel explores. Nonetheless, if, as Gilbert and Gubar maintain, an author is the father of his inventions, then Friel has engendered these characters and is responsible for how they interact in the worlds he has created for them. No Irish playwright's work is performed more than Friel's, either in Ireland or abroad; therefore, Friel's vision is a privileged one. Writers, male or female, with contrary views would find themselves writing against a vision as pervasive as Friel's. And because there are so few other playwrights of stature writing Irish women characters, a large proportion of Friel's audiences, inside and outside Ireland, probably accept, for the most part, his view of women; to do otherwise would require a well-developed critical awareness which the average theatre goer does not exert. Identifying and analyzing the gender roles Friel's women perform is necessary to reveal the message Friel's drama gives about being a *woman*, particularly about being an Irish woman.

One message is clear: Friel's women characters are defined primarily by their relationships as sisters, daughters, wives, mothers. The family relationship most represented by these twenty-seven women is *sister*. Friel defines seventeen of them as sisters, but the relationships he explores are not in any measure exclusively female. Only Angela and Berna in *Wonderful Tennessee* are lacking a brother; Angela's alliance with her brother-in-law Terry, however, shifts the sisters' focus to a man. And the relationship between Trish and her brother Terry in that play receives as much emphasis as the one between Angela and Berna. Virtually all of the sister relationships are focused, at least in part, on a male sibling: Cass McGuire has her Harry, after all, and Ellen is hanging on tenaciously to her brother, Claire's greengrocer in *Aristocrats*. Not only these exclusively male-female pairings are circumscribed by a male; where there are three sisters and four sisters and even five sisters, a large portion of the energy goes to the sole brother, as well. Helen, Miriam, and Tina in *Living Quarters* spend considerable time talking about their brother Ben whose relationship to their deceased mother had been unusually close; now Ben is having an affair with their young step-mother, an affair that, no doubt, triggers their father's suicide. In *Aristocrats*, the prospects of Judith, Anna, Alice, and Claire have been severely restricted because their brother Casimir, as is traditional, received all of the educational opportunities; Casimir, a somewhat silly but likable pedant, has been singularly unable to take advantage of his good fortune to be born a male. The choices open to his sisters are also traditional: Judith has been a slave to their father; Anna became a nun at seventeen; Alice emigrated with her husband and lives unhappily in London; and Claire gives up her dream of being a concert pianist and contemplates marrying a man twice her age with four children and a domineering sister. And the limited destinies of the Mundy sisters in *Dancing at Lughnasa* are about to become even more severely limited because of the changed status of their brother Father Jack. Even in this play where the sister relationships are the most finely drawn, great emphasis is placed on caring for this ailing, male sibling and helping him reclaim his privileged position as a priest. That men are valued more than women, even by women, seems unmistakable. Friel's sisters demonstrate well the male-identified woman.

Nine of Friel's women characters are defined as *daughters*; of those, eight are daughters of fathers. But including Father Jack as a type of father adds five more daughters to the list. Father Jack is more than ten years older than Kate, so, considering his age and his occupation, designating his influence as fatherly is appropriate. Molly Sweeney's is the only one described as a warm and caring father, but, nonetheless, he is too stingy to pay her fees for the blind school. Grace's father in *Faith Healer* is forever the judge; even in his dotage the words spill out of him accusing her of disgracing the family with that mountebank Frank Hardy, sentencing her to jail and then suspending the sentence because she comes from a good family, but threatening to impose the maximum penalty if she appears before him again. Grace finds no welcoming father the one time she leaves Frank and returns home; resisting the impulse to revile this cruel judge with obscenities in a final rejection, she goes back to Frank—to the van, the depravity, and the damp mattress. Similar to Grace's is the father in *Aristocrats*, who has also been a judge; his constant, direct condemnations of the disgrace Judith has brought to the family by having a child and his strange grumblings over the intercom keep his children on guard against yet another stinging criticism. And in *Living Quarters*, Frank Butler, the quintessential military man, simply expects his daughters to serve him much like he would those lower in rank, and, for the most part, his daughters don't question the relationship. The imbalance is striking. Whether Friel's fathers are cruel or cold or simply unconcerned, they give their daughters little comfort; and yet, in return, the daughters are expected to give unceasingly and uncomplainingly. And they perform on cue; Friel's daughters raise selflessness to an art.

Eleven are *wives*, two are betrothed, and one, Máire in *Translations*, is hoping to be. But no happy picture of married life develops from Friel's portrayals; whether it is Hanna in *Losers* whose passion for Andy changes to coldness after marriage or Crystal who tries desperately to hold onto Fox, marriage relationships seem irrevocably flawed. Trish in *Wonderful Tennessee* nearly expresses love for her husband, but this may be, in part, because George is dying. For all of the other wives, wedded bliss is an oxymoron. Alice in *Aristocrats* and Angela in *Wonderful Tennessee* lead lives of quiet desperation; Alice escapes by drinking and Angela evades both her husband and her brother-in-law by singing sad songs to George's accompaniment. But despite their unhappiness, most remain passively in these bleak relationships: although Berna, Angela's sister, expresses the wish that Terry leave her, only Helen in *Living Quarters* deals with the stigma of divorce. Unceasing, unrewarding work is apparently the lot of a wife: Miriam in *Living Quarters* responds uncomplainingly, but Sarah in *The Gentle Island* is confronted with the expectations of not only her husband but of her male in-laws as well. And then there are wives who suffer deprivation and abuse: after life with Frank, Grace in *Faith Healer* has no inner resources left to enable her to survive, and Molly Sweeney loses her own self as a result of the pygmalion aspirations of the men in her life. Even the two betrothed women seem headed for disaster: Mag in *Winners* is tied to a young man who ridicules and rejects her, and Claire in *Aristocrats* must face, if she marries, the grim combination of her greengrocer's unconcern and his sister Ellen's domination. The message resounds: marriage is, at best, an enterprise to avoid. Friel's wives get high marks as long sufferers.

Only eight of Friel's women are *mothers*, and they are overwhelmingly mothers of sons. Friel, however, explores many types of nurturing relationships which all seem to be rife with problems and few rewards. Many of his sisters are primarily nurturers: in *Dancing at Lughnasa*, Agnes mothers Rose, but probably unwisely; and Friel defines Máire, in *Translations*, tirelessly taking care of the ten below her, more as an overwhelmed mother than as a sister. The number of *aunts*, another type of substitute mother, is six. Although Michael's mother Chris has been unable to provide a father, the Mundy sisters—Kate, Maggie, Agnes, and Rose—have warm relationships with their nephew in *Dancing at Lughnasa*; but consistent to their characters, Maggie teases and Kate disciplines. Cass McGuire and also Berna in *Wonderful Tennessee*, however, are admittedly unsuccessful in their efforts to nurture their nephews. The actual mothers fare no better: Crystal tries but cannot protect her son; Mrs. Ryan in *The Mundy Scheme* humors her son to his detriment; and Judith in *Aristocrats* kept her son in an orphanage for eight years. Then there are failed mothers like Grace in *Faith Healer* mourning her stillborn child. Whether the adulterous, incestuous Anna in *Living Quarters*, literally a step-mother, can be classed as a mother is questionable. Only Angela in *Wonderful Tennessee* and Miriam in *Living Quarters* have children who, although absent from the action, seem to be by their mothers' reports relatively well-adjusted. Nonetheless, Friel paints, overall, an ambiguous, ambivalent picture of the Irish mother. Friel's mothers take the warmth out of nurture. But then Friel shows all of these family relationships—sister, daughter, wife, mother—to be limiting, systematically destroying hope, passion, purpose.

Fintan O'Toole raises and partially answers objections my discussion of Friel's women characters may provoke:

> Whenever anyone talks about issues of gender in relation to the theatre there is an air of barely suppressed exasperation in the response. Sure enough, the standard response goes, it would be nice to have more women playwrights, but does it make any real difference to the plays? Haven't male playwrights created superb

women characters? What does it matter who the writer is, so long as women are represented on stage? It is undoubtedly true that male playwrights in Ireland have written some splendid parts for women. From Synge and O'Casey to Friel and Murphy, there are complex, subtle and sympathetic portrayals of the lives of women. But there is nevertheless a real sense in which the perspective on those lives remains a male one. In particular, it says a lot about the overwhelming male domination of Irish playwriting that, while the theme of fathers and sons is perennial, that of mothers and daughters is rare. The plain fact is that the one area of family relationships that is exclusively female is very seldom represented on stage. (*The Irish Times*, 20 September 1994, 10)

O'Toole asks these questions at the beginning of his review of yet another Irish play about fathers and sons, *The Long Black Coat* by John Waters.

This primary women's relationship is largely undeveloped in Irish drama; the only mother-daughter relationship Friel explores in these thirteen plays is in *Losers* between Hanna and the disembodied bell-ringer wielding her invalid's tyranny from the upstairs bedroom. The mothers of Friel's women are, for the most part, either missing entirely or distant, insubstantial figures. For instance, when they were children, both Grace in *Faith Healer* and Molly Sweeney had mothers who were in and out of mental institutions. Certainly, there are hints of women nurturing each other as sisters, but even these relationships are characterized more by distance than by closeness. Friel is clearly standing outside, as he would have in life, observing these women and how they interact with each other. His male focus does not simply limit the possible range of women's relationships, however; the greatest limitations come in the psychology of his women.

Friel has, indeed, placed on the stage an array of compelling women, but their limited personality spectrum ranges from crazy to merely difficult. Some are truly crazy like the manic-depressive Claire in *Aristocrats* and the tranquilized Berna in *Wonderful Tennessee*. Others are driven to craziness like the violent Sarah in *The Gentle Island* and the brooding Grace in *Faith Healer*. Then a few are deeply disturbed due to their circumstances like the alcoholic Alice in *Aristocrats* and the grieving Helen in *Living Quarters*. And some are excused for becoming unhinged like Cass McGuire because she is old and Molly Sweeney because of the misguided operations. But Molly who is usually described as angelic becomes monstrous to Frank when she dances uncontrollably or insists on swimming during a storm. Here then are the fruits of the male gaze; if these women cease to be angels, they quickly become monsters. Few among Friel's twenty-seven women characters could be characterized as psychologically healthy; instead, a parade of passive, frustrated, aggressive, embittered, angry, depressed, slightly crazy women characters march across his stage. Where are the active, competent women, those successfully managing homes and families and rewarding jobs, those exploiting the range of possibilities open to them, those equal to their challenges, those happily enjoying life? Success may not be what drama is made of, but surely a few of these twenty-seven women could have demonstrated the fuller, healthier lives women have lived, both now and in the past. Surely, a few more could have surmounted the difficulties Friel created for them and survived, stronger and better for the experience.

Despite the awkward, limited portrayals and, at times, unbelievable situations, however, the vitality of Friel's women keeps bubbling to the surface, a proof of his ability as a writer. The vitality of these women, as I have argued earlier, develops because it is Friel's style to write open-ended characters which leaves space for his actor-collaborators to enrich their portrayals with distinct, non-stereotypical identities. Of course, it could also be argued that all Friel is doing is sympathetically and honestly showing the limited circumstances of his women characters and, by extension, Irish women as a whole. And to take the argument still further, that, in a strange, paradoxical way through the power of his considerable artistic skill, Friel thus saves both his characters and women in general from limitation and obscurity by telling their tortured stories. Friel, therefore in this scenario, is committing an act of love.

The question then seems clear: Does Friel simply present the limited roles as they exist or does he in the representation codify the gender role *woman* and perpetuate the limitations? Does he merely chronicle or does he as the chronicler change the outcome of the story? Or to recast Brendan Kennelly's questions: Does Friel define the limitations of these women he is trying to imagine? Or do these imagined women define Friel's limitations in imagining? And to reprise my own earlier questions: Does the very existence then of those Friel-imagined women further define the limitations of all women? Do these heightened, artistic representations somehow become an obstacle to be overcome by flesh and blood women?

To answer these questions, it would be fruitful to return to the issue that is most difficult for men to understand—women's passions. How does Friel handle the passionate natures of his women characters? Are they defined as either unaware angels or uncontrollable monsters? Is their sexuality treated as an understandable, integral aspect of their characters or as a fearful anomaly? This discussion of Friel's women characters demonstrates his difficulty in defining his characters as sexual beings. Only the Mundy sisters in *Dancing at Lughnasa* are able briefly to become fully embodied women. In the play, Gerry Evans, the father of Chris's son Michael, explains to Chris why he's going to Spain to fight: "It's somewhere to go—isn't it? Maybe that's the important thing for a man: a *named* destination—democracy, Ballybeg, heaven. Women's illusions aren't so easily satisfied" (51). Friel seems to despair of fulfilling those illusions, those overwhelming, mysterious passions. Yes, Friel's characters reveal his limitations in imagining. But the skill of Friel's portrayals also helps perpetuate his limited view of the gender role *woman*; thus his drama changes the way women view themselves. And yes, women must then work to overcome the constraints of Friel's artistic representations if they are to define themselves as competent, successful, and psychologically healthy.

But it is not only men who have difficulty writing about women's passions. Although Woolf successfully kills the angel in her house, she claims in "Professions for Women" to have never succeeded in "telling the truth about my own experiences as a body" (238). Speaking personally, no doubt, Woolf describes the difficulty a woman writer encounters when, in order to speak truthfully about her experience, she must write about herself as a sexual being: "She was indeed in a state of the most acute and difficult distress. To speak without figure, she had thought of something, something about the body, about the passions which it was unfitting for her as a woman to say. Men, her reason told her, would be shocked. The consciousness of what men will say of a woman who speaks the truth about her passions had roused her from her artist's state of unconsciousness. She could write no more" (*Ibid.*). Woolf too is stymied by the male gaze. She may have killed the angel, but she is still left prey to her passions which she knows men find monstrous.

The power to decide what is appropriate is how the male gaze robs women of their experience. And the theatre by replicating artistically gender roles in which men are the active subjects and women are the passive objects reaffirms gender positions taught by a male-biased culture. Reclaiming women as active, passionate beings, however, can work as a corrective. In *The Feminist Spectator as Critic*, Jill Dolan explains the need to rediscover women's desire: "left passive in a narrative articulated by men who control its linguistic, social, political, and psychological power, women become objects pursued for the fulfillment of male desire. If male desire is the underlying principle driving narrative, then to disrupt the cinematic and narrative patterns that rob women of their subjectivity, women's desire must somehow find its place in representation." (Dolan: 49). And this then explains the power of the Mundy sisters' Act I dance; they break out of that male-controlled narrative. As it turns out, this brief dance is the only time in the play that they escape the male filter, but the possibility bubbling just below the surface keeps the audience hungering for another exuberant episode. Mary Eagleton asserts that "female desire, what women want, is so repressed or so misrepresented in a phallocentric society, its expression becomes a key location for deconstructing that control" (Eagleton: 205).

Observing this dance dispels any question of its authenticity; the scene is pure theatre because of its genuine representation. The sisters' overwhelming desire is undeniable as they become sexual beings in their own right, as they become subject rather than object. The power of the scene is in its raw passion. Friel's mother and aunts, no doubt, confused him with their open, although momentary, sensuality, and writing the play is possibly Friel's attempt to understand the dancing. Placing Michael on stage as his stand-in is at least Friel's recognition that this play is his own particular view of the events of that magic summer. Women have actually expressed relief that rather than Friel presenting these women as he usually does—"This is the way they are"—Michael's presence makes it clear that here Friel is saying—"This is the way I see them." In contrast to his other work, *Dancing at Lughnasa* is an open, honest representation of the male gaze. But, nonetheless, I don't believe for a moment that these erotic interludes were because of the radio or because of Lughnasa or because Father Jack returned from Africa; these women, very much like all women, were passionate beings caught in a culture that told them they should be asexual. They broke free in the only way they could. And the actors portraying these sisters understand this need to dance with utter abandon in a way Friel never could—thus these stunning moments of pure theatre. Friel can write the scene; he can even identify the emotion; but it takes women to embody such action, such orgasmic pleasure, such *jouissance*. These women, both the original Glenties five and the actors portraying them, are writing the body in the fullest sense of the term.

*Dancing at Lughnasa* is full of dancing—Rose's uncoordinated jigging, Father Jack's pagan shuffling, Gerry's smooth ball-room turning, and the sister's abandoned reeling. David Richards claims that "Mr. Friel is dancing, too. Sometimes he reels his characters in, so he's swaying with them lovingly, cheek-to-cheek. Sometimes he twirls them away from his side, as if to send them spinning out into the world. At the last minute, however, he invariably catches them by the hand and gracefully pulls them back—partners in memory" (*New York Times*, 3 November 1991). Richards misunderstands the motivation for the seeming grace with which Friel reels in the Mundy sisters. Yes, Friel dances with his characters, but at that moment in Act I he can't keep up with their whirling, twirling motion. The five Mundy sisters take over his stage; they control for an instant their own story.

# NOTES

1. Contrary to the widely circulated rumor that the recording used for the dance was by the Chieftains, Patrick Mason told me that a ceili band was organized solely to record "The Mason's Apron" for the production. Unlike the usual ceili band, however, this one included the bodhrán, an Irish traditional drum, to emphasize the beat.

2. Page numbers to Friel playscripts refer to the editions listed in the references. The year of first production is given in the text.

3. Another good example of pure theatre in Friel's work is Scene Two, Act Two of *Translations* (1980). Máire and Yolland yearn to express their feelings although their only common language is their passion for each other. That desperate reaching across language and cultural barriers is central both to their relationship and to the theme of the play itself. The scene has the power to lift both the lovers and the audience above the limitations of language to a realm of sensation and sensibility. This extraordinary scene is described in review after review: "A love scene, supposedly bilingual . . . is one of the finest Friel has written" (*Evening Herald*, 24 September 1980); "Marvelous passages . . . particularly a love scene . . . the rhythmic evocation of the languages at odds with each other is both touching and humorous" (*The Times*, 26 September 1980); "The old story that love conquers all comes through in a very moving love scene where the English soldier uses the Irish names of townlands to communicate with his beloved 'Máire' while she in turn uses what few English words she knows" (*Derry Journal*, 26 September 1980); "Its most powerful scene is one in which two young people move towards love without either being able to understand a word that the other is saying. Friel here seems to be using language with infinite care, to suggest that language itself may be of little importance" (*The Irish Times*, 25 September 1980); "The work has a love scene which is unique in dramatic literature. It is very remarkable, very beautiful, and extremely touching, and it provides, to a considerable degree, a symbolic shorthand of what the play as a whole is about" (*Irish Independent*, 26 September 1980). And thus this scene is the very raison d'être of the play.

4. In an early play *The Loves of Cass McGuire* (1966), Friel demonstrates this ability to make space available to his actors. Cass McGuire repeatedly interrupts the play: "The story begins where I say it begins" (15). She tries to control the telling of her own story: "What's this goddam play called? *The Loves of Cass McGuire?* Me! Me! And they'll see what happens in the order I want them to see it" (16). Past and present blend in Cass's mind; time becomes fluid as she reconstructs the action and a more pleasing, fantasy view of events increasingly

takes precedence. Having Cass talk directly to the audience is a good example of a gap that Friel creates in his texts. Providing space such as this to stand outside and comment on the action allows more room for unique character development by any actor playing the role. Throughout the play, Cass aggressively calls her playwright to account: "*The Loves of Cass McGuire*—huh! Where did he get that title from anyways?" (26). Commenting like this, deliberately engaging the audience, was a revolutionary technique when Friel first introduced it. The unloved Cass speaks for the audience when she focuses on the irony of such a title. The permission Friel gives many of his characters to criticize their playwright is another example of space in a text.

5. The fifteen percent figure for the number of women playwrights comes from the 1983 British Alternative Theatre Directory. No corresponding publication gives separate information for Ireland, but informal data indicates an even lower percentage. The seven percent figure for productions of plays by women was arrived at through a 1983 survey; of those, Agatha Christie's plays accounted for nearly half of the productions. There is no indication that these low percentages have improved during the past ten years (Wandor: 104).

6. *Living Quarters* (1977) is a remarkable play structurally. Sir, a calm, tolerant character, acts as stage manager, referee, and confidant. Except for a few instances when he enters the playing space to move things or participate directly, Sir sits outside the main action holding the ledger, referring to it frequently, reading the stage directions aloud, introducing the characters, conversing with the actors, and helping move the play along to a fuller disclosure of the events leading up to the suicide of Frank—father, friend, and husband. The ledger is "a complete and detailed record of everything that was said and done that day . . . in it must lie the key to an understanding of *all* that happened" (9). Repeatedly, Friel bends stage conventions so actors can move fluidly in and out of scenes, walk across walls, interrupt the action to argue against particular ways of playing the scene or specific interpretations of their characters. Time becomes relative as reminiscences take over. A kind and paternal Sir keeps pulling the actors back to the present task, literally setting the stage for the next scene, and quietly shooing actors off stage when they are not needed. This play demonstrates both how Friel creates space in a text and how a character can play the role of the camera's eye. Sir, a stand-in for Friel, identifies the shots, frames the action, adjusts the focus, and all through a benevolent male gaze.

# REFERENCE

## Playscripts:

———. *Aristocrats*. Dublin: Gallery Press, 1980.

———. *Crystal and Fox*, in Two Plays by Brian Friel. New York: Farrar, Straus and Giroux, 1970.

———. *Dancing at Lughnasa*. London: Faber and Faber, 1990.

———. *Faith Healer*. London: Samuel French, 1980.

———. *The Gentle Island*. Loughcrew, Co. Meath, Ireland: Gallery Press, 1993.

———. *Living Quarters*. London: Faber and Faber, 1978.

———. *Lovers: Winners, Losers*. Dublin: Gallery Press, 1984.

———. *The Loves of Cass McGuire*. Loughcrew, Co. Meath, Ireland: Gallery Press, 1990.

———. *Molly Sweeney*. Loughcrew, Co. Meath, Ireland: Gallery Press, 1994.

———. *The Mundy Scheme*, in *Two Plays by Brian Friel.* New York: Farrar, Straus and Giroux, 1970.

———. *Translations*. London: Faber and Faber, 1981.

———. *Wonderful Tennessee*. London: Faber and Faber, 1993.

## Works Cited:

Austin, Gayle. *Feminist Theories for Dramatic Criticism*. Ann Arbor, University of Michigan Press, 1990.

Bem, Sandra Lipsitz. "In a Male-Centered World, Female Differences Are Transformed Into Female Disadvantages," *The Chronicle of Higher Education*, XL, No. 50 (17 August 1994), B1-B3.

Butler, Judith. "Performative Acts and Gender Constitution: An Essay in Phenomenology and Feminist Theory." In *Performing Feminisms: Feminist Critical Theory and Theatre*, Sue-Ellen Case, ed., 270-282. Baltimore: Johns Hopkins University Press, 1990.

de Beauvoir, Simone. *The Second Sex*. Trans. and ed. H. M. Parshey. 1949. London: Jonathan Cape, 1953; rptd. Harmondsworth: Penguin, 1974.

Dolan, Jill. *The Feminist Spectator as Critic*. Ann Arbor: University of Michigan Press, 1988.

Donovan, Katie, A. Norman Jeffares, and Brendan Kennelly, eds. *Ireland's Women: Writings Past and Present*. Dublin: Gill & Macmillan, 1994.

Eagleton, Mary, ed. *Feminist Literary Theory: A Reader*. Oxford: Basil Blackwell, 1990.

Gilbert, Sandra M., and Susan Gubar. *The Madwoman in the Attic: The Woman Writer and the Nineteenth-Century Literary Imagination*. New Haven, Yale University Press, 1979.

Jankowski, Theodora A. *Women in Power in the Early Modern Drama*. Chicago: University of Illinois Press, 1992.

Mulvey, Laura. "Visual Pleasure and Narrative Cinema." *In Art after Modernism: Rethinking Representation*, Brian Wallis, ed., 361-373. Boston: David R. Godine, 1984; reprinted from Screen 16 (Autumn 1975): 6-18.

Wandor, Michelene. "The Impact of Feminism on the Theatre: New Women Playwrights and Problems of Patronage." In *Feminist Literary Theory: A Reader*. Mary Eagleton, ed., 104-106. Oxford: Basil Blackwell, 1990.

Woolf, Virginia. "Professions for Women." In *The Death of the Moth and Other Essays*. New York: Harcourt Brace, 1942, 236-238.

# LANGUAGE PLAY: BRIAN FRIEL AND IRELAND'S VERBAL THEATRE

## Richard Kearney

There has been much discussion in recent times about the *verbal* character of Irish theatre. Some argue that since the Irish are "great talkers" off stage it is both natural and logical that their "way with words" should be creatively explored and exploited on stage. Others claim that the Irish dramatist's preoccupation with language is a curse which hampers the genuine medium of theatre: the immediate, physical presence of actors performing in front of an audience. The critical response to Irish drama could be summed up in the protest—too much talk and not enough action! But what exactly does this aesthetic choice between talk and action *mean?* To what extent does it reflect the perennial philosophical conflict between the claims of mind and body, between intellectually interpreting our world in words and concretely incarnating it in sensory praxis? And how, if at all, does this opposition relate to the cultural and socio-historic nature of a specifically Irish experience? I propose to examine here some of these implications of the verbal tradition of Irish theatre with particular attention to the work of Brian Friel.

### THE NATIVE TRADITION OF VERBAL THEATRE

The indigenous movement of verbal theatre boasts of an august lineage extending from Goldsmith, Wilde, Shaw, Synge, Yeats and O'Casey to such contemporary dramatists as Murphy, Kilroy, Leonard and Friel. All of these authors share a common concern with the play of language. Or to put it in another way, they have created language plays where words tend to predetermine character, action and plot. Oscar Wilde stated his own commitment to language with characteristic pertness when he wrote:

> It is very much more difficult to talk about a thing than to do it. There is no mode of action, no form of emotion that we do not share with the lower animals. It is only by language that we rise above them . . . (Action) is the last recourse of those who know not how to dream. [1]

Synge confirmed this predilection for words when he argued that "in a good play every speech should be as fully flavoured as a nut or an apple." *The Playboy* proves his point. This drama is a powerful example of native language resources brought to full fruition in the speeches of its characters. But it is a language play in another sense also. *The Playboy* is a drama about the power of words to transform oneself and one's world. "By the power of a lie," that is by his own fantastic story of fictional parricide, Christy Mahon ceases to be a "stupid lout" spinelessly subservient to his tyrannical father and becomes instead the "only playboy of the western world." Deploying words in an imaginative and poetic way Christy persuades himself and others to believe in his fiction. And the fiction recreates reality according to its own image. As Blake put it: "the firm persuasion that a thing is so, makes it so." By playing out his imaginary scenario of heroic rebel, Christy actually *becomes* a great lover and a great athlete. When his father eventually intrudes upon the scene, the verbal fiction is momentarily shattered. Christy is accused by Pegeen Mike of being a fake who in reality possesses "no savagery or fine words in him at all." The accusation is highly significant for it epitomizes Pegeen's own failure of imaginative nerve before the apparent discrepancy between narrative word and real world. "A strange man is a marvel with his mighty talk," says Pegeen, "but there's a great gap between a gallous story and a dirty deed."

Christy resists such scepticism however. His fall from grace is no more than provisional. Tenaciously reaffirming the triumph of fiction over fact, he proclaims himself a hero in spite of Pegeen's rebuke. "You've turned me into a likely gaffer in the end of all," he retorts. Father and son set off on the roads to have "great times . . . *telling stories* of the villany of Mayo and the fools is here." The marvel of "mighty talk" vanquishes the daily treadmill of mediocrity. And Pegeen is compelled tragically to acknowledge that what she has lost is not the "small, low fellow, dark and dirty" that Christy *was,* but the playboy of the western world he has *become* through the power of a lie.

Synge's theatrical portrayal of the transfiguring power of the word is representative of the mainstream of the Irish dramatic movement. In a study entitled *Anglo-Irish Playwrights and the Comic Tradition,* Tom Kilroy, one of Ireland's eminent contemporary dramatists, argues that this indigenous fascination with the play of language is a direct response to the Anglo-Irish experience of a displaced or de-centred cultural identity. Writing of Goldsmith, one of the most influential inaugurators of the native dramatic tradition, Kilroy remarks that his works are informed by an interplay between two contrasting *styles* of language: a "low" style imbued with natural integrity and imaginative feeling and a "high" style marked by pretentiousness, hypocrisy and snobbery. The tension between these opposing cultures of language provides his plays with their singular verbal intensity. Goldsmith, he concludes, "had an acute ear for the way in which language betrays a distortion of personality and a benevolent discernment of how metropolitan culture produces such artificiality. The perspective from which he perceived this is that of a figure off-centre, personally awkward in a society which measured correct bearing with calibrated accuracy, feckless in a society dedicated to thrift and efficiency.[2]

## A THEATRE OF THE SENSES

In recent years there have been several spirited attempts to challenge and unseat the primacy of verbal theatre in Ireland. Tom MacIntyre's experiments with mime in *Jack be Nimble* and with dance in *Doobally/Blackway* were, in large part, motivated by the conviction that the Irish preoccupation with verbal theatre has neglected the more fundamental aspects of dramatic art, namely the rituality of performance and the carnal, visual immediacy of movement and gesture. MacIntyre believes that these latter qualities of theatrical performance provide better means of expressing the root dimensions of human emotion—the subterranean, "black way" of our preverbal and preconscious experience.

This plea for a more *embodied* form of drama has gained considerable momentum in Ireland with the emergence of performance art or such experimental groups as *Red Rex* (MacCabe and Keogh), *Operatic Theatre* (Coleman, Fouere and Doyle), *Animals Don't Tapdance* (McKenna and Byrne) and *The Dublin Mime Company.* Such groups are committed to a drama of the senses. As Roger Doyle explained with respect to the work of *Operatic Theatre:*

> Theatre *is* freeing itself from the bondage of the word . . . . The communication is now in the actors not in the words they speak. You cannot really begin to describe it in conventional terms. If you move away from verbal theatre, you move away from verbal explanation. The idea is to bring visual life back into the theatre. Theatre does not have to be a written medium. Too often the word is mistaken for the actor. This creates a block in the audience's

perception of the performance. They think that if they don't hear all the words, they won't understand. There has been too much emphasis on declaiming lines and not enough on the rhythm of word sounds.

Olwen Fouere, another member of this group, expounds their innovatory project as follows: "Words may even distract from the inner life of the show. . . . They are such a limited way of communicating. They reach an audience only through the intellect. The body and the voice *without any words* have much more potency on stage."[3] It is surely significant that the alternative dramatic model advanced by the *Operatic Theatre* group draws from the combined efforts of a sculptor (Coleman), an actress (Fouere) and a musician (Doyle). Not a wordsmith amongst them.

This challenge to the hegemony or verbal theatre in Ireland is perhaps most cogently formulated by David McKenna, the director and critic, in a recent manifesto entitled *The Word and the Irish—A New View of Theatre as Performance*. He opens with the following salvo: "Irish theatre began with the word, the word, unfortunately, of a Great Poet (W. B. Yeats) and it has been dominated by the word ever since."[4] McKenna decries the fact that in Ireland the writer has invariably been considered as the "unique starting point of the process" of drama. This prejudice, he submits, has been the major cause of the "lack of attention paid to the performer in Irish theatre, an oversight which has produced a stagnant and repetitive relationship between actor and audience." Adverting to the ways in which theatre has been developing internationally in terms of experimental performance, largely due to the pioneering work of Stanislavsky, Artaud, Piscator, Brecht and Brook, the author regrets that "in Ireland we have been *telling stories.*" McKenna attributes much of the blame to Yeats' underestimation of the preverbal "dionysian spirit" and "sensual exchange" which he believes are the very flesh and blood of powerful drama. As one of the most decisive and formative influences on modern Irish theatre, Yeats "left the field to the story-tellers. These people produced charming tales, mostly of rural life, ranging from the whimsical and commercial to the magical and superstitious. The Abbey Theatre was their hearth. . . ." The manifesto concludes by indicting the Abbey's legacy of "processing well-spoken automatons . . . shrouded, hobbed, muffled" and untrained in those "gestures which create a tangible dramatic world." (To be fair to Yeats, however, it must also be remembered that he was not only a poet of words but an experimental playwright whose Noh plays introduced dance, ritual, music and gesture into Irish drama).

***********

The Dublin Theatre Festival of 1982 provided a telling sample of the widening rift between the theatre of the Word and the theatre of the Senses. At least six of the major performances gravitated towards the latter category. These included: Peter Sheridan's *Rock and Roll Show* in which the media of music and dance took precedence over dialogue; Vincent O'Neill's *Metamorphosis,* a mime adaptation of Kafka's story; Reinhild Hoffman's *Wedding,* where the narrative was subordinated to a balletic choreography set to a musical score by Stravinsky; *I Didn't Know The Continent Was So Beautiful,* a visual comedy presented by Theater Radeis drawing from such non-verbal media as circus mimicry, surreal cabaret and the slapstick of silent movies. But the shift away from verbal theatre was perhaps most conspicuously represented by the ecstatic response to the Polish production of *Anna Livia* and the Brazilian production of *Macunaima.* Despite the fact that these two plays were performed in foreign languages—Polish and Portuguese respectively—they commanded full houses and rave reviews. Their success was taken as proof of the ability of modern theatre to transcend the language barrier and to communicate in the international media of "cabaret . . . sex, nudity and comicality."[5] Lazimierz Braun, the director of *Anna Livia,* stated the radical implications of his experimental drama in a program note: "How are we to understand one another? I personally believe in the universality of the language of the theatre. I believe that the theatre will express itself *above and beyond words . . .* We are speaking to you through pictures, rhythms, melodies." *Macunaima,* based on the fantastical wanderings of a Brazilian mythic hero, was hailed by *The Times'* critic as a "triumphant production which flows from image to image like the floats and dancers of a carnival parade, never being much harder to understand." And a critic from the *Sunday Independent* celebrated the novelty of "audiences sitting enthralled through a performance in a language they did not know and yet they understood."

These critical reactions are highly significant. They signal an unprecedented enthusiasm for the non-cerebral communication of direct sensation, for a wordless theatre of pure experience untrammeled by intellectualizing interpretations. In this respect they could be said to echo Beckett's desire for a silent drama freed from symbolic interference. Indeed Beckett's retort to the prying academics bent on a metaphysical deciphering of his plays, could serve as a guiding maxim for the new Theatre of the Senses: "No symbols where none intended."

## BRIAN FRIEL'S LANGUAGE PLAYS

The proponents of a Theatre of the Senses have thrown down the gauntlet. They have delivered an unambiguous challenge to the native Irish tradition of verbal theatre, the implications of which are crucial and far reaching. In the remainder of this article I propose to examine the recent work of Brian Friel who may be considered one of the most talented exponents of the language play. I thereby hope to interrogate the *crisis of the word* which contemporary Irish theatre, and indeed Irish culture as a whole, is presently experiencing.

Brian Friel's plays in the eighties have become increasingly concerned with the problem of language. So much so that they constitute not just a theatre *of* language but a theatre *about* language. Words have become both the form *and* the content of his dramas. And this replay of language within the plays themselves may well indicate a critical process of self-reflection wherein the native movement of verbal theatre is beginning to take stock of itself, to put itself into question and reassess its own assumptions.

*Faith Healer* (1980) is a story about the art of story-telling. It portrays the attempts made by three characters, a faith healer (Frank), his wife (Grace) and his promotion agent (Teddy) to give order and sense to their shared past by recollecting it in the present. But they cannot achieve a common version of events. Each character is separated by the subjective and fictive interpretation he/she brings to bear on his/ her own experience of the past.

The play, however, is not so much about the characters themselves as the artistic performance and inspiration in which they are engaged. Coleridge defined the magical power of art to transform reality as a "willing suspension of disbelief." Friel calls it, simply, *faith*. Frank's "performance" can only work when the healer and the healed come together in a ritual of mystic oneness—when they agree to play the language game of faith. The problem arises when the rules of the game are obfuscated or forgotten or interpreted in different ways by different players; in short, when the healing word no longer communicates a common message.

With *Translations* (1981) and *The Communication Cord* (1982) Friel's exploration of the transforming and deforming potencies of the word shifts from a personal to a communal/historical perspective. *Translations* deals with the ways in which the consciousness of an entire culture is fractured by the transcription of one linguistic landscape (Gaelic and classical) into another (Anglo-Saxon and positivist). This demise of a communal continuity of language coincides significantly with the historical demise of the old Gaelic society in the famines of the 1830s and 40s . *The Communication Cord* features the futile and sentimental efforts of the modem Irish bourgeoisie to purify the dialect of the tribe and reinstate the antique pieties of a lost culture.

\* \* \* \* \*

Friel's critical obsession with the workings of words betrays more than an aesthetic interest in the instruments of his own profession. Though not wishing to minimize the aesthetic problem of language, Friel insists that he is also responding to the contemporary crisis of identity in Irish culture. "The whole issue of language is very problematic for all of us on this island," he explains.

I had parents who were native Irish speakers and also two of our four grandparents were illiterate. It is very close you know. I actually remember two of them. And to be so close to illiteracy and to a different language is a curious experience. In some ways I don't think we've resolved it on this island for ourselves. We flirt with the English language, but we haven't absorbed it and we haven't regurgitated it.[6]

Friel insists that the *aesthetic* and *cultural* dimensions of the language crisis entail a third and equally fundamental one—the *political.* He is refreshingly candid in his pronouncements on this aspect of his writing: "It is back to the political problem—it is our proximity to England, how we have been pigmented in our theatre . . . with the use of the English language, the understanding of words, the whole cultural burden that every word in the English language carries is slightly different to our burden."[7] Friel compares his own sentiment of linguistic difference and dissent to Stephen's declaration in *A Portrait* that he cannot, as an Irishman, write or speak in the English language without "unrest of spirit," without holding its words at bay. For the ruled the lexicon of the ruler is at once familiar and foreign. It remains an adopted tongue.

But Friel is not only an *Irish* writer; he is more specifically a *northern* Irish writer. And this geographical distinction accentuates his sense of cultural, political and linguistic alienation. Though he repudiates the colonial identity of Britain, he also feels an outsider in the Republic. This sentiment of permanent dislocation and dispossession carries with it both a liberty and an urgency to question the prevailing notions of cultural belongingness and to recreate new ones. "If you have a sense of exile," Friel confesses, that brings with it "some kind of alertness and some kind of eagerness, some kind of hunger. If you are in possession you can become placid about things." [8]

The festering wound of the North is a constant reminder for Friel that the body politic of the Irish nation is deeply hemorrhaged. An amputated Ulster acts as a phantom limb haunting his work. Friel's residence is fundamentally dual, not only because he is an Irish dramatist working in the English language, but also because he is not fully at home either north or south of the Irish border. "You cannot deposit fealty to a situation like that of the North which you don't believe in," he declares. "Then you look south of the border and that enterprise is so distasteful in many respects. And yet both places are home in some way. It may be an inheritance from a political situation."[9] Friel's border mentality epitomizes the dual personality of the Catholic minority in the North. And this duality is undoubtedly accentuated by Friel's own formative memories of his childhood in

Glenties, the Donegal border town which was to serve as the setting for his language plays (under the pseudonym of Baile Beag).

But while the diagnosis is to a large extent political, the prognosis for Friel is of a cultural order. The division within the four political provinces of Ireland will only be overcome when *a fifth province* of the imagination has been created "to which cultural and artistic loyalty can be offered." [10] The creation of this fifth province calls for the creation of a new vocabulary, a new mode of communication which will acknowledge, and perhaps ultimately mediate between the sundered cultural identities of this island. A common sense of purpose, or at least the identification of a common problem, which is the *sine qua non* of any genuine community, may, he believes, be retrieved by discovering a common voice. The search for this common voice lies at the root of Friel's dramatic obsession with words. His language plays are not confined to semantic matters. It is not by ignoring the four political provinces that the fifth province is produced but by creatively reinterpreting the possibilities of their interrelationship.

> I think that the political problem of this island is going to be solved by language . . . Not only the language of negotiation across the table, but the recognition of what language means for us on this island. . . . Because we are in fact talking about the marrying of two cultures here, which are ostensibly speaking the same language but which in fact are not. [11]

By recognizing the inadequacy and indeed redundancy of the idioms and shibboleths that have satisfied and separated us up to now, Friel's plays open up possibilities of finding "a different voice" which might enable us to understand ourselves in a new way. This linguistic overhaul, he hopes, "should lead to cultural state, not a political one . . . out of that cultural state, the possibility of a political state follows." [12]

There is, however, yet a further dimension to Friel's dramatic obsession with language, a fourth dimension which grounds and underpins the other three— *aesthetic, political, cultural.* This fourth dimension might best be described as *ontological* for it concerns the very way in which language determines our innermost being-in-the-world. I employ this Heideggerean terminology advisedly, following Friel's own invocation of Heidegger's ontological definition of language in his prefatory program note to *Translations:* "Man acts as if he were the master of language, while it is language which remains mistress of man. When this relation of domination is inverted, man succumbs to strange contrivances." This citation is taken from an essay entitled, "Poetically Man Dwells," published in Heidegger's major philosophical work on language, *Poetry, Language, Thought.* [13] The passage from which Friel quotes proceeds as follows: "It is language that speaks. Man begins speaking and man only speaks to the extent that he responds to and hears language addressing him, concurring with him. Language is the highest and foremost of those assents which we human beings can never articulate solely out of our own means." Heidegger argues here that man can only have a genuine rapport with the Being of the world if he obediently listens to *(ob-audire)* language, abandoning his habitual tendency to master it by reducing words to his own willful contrivances. Man being-in-the-world becomes authentic when he ceases to abuse language as a strategic instrument for the manipulation of people and objects and responds to it instead as that which it truly is: the house of Being in which man may poetically dwell. Heidegger warns against the contemporary decadence of language evident in the prevailing habit of taking language for granted as a mere tool for conveying information and representing objects. This modern eclipse of the original vocation of language to reveal the deep mysteries of Being has provoked a crisis of human alienation of unprecedented proportions. A conversion in man's historical, political or cultural being can never occur, Heidegger insists, without a prior conversion in that innermost region of our existence which is nothing less than our ontological rapport with the very essence of language itself.

> It is because language is the house of Being, that we reach what is by constantly going through this house. When we go to the woods, we are already going through the word *woods*. When we go to the well, we are always already going through the word *well* . . . All beings are, qua beings, in the precinct of language. This is why the return from the realm of objects and representation into the innermost region of the heart's space can be accomplished, if anywhere, only in this precinct. [14]

Friel's trilogy of language plays—*Faith Healer, Translations* and *The Communication Cord*—constitute an impressively sustained attempt to bring about just such a conversion in our ontological attitude to language.

### FAITH HEALER

In *Faith Healer* Friel's exploration of the enigmatic labour *of* language focuses primarily on its *aesthetic* power to recreate reality in fiction. His choice of the dramatic medium—a faith healer's performances and incantations—as the subject of the play, reflects Friel's critical concern with the *modus operandi* of his own professional activity as a playwright. The word-player is holding a mirror up to himself, examining his own conscience as it were.

Friel does not shy away from these implications of the play. He freely concedes that *Faith Healer* is "some kind of metaphor for the art, the craft of writing . . . and the great confusion we all have about it who are involved in it. How honourable and dishonourable it can be."[15] Since writing is a pursuit that requires one to be introspective, it can lead to great selfishness. So that the natural impulse to pursue one's own creative talents is constantly invigilated by the "third eye" of self-consciousness. But this in turn, Friel admits, can be a dangerous thing "because in some way it perverts whatever natural freedom you might have, and that natural freedom must find its expression in the written word. So there's an exploration of that . . . element of the charlatan that exists in all creative work."[16]

In *Faith Healer* Friel's attitude to the creative word vacillates between the despondency of a sceptic and the ecstasy of a believer. The play teases out that subtle knot in which religious and aesthetic faith are intertwined. It is not so much a matter of rehearsing anthropological theories about the origins of drama in primitivistic ritual as a keen probing into that deep psychic need for marvel and miracle to which both religion and theatre have always responded in their distinctive ways. *Faith Healer* has a singularly perennial ring about it.

The play begins with Frank Hardy's incantation of an endless list of paltry towns and villages in which he has performed his art of healing: Aberarder, Aberayron etc. The names are reeled off like the litany of an ancient pilgrim mindlessly reciting his rosary beads of memory. The assonantal place-names are repeated, Frank tells us, for their purgative powers of "mesmerism and sedation." They serve now as "relics of abandoned rituals" in a secular age. Frank is the messianic highpriest of his own imagination, recruiting the lingering pictics of senescent rural communities where mundane despair is beginning to replace orthodox religious belief. He is a hybrid creature possessing both the compassion of a Christlike healer devoted to the infirm and the commercialism of a meretricious mountebank. He is an artist in straits, the evangelist of a message that has fallen into disrepute. Frank describes his own art of faithhealing accordingly as a "craft without an apprenticeship, a ministry without responsibility, a vocation without a ministry."

But while acknowledging that his art is obsolescent, Frank still clings to the conviction that it responds to an ineradicable need in himself and in his audience to be made "whole and perfect," to be released from what they are into what they might be. People still hunger for the fiction of a life transformed. And so the show goes on. One half of Frank knows that he is a con man of many masks, but the other remains faithful to the suspicion that he is endowed with a unique and awesome gift which possesses him and compels him to put it to the service of others. "Was it chance?—or skill?—or illusion?—a delusion?" he asks himself bemusedly. "Precisely what powers did I possess? Could I summon it? When and how? Was I its servant? Did it reside in my ability to invest someone with faith in me or did I evoke from him a healing faith in himself? . . . Faith in faith?" Put in the terms of Heideggerean ontology, Frank's equivocations amount to the fundamental question: Am I the manipulative master or the obedient servant of the healing word?

*Faith Healer* is a play in four acts which records this questioning crisis of faith as it is experienced by three characters—Frank the Irish miracle worker and his two English traveling companions, Grace his mistress and Teddy his stagemanager. All three deliver monologues in which they bear witness like modern day gospellers to the wanderings, homecoming and sacrifice of the Fantastic Frank Hardy.

Grace recounts how Frank performed his art "in such complete mastery that everything is harmonized for him . . . that anything is possible." Her "proud testament," as she significantly if half ironically terms it, pays particular reverence to his hypnotic play with words—"releasing them from his mouth in that special voice he used only then, as if blessing them or consecrating himself." But Grace's testament is also tinged with resentment. She is jealous of the way in which Frank's single-minded quest for artistic completion erased and obliterated her from his orbit of concern as he withdrew into the inner sanctum of his "private power." This memory of exclusion prevents Grace from invoking the litany of placenames with the same impersonal devotion as Frank. She halts at the name Kinlochbervie. In this tiny sequestered village in Scotland their still-born child—a tangible symptom of their diseased life—was brought into the world and buried. Though she may grant to Kinlochbervie its ritual fitness in the aesthetic scheme of things— "a nice name, a complete sound"—she cannot dispel the tragic reality which it connotes. This is where Grace's narration of the past parts company with Frank's. The gruesome memory of her child's death is retractory to the healing power of fiction. Frank's faith, by contrast, can only survive intact by erasing this memory from his mind.

The bitter intrusion of this memory causes Grace's faith to lapse. For a few brief moments she casts a cold eye on Frank's addiction to his own imaginative script. She recalls how Frank would humiliate her by constantly changing her name and rearranging the facts of her life (where she was born, how they met etc.) to suit his own scenario. His talent for healing others on stage was evenly matched by his "talent for hurting" her in life. He had chosen, in Yeats' phrase, perfection of the work over perfection of the life. Not content to fictionalize only the characters of his performance, Frank dragged all of his family and friends (father, mother, wife, child, Teddy) into the quarrel between himself and his art. Each person became grist for his metamorphosing mill.

Grace concedes this painful fact but she cannot wholly consent to it. Indeed, her account of her torturous wanderings with Frank gives us a good idea of how Pegeen Mike might have mused to herself had she left her homeland of Mayo and taken to the roads with her story-telling playboy:

> It wasn't that he was simply a liar—I never understood it—yes, I knew that he wanted to hurt me, but it was much more complex than that, it was some compulsion he had to adjust, to refashion, to recreate everything around him. Even the people who came to him . . . yes, they were real enough, but not real as persons, real as fictions, his fictions, extensions of himself that came into being only because of him. And if he cured a man, that man became for him a successful fiction and therefore actually real . . . But if he didn't cure him, the man was forgotten immediately, allowed to dissolve and vanish as if he had never existed.

Teddy is the third member of the performing trinity. He is described by Grace as a "dedicated acolyte to the holy man." But Teddy's apostolic posturings are tempered by his clowning humanity. The cockney comic in him keeps the religious votary in check; and if Teddy canonizes Frank it is not as a member of the ancient communion of saints but of the new communion of stage and screen idols which includes Fred Astaire, Lillie Langtry, Laurence Olivier, Houdini, Chaplin and Gracie Fields. Teddy is the odd man out, an Arnoldian enthusiast bemused by Frank's 'celtic temperament' and bewildered by his turbulent exchanges with Grace. As entrepreneurial mediator between Frank and his fictions, Teddy is determined to remain aloof and uninvolved, following his chosen thumbrule that friends is friends and work is work and never the twain shall meet. But Teddy's entire monologue belies his own rule and testifies to his incorrigible incapacity to separate his professional commitment to Frank and Grace from his personal commitment to them as real people. Life and art are as inextricable for Teddy as for Frank and Grace.

Friel deftly underscores the discrepancies between the three narrators' accounts of their shared past. The conflict of evidence is particularly obvious in their different versions of the death and burial of the still-born child. We see clearly how fiction is deployed by each character as an indispensable strategy of psychological self-survival. Friel's juxtaposition of the three diverging testimonials reveals how all three are caught up in their own fictive reenactment of the past, condemned to their own stage performance. The monologue format is ingeniously exploited by Friel as an exact correlative of their solitary confinement. They have ceased to communicate with each other; the confessional mode of private address has become the last resort of their language.

By means of this play-within-a-play technique, Friel reiterates one of the cardinal themes of modernist theatre developed by Pirandello, Genet, Sartre, Beckett and others: the performer can never be released from his performance and his very existence as a player of roles depends on both author and audience keeping faith with his fiction. Theatre is an *interpretative* art whose very interpretation involves mediation. The final poignant words of Grace's monologue are directed not solely to Frank but to Friel and the spectator as well—"O my God, I'm one of his fictions too, but I need him to sustain me in that existence." There is, as Sartre would say, *no exit . . . .*

*Faith Healer* terminates with Frank, in the last of the four monological testaments, deliberating on his first and final performance of the "miracle" in his native townland of Ballybeg in Donegal. Frank had intended his return from exile to be a glorious homecoming, the ultimate fulfillment of his promise—"a restoration . . . an integration, a full blossoming." Frank's valedictory speech is replete with mock-heroic allusions to the New Testament. He talks of those rare performances when he could have moved mountains; of how only one of the many that were cured came back to thank him; of Grace's father, the disbelieving Yorkshire judge, dismissing his faithhealing as chicanery; of the triumphal homecoming to Ballybeg; the miracle of the healed finger performed with the wedding party in the pub; and the Gethsemane reckoning in the yard, with Grace and Teddy asleep, when he prepared for his sacrifice, "both awed and elated . . . as if he were entering a church."

The apocalyptic overtones of Frank's portrayal of himself as an innocent lamb being led to the slaughter are unmistakable. As he walks towards his faithless executioners, a prophet unrecognized in his own country, Frank speaks of being possessed of a strange intimation "that the whole corporeal world—the cobbles, the trees, the sky, those four malign implements—somehow they had shed their physical reality and had become mere imaginings, and that in all existence there was only myself and the wedding guests." This intimation, he goes on, gave rise in turn to a still deeper sentiment that "even we had ceased to be physical and existed only in spirit, only in the need we had for each other. And as I moved across that yard towards them and offered myself to them, then for the first time I had a simple and genuine sense of homecoming . . . and the maddening questions were silent."

This passage is a veritable tour *de force,* the pathos it evokes extending into the deepest reaches of symbolic association. Apart from its manifest biblical connotations, the passage also sends reverberations rippling through the Irish literary subconscious. One thinks of Yeats' enigmatic lines in the *Second Coming* or in *Ben Bulben* when he invokes the transfiguring potency of apocalyptic violence:

Know that when all words are said
And a man is fighting mad,
Something drops from eyes long blind,
He completes his partial mind,
For an instant stands at ease,
Laughs aloud, his heart at peace.
Even the wisest man grows tense
With some sort of violence
Before he can accomplish fate . . . .

One is also reminded of the "terrible beauty" symbolism of the Irish nationalist ideology of martyrdom and blood-sacrifice (e.g. Pearse's appeal to bloodshed as a "cleansing and sanctifying thing"). Viewed in this perspective, the complex relationship of conflict and complicity between Frank, Grace and Teddy might even be construed as a veiled allegory of Anglo-Irish relations.

Friel's casting of Frank as a hapless *Salvator mundi* retains, however, its primary function as a metaphor for the self-destructive impulses of the creative artist overobsessed with his own art. The story-teller who sacrifices life to fiction, Friel concludes, risks becoming the victim of his own perilous script, the dummy of his own ventriloquism. Placed in the context of the Irish dramatic tradition, *Faith Healer* may be read accordingly as a cautionary tale in response to the romantic optimism of the *Playboy*. For if the belief in the power of a lie made Christy into a likely gaffer in the end of all, it makes Frank into a mutilated corpse.

And yet one cannot escape the feeling that Friel's verdict on his own aesthetic profession as playwright is somewhat equivocal. A tentative plea of not guilty is lodged somewhere between the final lines. We are left with a sneaking admiration for these possessed players prepared, quite literally, to lay down their lives for their faith. Nor are we allowed to easily forget that if nine times out of ten, Frank failed to perform the miracle, one time in ten he *did* succeed in making the crippled whole and the faithless faithful. In these exceptional moments of dramatic magic, the healing touch worked. It is not as Beckett's Didi commented of the two crucified thieves in *Godot* (one of whom was saved)—"a reasonable percentage." But it is a percentage nonetheless. And one sufficient to sustain Friel's act of faith in his own writing and the audience's response of faith in the transforming power of his dramatic lie.

## TRANSLATIONS

With *Translations* Friel's exploration of language play takes a new turn. He moves beyond the critical examination of his own aesthetic conjuring with words to the broader question of the socio-cultural role of language in the historical evolution of a community.

*Translations* begins where *Faith Healer* ends—in the Donegal town of Ballybeg. Only now it goes by its original Gaelic name of Baile Beag. Friel has wound the clock back a century, recreating the life and circumstances of this small Donegal community as it faced into the social and linguistic upheaval provoked by the Great Famine of the 1840's. The year is 1833 and the old Gaelic language and culture are enjoying their last lease on life. The play relates the fortunes of a hedge school master, Hugh—Frank Hardy's spiritual and tribal ancestor—and his motley crew of scholarly disciples: the sixty-year-old "infant prodigy," Jimmy Jack, fluent in Latin and Greek; Hugh's son and assistant, Manus; and the quasi-illiterate peasant pupils, Sarah, Máire and Doalty. The hedge school fosters an harmonious compound of Gaelic and Classical cultures. "Our own culture and the classical tongue," boasts Hugh, "make a happy conjugation." Athena and Grainne, Apollo and Cuchulainn rub shoulders here with unpretentious ease. The poetic imagination still reigns supreme, roaming from Baile Beag to Athens and Rome in the breath span of a single verse.

But this cultural sanctuary is abruptly threatened by the arrival of a detachment of Royal Engineers from the British Army sent to make an Ordnance Survey map of the local landscape. This military mission is disguised as a benign exercise in geographical linguistics, its ostensible purpose being the transcription of Gaelic placenames into their English equivalents. Friel's play documents the nefarious consequences which this seemingly innocuous administrative project has upon the indigenous community. Special attention is given to the decisive role in this cultural genocide played by Owen, the school master's second son. Recently returned from the anglicized capital, Dublin, Owen enlists in the Survey project as translator and mediator between the two opposing languages, only to find himself spiritually spread-eagled in the collision of cultural loyalties.

The play opens with two crippled beings struggling towards communication: Manus, the master's lame and loyal son, is trying to teach a local dumb girl, Sarah, to speak. After much encouragement, she succeeds in repeating the sentence—"my - name - is - Sarah." Manus hails this miraculous act of speech as the unlocking of a hitherto hidden landscape of consciousness. "Marvellous", he expostulates, "soon you'll be telling me all the secrets that have been in that head of yours all these years." While Manus is shepherding Sarah into speech, Jimmy Jack is reciting, chorus-like, the Greek legend of the goddess Athene magically touching and transforming Ulysses with her wand. Friel provides us here with an Hellenic tale of faith-healing which subtly counterpoints the reciprocal act of communication whereby Manus and Sarah cure each other of the paralysis of solitude which their respective forms of crippledom embodied. Jimmy's facility with languages is a token of his attunement to the original harmony between word and world—what the Greek philosophers called the *harmonia* of the *Logos*. We are told that for him the world of the gods and ancient myth is "as real and as immediate as everyday life in the townland of Baile Beag." Jimmy represents that declining old order where man still felt at one with the divine (he talks of gods and goddesses "as if they lived down the road" ) and where language was still a cohesive rather than a divisive force in the community. For Jimmy speech equals communication equals community.

The other characters in the opening act of the play are also defined in terms of their attitude to language. The first we hear of the master, Hugh, is that he is off at a christening, helping to choose a name for a baby. The choice of name is impatiently awaited by the community as a means of deciding the dubious identity of the child's father! Hugh is thus casually introduced as a minister of names, and by extension, a transmitter, guarantor and guardian of the community's cultural identity. Moreover, by professionally imparting to his students the scholarly art of translating Gaelic words into Latin and Greek, Hugh permits the community to communicate with cultures other than its own. It is of course significant that the classical tongues cultivated by the master represent *past* civilizations, now dead and gone. A hint of what is in store for his own Gaelic tongue and civilization, Hugh's vision is sighted on a vanished and vanishing kingdom. He is an inquisitor of origins and etymologies who speaks in the past tense. He is backward looking for the simple reason that the future holds no hope for his language.

When Hugh finally arrives on stage, he proudly announces the identity of the child disclosed at the "ritual of naming"—or *caerimonia nominationis* as he hastens to add. He then proceeds to quiz his pupils on the Greek and Latin etymologies of the word baptize— *baptizein,* to dip; *baptisterium,* a bath etc. When his pupils apprise him of the departure of one of his students from the school, he extends the importance of the naming motif with the humorous quip: "Nora Dan can now write her name—Nora Dan's education is complete!"

But Nora Dan may well be one of the last graduates of Hugh's hedge school education. English—the new colonial language of commerce and maps—is already making deep incursions into the old system of learning. Several of the young peasants greet the arrival of this new tongue as holding out the promise of a new beginning. Máire is one such peasant pupil seduced by the allure of English words. She only knows three snatches which an aunt has taught her to recite by rote. Though still not having an idea what the words actually mean, she is prepare nonetheless to trade in her limited knowledge of the classics for more of the same: "I don't want Greek. I don't want Latin . . . Fit me better if I had that much

English." Máire belongs to the emerging generation of aspiring peasants tired of treading the timeless mudtracks of oppressed Gaeldom. She dreams of finer things to come, approvingly citing the opinion of Dan O'Connell, the "Liberator," that the sooner "we all learn to speak English the better . . . The old language is a barrier to progress."

Máire has secured passage money to the New World and knows full well that the only *useful* language for her now is English. She sits on the hedge school floor excitedly scanning the map of America for the English placenames of her future abode. But the lens of her youthful fascination soon focuses on a more literal map nearer to home. The British soldiers "making the maps" for the Ordnance Survey in the neighbouring fields have not escaped her attention. Máire's unsuspecting enthusiasm for the arrival of the Royal Engineers is, however, offset by two discreet allusions to the threat which their colonial culture represents to the native Gaelic-speaking community. First, we are casually informed that the hedge school is to be replaced by a progressive National school where every subject will be taught through English. And second, we learn of the imminent danger of a potato blight—"just beyond where the soldiers are making the maps—the sweet smell was everywhere."

The next character to make an appearance at the hedge school is the master's second son, Owen. He is something indeed of a prodigal son returning from his travels with a reputation of great business successes (Máire claims she heard stories that he owned "ten big shops in Dublin"). Owen is accompanied by two English officers—Captain Lancey and Lieutenant Yolland—in whose employ he is presently engaged as a "translator."

(Hugh has already prepared us for the arrival of the English speakers. Having met with Captain Lancey on his return from the baptism, Hugh had pointed out to the Royal Engineer that his alien tongue "couldn't really express us" and was only employed in the community on rare occasions for "purposes of commerce," a use, Hugh comments with ocular disrespect, to which the English language "seemed particularly suited." Hugh mischievously informs the officers that his people are not familiar with their literature, feeling "closer to the warm Mediterranean. We tend to overlook your island.")

Owen arrives first at the school—like an Indian scout preparing the way for the ensuing cavalry. He greets his father, brother and the local pupils with genuine affection and camaraderie. It is after all his first homecoming to Baile Beag. And it is no less festive than that of Frank Hardy a century later. Owen immediately enters his father's game of translating Irish into Latin and vice versa, thus reminding his people that he is still one of their own, still familiar with the rules of their language play. Owen is a master of what Kavanagh called "the wink and elbow language of delight." There follows a particularly poignant exchange between Owen and Sarah. Echoing the earlier act of communication between his brother and the dumb girl, Owen asks her name. When she falteringly replies that it is Sarah Johnny Sally, he spontaneously adds: "Of course! From Bun na hAbhann! I'm Owen Hugh Mor from Baile Beag." Owen thus subscribes to the password of the tribe, uttering once again that communal dialect which identifies its members at birth according to their native origins—the name of their parents and local birthplace.

Owen does not try to hide the fact that he is on the pay roll of the Ordnance Survey expedition. On the contrary, he announces his brief as civilian interpreter with good-humored candour: "My job is to translate the quaint, archaic tongue you people persist in speaking into the King's good English." Owen then introduces the two officers who have been waiting in attendance. Captain Lancey is a hardnosed military expert with little or no culture. He mistakes Jimmy's Latin for Gaelic and is only interested in language in so far as it may prove a useful instrument in the colonial conquest of a landscape by means of a mechanistic mapping system. Lancey's attitude perfectly epitomizes the British Empiricist philosophy of language as a crude reductionism of things to signs. "A map is a representation on paper," he explains, subverting Hugh's pedagogical role. "His Majesty's Government has ordered the first ever comprehensive survey of this entire country—a general triangulation which will embrace detailed hydrographic and topographic information and which will be executed to a scale of six inches to the English mile." Nor does Lancey leave us in any doubt that this apparently inoffensive task of cartographical translation involves an ulterior purpose—the colonial and commercial exploitation of the native community as a whole. "This enormous task," he blandly reveals, "has been embarked on so that the military authorities will be equipped with up-to-date and accurate information on every corner of this part of the Empire . . . and also so that the entire basis of land valuation can be reassessed for reasons of more equitable taxation." Lancey betrays himself to be a patronizing hypocrite, however, when he presents the entire exercise as a token of British altruism, undertaken to "advance the interests of Ireland." The Irish people are privileged, he ironically affirms, since no such survey will be undertaken in England! In short, Lancey's formal address exposes the devious uses to which his language is being put as an imperial ploy to patronize, deceive and conquer.

But Friel's depiction of the adversary resists the temptation to crude caricature. If Lancey is cast as a disingenuous and cheerless servant of the Crown, his subordinate officer, Yolland, impresses immediately as a sensitive and romantic youth. Yolland is a "soldier by accident" whose birthplace was, significantly, only four miles away from that of William Wordsworth—a reliable signal, as it transpires, of his own spiritual identity. He takes his note from the temper of his native environment across the waters: an imaginative disposition which enables him to empathize with this strange Gaelic culture into which he has been dispatched. Yolland is a self-proclaimed hibernophile enamoured of the local people and modestly perturbed by his inability to understand their language. Struggling for words, in a manner reminiscent of Sarah's stammering towards speech, Yolland's opening address is in stark contrast to that of his military superior: "I - I - I've nothing to say really . . . I feel very foolish to - to - to be working here and not to speak your language . . . . I hope we're not too - too crude an intrusion on your lives."

In all this, Owen plays a double language-game, commuting with apparent ease between the two parties. But the ease is no more than apparent. In reality, Owen's linguistic duality entails a fundamental duplicity. He mistranslates Lancey's message, winnowing off its mercenary implications in order to make it more palatable for the locals. Yet at the same time Owen is sufficiently circumspect to withhold his real name (and by extension, *identity)* from the English officers, operating under the pseudonym of Rolland. Owen is both a mistranslator and a misnomer, double-timing as it were in his efforts to keep in with both sides of the colonial schism. In response to his brother's objection that there is nothing incorrect about the existing Gaelic placenames, he declares—"They're just going to be standardized . . . where there's ambiguity, they'll be anglicized." Owen's description of this linguistic transposition is in fact a self-description, accurately foreshadowing his own fate. Friel touches here, with characteristic and unpretentious irony, on the crisis of cultural ambiguity which so indelibly hallmarks the modern Irish Psyche.

***********

In the second act of the play, Friel provides us with two dramatic instances of personal and cultural translation. The first is a translation of labour (between Owen and Yolland); the second a translation of love (between Yolland and Máire).

The act opens with Yolland and Owen, bent over a Name Book and large map, embarked upon their task of transliterating the Gaelic toponymy of Baile Beag into an English alternative. The translation of names also involves a translation of namers; the roles of colonizer and colonized are reversed, as Yolland and Owen undergo an exchange of identity.

While Owen is patently engrossed by the mapping process, Yolland is lost in a world of dreams, savouring each Gaelic word upon his tongue, reluctant to "traduce" it into its Anglo-Saxon equivalent. So that when Owen offers the practical suggestion of rendering *Bun na hAbhann* (in Irish, mouth of the river) as

*Burnfoot*, Yolland's reaction is one of protective deference towards the original: "Let's leave it alone. There's no English equivalent for a sound like that." But it is not just the sound that is at stake. It is the stored heritage of local history which each Gaelic name recollects and *secretes*. The translation of these placenames closes off rather than discloses their mnemonic secrets, distorts rather than restores their original identity.

Yolland describes his first encounter with the Gaelic language as a quasi-mystical revelation. The language divide is experienced by him as a threshold demarcating fundamentally heterogeneous modes of consciousness. He speaks of discovering a new continent of feeling, belonging to "a totally different order. I had moved into a consciousness that wasn't striving nor agitated, but at its ease and with its own conviction and assurance."

But the threshold is also a frontier. It cannot be crossed with impunity, as Yolland will discover to his cost. Already he has intimations of the ultimately impenetrable barrier of words which no translation, however well-intentioned, can traverse. "Even if I did speak Irish," concedes Yolland, "I'd always be an outsider here, wouldn't I? I may learn the password but the language of the tribe will always elude me, won't it? The private core will always be . . . hermetic, won't it?" Owen's reassuring rejoinder—"you can learn to decode us"—has an ominous ring, its scarcely veiled sarcasm reflecting his private complicity with his own native tribe. In short, the commercial collusion between Planter and Gael cannot be quarantined against the cultural-linguistic conflict which opposes them.

If language unites people by permitting communication, it divides them by cultivating the possibility of separate cultural and tribal identities. This paradox is a heritage of the *felix culpa* of our first parents: their fall from the Edenesque *Logos* which enabled God and man to speak with one voice. And this original sin of language—the sin of speaking in a multiplicity of conflicting tongues—finds its ultimate nemesis in the subsequent biblical account of the Tower of Babel. In his study, *After Babel*, George Steiner writes of the literary history of translation as a series of attempts to build bridges between the disparate tongues of our fallen humanity. Friel has been deeply impressed by Steiner's disquisition and succeeds in *Translations* in dramatically extrapolating some of its scholarly insights. In an appendix to this essay, I have provided a short inventory of several key passages from *After Babel* which Friel has reworked in his own original idioms. What bears interest in this creative partnership of minds—itself a felicitous translation or exchange between English and Irish cultures—is the way in which Friel brilliantly contrives to refashion Steiner's academic research in the form of a drama concretely situated in his native cultural and historical context. Friel's play serves in this respect as a fine example of how literary theory may be reclaimed as literature, of how criticism may be retranslated into imaginative practice.

Yolland cannot help recognizing that the whole business of toponymic translation constitutes an "eviction of sorts," an "erosion" of the traditional Gaelic pieties in the name of Imperial Progress. But Yolland's disapproval of colonial conquest is counterbalanced by his naive and positivistic belief that there might exist an ideal system of translation where the atavistic obstacles thrown up by tribal dialects could be transcended. Yolland is hankering after a prelapsarian naming process, similar to that of Adam when he named the animals, capable of achieving an exact correspondence between word and thing. When Owen finally confesses to Yolland that his real name is not *Rolland* but *Owen* or better still *Oland*—by way of a perfect compromise or synthesis between the nominal differences of Irish (Owen) and English (Yolland)—they celebrate their newfound confraternity of naming as follows:

> *Owen:* A christening! . . .
> *Yolland:* A thousand baptisms! Welcome to Eden!
> *Owen:* Eden's right! we name a thing and—bang!—it leaps into existence!
> *Yolland:* Each name a perfect equation with its roots.
> *Owen:* A perfect congruence with its reality. Take a drink.
> *Yolland:* Poteen—beautiful.
> *Owen:* Lying Anna's poteen.
> *Yolland:* Anna na mBreag's poteen . . . I'll decode it yet.

Once again, Friel reminds us that the magical equation of word and world is achieved by the power of a lie! The fact that Owen and Yolland consecrate their new transliteral unit (as *Oland*) with Anna's illusionist brew is itself a hint of the disillusioning reality to follow.

Friel juxtaposes this "translation of labour" sequence between Owen and Yolland with a scene featuring a "translation of love" between Yolland and Máire. In this second exchange Friel highlights the tragic impossibility of ever attaining an ideal system of language capable of decoding semantic differences into some common, transcultural identity. Yolland and Máire meet at the local dance. Ever since Yolland arrived in the village they have been admiring each other from a distance. Now at last together they try to transcend this distance, stealing away to the fields so that they might communicate their mutual love. But if their love is mutual their dialect is not. Máire begins by speaking Latin which Yolland mistakes for Gaelic. Then she stammers forth the only three English words in her possession—water, fire, earth. But even though Yolland congratulates Máire on her "perfect English," his lie of encouragement cannot alter the fact that they continually misunderstand each other's words. Finally they do appear to reach some level of communication by lovingly reciting to each other the litany of Gaelic placenames. The irony is of course that this common source of semantic agreement is precisely the issue which so tragically divides their respective tribes. Their commonly uttered words still consign them to separate worlds as Friel himself indicates in a textual note: "Each now speaks almost to himself/herself." (One recalls Frank's and Grace's equally discrepant invocation of placenames in *Faith Healer*). As each name is intoned by one lover and antiphonally echoed by the other, they move closer together and embrace. This climactic touch serves as a sort of dramatic leitmotif reiterating once again the opening exchange between Manus and Sarah. The order is reversed, however, in so far as speech now becomes touch whereas in the former scene touch had become speech.

When Yolland and Máire finally kiss, their epiphany of loving silence is no more than a provisional reprieve from the sentence of language. At that very moment Sarah enters. Shocked by what she witnesses she rushes off calling out the name of Máire's suitor—"Manus!" Thus in a cruel twist of dramatic irony, Sarah's initial transition from silence to speech—her initiation into the naming process in the opening love scene between herself and Manus—becomes the condition for the betrayal of love.

According to the local code of the community, Máire has been promised to Manus and this tacit tribal contract cannot be gainsaid or "decoded" by an outsider—even in an act of love. As Jimmy Jack explains in his final speech, enunciating his own fictitious betrothal to the Goddess Athene, "The word *exogamein* means to marry outside the tribe. And you don't cross those borders casually—both sides get very angry. Now, the problem is this: Is Athene sufficiently mortal or am I sufficiently godlike for the marriage to be acceptable to her people and to my people?" Whatever is done about transgressing the mythological boundaries between the human and the divine, the real boundaries between one human code and another cannot be ignored with impunity. Yolland is assassinated by the Donnelly twins—renegade pupils from the hedge school; and Captain Lancey promises retribution and revenge on the whole community—he orders their livestock to be slaughtered and their abodes leveled.

Friel's irony excels itself at this point: Lancey's threat to destroy the very locality which his own Ordnance Survey was proposing to civilize and advance, renders the whole "translation" process null and void. Nominal eviction has been replaced by its literal equivalent. This reversal of plot also extends to a reversal of character. Summoned before a local gathering, Owen is now compelled to give a literal translation of Lancey's bellicose and punitive intentions, his compromising role as go-between now made embarrassingly plain. For the dubious benefit of his own tribe, Owen is forced to *retranslate* Lancey's English rendition of the names of the local villages to be destroyed back into their Gaelic originals. Owen's own labour of words has backfired; he is hoisted with his own petard.

Máire also becomes a victim of this reverse play of language. Exposed in the abrupt polarization of the two rival tribes, she can no longer feel at home in her own community and yet has no other home to go to now that Yolland is dead. Employing again his dramatic technique of inverse repetition or leitmotif, Friel reinvokes the idiom of mapping to emphasize Máire's dilemma. Tracing out an imaginary map on that very spot on the hedge school floor where Owen's Ordnance Survey map had been spread, she lists off the placenames of Yolland's native Norfolk which he had taught her to recite during their love-duet the previous night—Winfarthing, Barton, Bendish, Saxingham etc. "Nice sounds," she muses, as Yolland had done before her with reference to Gaelic names, "just like Jimmy Jack reciting Homer." But there is a fundamental difference between the recitation of Jimmy Jack and that of Máire and Yolland. Since the Greeks had no historic quarrel with the Gaels their two tongues could peaceably conjugate in a way that English and Gaelic cannot. In one particularly striking moment, Máire recalls that Yolland's parting message to her was in fact a mistranslation: "He tried to speak in Irish, he said—'I'll see you yesterday'—he meant to say, 'I'll see you tomorrow'." This mistranslation is a poignant symptom of the tragic historical fact that in the colonial conflict between England and Ireland the time was out of joint. Or to put it in another way, linguistic discrepancies are the inevitable consequence of historical ones.

These reversals of *plot, persona,* and *time,* are reinforced by a more generalized reversal of *perception.* The radical disarticulation of language brought about by the various abortive attempts at translation, also expresses itself at the basic level of the characters' distorted perception of the world about them. The last scene of the play is littered with mistaken identities, and misidentifications, on a par with the most convoluted comedies of Wilde or Shakespeare. Manus, who flees to Mayo, is mistaken for the assassins (the Donnellys); the fumes from the burning army tents are mistaken for the sweet smell of potato blight; Doalty is mistaken for the arsonist; a bacon-curing schoolmaster from Cork is mistaken for the village schoolmaster, Hugh—the National school replacing the old hedge school; and the anglicized Owen is mistaken for (again in the sense of taking over from) his inveterately Gaelic brother, Manus, as faithful son to their father, Hugh.

All these instances of misplacement and displacement serve to consolidate Friel's central message about the mis-taken substitution of Irish by English. But Friel, like Hugh, recognizes that this mistake is an irreversible, if regrettable, inevitability of history. "We like to think we endure around truths immemorially posited," Hugh explains with rueful wisdom, "but we remember that words are signals, counters. They are not immortal. And it can happen . . . that a civilization can be imprisoned in a linguistic contour which no longer matches the landscape of . . . fact." The rich mytho-poeic resources of the Gaelic language, Hugh stoically adds, were themselves a response to the painful historical circumstances which conditioned its development: "Yes, it is a rich language . . . full of mythologies of fantasy and hope and self-deception—a syntax opulent with tomorrows. It is our response to mud cabins and a diet of potatoes; our only method of replying to . . . inevitabilities." Thus in sober acknowledgment that what is done cannot be undone, Hugh determines to make a virtue of necessity by creatively refashioning the English language so as to make sense of the new landscape of historical fact. At one point Owen tries to revoke the repercussions of translation, dismissing the whole sorry business as "my mistake—nothing to do with us." But Hugh has had enough of self-deception. Pointing to the Name Book, he counsels his community to reclaim in and through the English language that which has been lost to it. "We must learn those new names," he soberly challenges, "we must learn to make them our own, we must make them our new home."

***********

If history has deprived the Irish of their native tongue, this will not prevent them from recreating their identity in a new tongue. Speaking in his capacity as poet, Hugh bequeaths to his community a legacy of challenge, the challenge of an Irish literature written in English, the challenge to persist in an *aesthetic* reconquest of that cultural self-image brutally vanquished by the *empirical* fact of colonization. We the audience recognize of course that the entire modern tradition of Irish writers of English—extending from Synge, Yeats and Joyce to Friel himself—has arisen as a response to just this challenge. We know that for the Irish writer this is his *heritage now.* The historical fatality of linguistic dispossession has not condemned the Irish imagination to dumb show. Our best writers have masterfully succeeded in reworking their adopted language so as to reflect upon and renew the original images of their cultural past. Indeed *Translations* is itself a paramount example of this very success. Hugh outlines a blueprint for this poetic retrieval of lost ground when he appeals for an authentic discrimination between the separate laws of history and imagination, or if you wish between the laws of empirical necessity and cultural freedom. "It is not," he insists, "the *facts* of history, that shape us, but *images* of the past embodied in language . . . We must never cease renewing those images; because once we do, we fossilise." Jimmy Jack, the otherworldly poet of the old order, has fossilized precisely because he was unable "to make that discrimination." The poets of the new order cannot afford the luxury of such indifference.

But Hugh's lesson in aesthetics also serves as a history lesson. Friel would seem to be cautioning us against the temptation of becoming political prisoners to historical fact. "To remember everything is a form of madness," Hugh warns, implying a preference for a more discerning use of memory capable of discriminating between the past that liquidates by spawning a narrow obsession with revenge, and the past which liberates into new possibilities of self-recollection. Recalling the rebel Uprising of 1798 when himself and Jimmy went forth to battle with pikes in their hands and Virgil in their pockets, Hugh humourously confesses that after several miles of marching they got drunk in a pub before staggering unheroically home. Hugh admits to the feeling of "perception heightened . . . and consciousness accelerated" which the prospect of violence induced in them. But in a precise inversion of Frank's apocalyptic vision at the end of *Faith Healer,* Friel shows Hugh opting for an alternative version of home-coming, an option for a more domestic and poetic form of self-survival. "Our *pietas* was for older quieter things," Hugh recounts, "the *desiderium nostrorum*—the need for our own." If Frank condones the capitulation of words to violence, Hugh averts violence in the name of the recreative and recollective powers of words.

To rephrase this alternative in terms of a Yeatsian parallel, we would say that while *Faith Healer* mirrored the apocalyptic tones of *Ben Bulben, Translations* moves closer to the ancestral solace of *A Dialogue of Self and Soul:*

> Why should the imagination of a man
> Long past his prime remember things that are
> Emblematical of love and war?
> Think of ancestral night that can . . .
> Deliver from the crime of death and birth.

A cultural fidelity to the images of the past, Friel seems to suggest, is not necessarily reducible to the facts of history. There may be other more complicated ways of recovering what has been lost and settling one's score with history. One of these ways is the poetic possibility of forging a new language of our own, or recreating a new home where the secrets of the old heritage may be restored. Any attempt at such a cultural translation and transition is, of course, freighted with risk and danger: the risk of losing everything, the danger of self-annihilation. But given the ominous alternatives, it may be a risk worth taking. Perhaps this is why Hugh agrees at the end of the play to teach Máire English. He frankly concedes the necessity for change, telling Máire that the word "always" is a silly one. But Hugh will not, and cannot, guarantee that her acquisition of the art of translation will permit her to transport the secret heritage of the old culture into the new one. His parting verdict on translation promises neither too little nor too much. "I will

provide you with the available words and the available grammar," he assures
Máire, "But will that help you to interpret between privacies? I have no idea."

## THE CONFLICT OF LANGUAGE MODELS
## (ONTOLOGY VERSUS POSITIVISM)

Friel's work operates with two basic linguistic models—one ontological, the
other positivistic. The former treats language as a house of Being; the latter treats it
as a mechanical apparatus for the representation of objects.

As we had occasion to remark above, Friel's ontological approach to language
is, philosophically speaking, akin to that of Heidegger. Here language is celebrated
as a way to truth in the Greek sense of the term, *A-letheia*, meaning un-
forgetfulness, un-concealing, dis-closure. Language tells us the truth by virtue of its
capacity to unlock the secret privacies of our historical Being (the "interiority of
the heart's space"). In *Translations* Friel identifies this ontological vocation of the
Word with the Gaelic and Classical languages. It manifests itself in the local
community's use of naming to release the secrets of their psychic and historical
landscape or in Hugh's excavations of Latin and Greek etymologies. Friel's play
illustrates Heidegger's claim that language is the house of Being not only in so far
as it permits us to dwell poetically in our world but also in that it grants us the
power to recollect our past, to divine our forgotten origins. (It is perhaps not
insignificant that Friel's collection of stories published just two years after
*Translations* is called *The Diviner*). Language houses Being by recalling things out
of their past oblivion, thus attuning us once again with our lost identities, enabling
us to re-member *(an-denken)* our alienated, dismembered selves. Poetic words are
not, Heidegger teaches us, as also does Hugh, "copies and imitations," they are
"imaginings that are visible inclusions of the alien in the sight of the familiar."[7]

Friel opposes this *ontological* model of language to the *positivist* use of words
as agents of pragmatic progress. This alternative positivist model is perhaps most
closely associated with the philosophy of British Empiricism, which served in
recent centuries as the ideological mainstay of British colonialism; though it has
found a more contemporary ally in the scientific structuralism of Levi-Strauss and
others. Positivism maintains that words are mechanically given *(positum)*—no
more than objects in a world of similar objects. They are eminently unmysterious
entities to be used as instruments for the representation, mapping or classification
of reality. And the reductionist goal of positivism is to produce an exact decoding
of the world by establishing a one-to-one correlation between *words* and the *facts*
of empirical experience. Language is thus reduced to a utilitarian weapon for the
colonization of Being. It murders to dissect.

John Locke was one of the most notable proponents of British Empiricism.

He believed that only such a philosophy of perception and language could prevent our thoughts from straying "into the vast ocean of being" and thereby remove the metaphysical "rubbish from the way of knowledge." A keen defender of the right of proprietors—which he saw as an inalienable right of man and an essential prerogative of any gentleman's son—Locke construed language according to an equally proprietal epistemology. He promoted the ideal of a perfectly transparent language resulting from the accurate mapping of words onto empirical sensations. The domestication of reality by means of this rigid conformity of words to sensory objects would lead, he believed, to a rigorously scientific knowledge. Naturally there was to be no quarter given to poetic or ontological language in this scheme of things. And in *Thoughts Concerning Education,* Locke advises parents who were unfortunate enough to have children born with a poetic propensity, to "labour to have it stifled and suppressed as much as may be." This empiricist view of language is caricatured by Friel in *Translations* as the reduction of a living, ontological landscape to the proprietal proportions of a six-inch map. The following comment from Lord Salisbury which Friel places alongside his quotation from Heidegger in the prefatory notes to the play, clearly reveals the author's satiric intentions: "The most disagreeable part of the three kingdoms is Ireland; and therefore Ireland has a splendid map." Once exposed to the linguistic lens of empiricism, the landscape ceases to *be* and becomes merely *useful*; language as *evocation* is replaced by language as *information*.[18]

Another positivist model of language to have gained widespread currency in recent years is linguistic structuralism. The two most influential exponents of this model are Ferdinand de Saussure and Claude Levi-Strauss. The structuralists may be classed as "positivistic" to the extent that they attempt to reduce language to a mechanistic system of formal substitutions, to a skeletal logistics of signs. "Language is a *form* not a *substance*," ran Saussure's celebrated maxim. And it was on the basis of this maxim that structuralist linguists could argue that the entire complex of language be considered as an impersonal system of coded relations between its constituent units (semantic or phonetic) with no ontological rapport whatsoever with nature, history or the human subject. Words are thus treated as neutral or objectified units of exchange in an abstract network of coded messages. The ontological question of the *authenticity* of language as a disclosure of personal or historical meaning no longer arises. The flesh of *subjectivity*—the "interiority of the heart's space"—has been stripped away to leave the clean, bare bones of *structure*.

Levi-Strauss' original contribution to structuralism lay in his equation of the codes of the language system (as an exchange of structural units) with the codes of kinship systems (as an exogamous exchange of women—or by extension, other consumer commodities—between different tribes). This primitive model of kinship as a mechanism of utilitarian and commercial substitution is, Levi-Strauss believes, the determining structure of all languages. In a passage remarkably apposite for a reading of Friel's language plays, Levi-Strauss claims that we should regard

> marriage regulations and kinship systems as a kind of language, a set of processes permitting the establishment, between individuals and groups, of a certain type of communication. That the mediating factor, in this case, should be the *women* of the group, who are circulated between classes, lineages, or families, in place of the words of the group, which are circulated between individuals, does not at all change the fact that the essential aspect of the phenomenon is identical in both cases" (*Structuralist Anthropology*). [19]

This structuralist model of language bears particular relevance to Friel's third language play, *The Communication Cord.*

### THE COMMUNICATION CORD

*The Communication Cord* is in many respects the logical sequel to *Translations*. Friel has made quite plain his wish that the two plays be considered "in tandem," [20] as consecutive forays into the whole complex of our language culture.

If *Translations* set out to chart the transition of a language from its ontological past to its positivist present, *The Communication Cord* operates in reverse order: it portrays the attempt to retrace language from its contemporary orphanage and uprootedness back to its pristine ancestry. Both plays conspire to present us with a fascinating genealogy of the process of human speech, the ways in which we use words to progress or regress in history, to find or lose ourselves, to confute or to communicate. The fact that the former play is composed in *tragic* tones, while the latter is written as a *farce*, is in itself an indicator of Friel's tragicomic realization that there is no going back on history; that the best that can be achieved is a playful deconstruction and reconstruction of words in the hope that new modes of communication might be made possible.

Both plays situate the conflict of language models—ontological and positivistic—in the specific context of Irish culture. *Translations* deals with prefamine Ireland bracing itself for the final transplantation of Gaelic into English. *The Communication Cord* takes up the story more than a century later. It shows us modern Ireland taking stock of its linguistic identity and attempting to recover the ancient pieties of its prefamine heritage. While one play features the old language looking forward to its ominous future, the other features the new language looking back to its dispossessed origins. Or to use a photographic analogy, the negative plate outlined in the first play is graphically developed and exposed in the second.

The scene of the action in *The Communication Cord*—a "'restored'" thatched cottage in Ballybeg—is simply an inverted replica of the "'condemned'" school house of Baile Beag. In similar fashion, Tim Callaher, the central character of the play—a university lecturer in linguistics preparing a Ph.D. on communication—serves as an inverted mirror-image of his ancestral prototype, Hugh. Both are displaced scholars without tenure; both teach that the transmission of communal wisdom cannot be divorced from the ontological power of language. In fact, Tim's thesis is attempting to prove what was still self-evident for Hugh: that words which function as positivistic units or linguistic maps, based on agreed codes, are, at root, derived and often distorted forms of ontological "response cries." To put it in Heidegger's terms, Tim is resolved to return from the language of objects and representation (Owen's modern legacy) to the ultimate origin of words in the interiority of the heart's space (Hugh's lost legacy).

The distinctively ersatz character of the restored cottage betokens the futility of any literal quest for the lost grail of our cultural past. Adorned with the antiquarian accoutrements of churn, creel, crook, hanging pot, thatched roof and open hearth, the cottage is described by Friel in a stage note as "false . . . too pat . . . *too* authentic." It is, in short, an artificial reproduction, a holiday home of today counterfeiting the real home of yesterday.

This play about communication begins, significantly, with a failure of communication. Tim is saying that the door to the cottage is open, while Jack McNeilis, his friend, misunderstands him to say that it is locked. From the outset their language is at cross purposes. If Owen was Manus's alter ego in *Translations*, Jack is Tim's. Jack is a successful, suave, and self-assured barrister from Dublin. He possesses all those qualities of the modern Irish bourgeoisie which Tim lacks—efficiency, sexual confidence and above all, since language remains the key, a remarkable felicity with conversational repartee.

Jack's *nouveau-riche* family bought the rickety cottage in Ballybeg and refurbished its rustic charms in order to experience the "soul and authenticity of the place." Jack's description of this romantic return to the land is presented as a saucy parody of Hugh's genuine *pietas*. "Everybody's grandmother was reared in a house like this," Jack quips, claiming it to be the "ancestral seat of the McNeilis dynasty, restored with love and dedication, absolutely authentic in every last detail . . . This is where we all come from. This is our first cathedral. This shaped our souls. This determined our first pieties. Yes. Have reverence for this place." Jack's way of revering his "father's house" is, ironically, to recite a tedious inventory or "map" of all the objects contained in the cottage (fireplace, pot-iron, tongs, etc.). He employs naming according to the empiricist model of utilitarian representation in order to classify each thing as a use-item. For Jack, language is not a house of being but a filing cabinet of objects.

But if Jack and Tim's ultimate concern is with words, their ostensible concern is with women. They have come to the cottage for the purpose of amorous exchange—Tim with the girl of his fancy, Susan; Jack with his latest catch, Ivette Giroux from the French Embassy in Dublin. When Tim tries to express genuine reservations about his feelings for Susan, Jack reassures him that it's a "perfect match." He means of course a perfect *commercial* match: "you're ugly and penniless, she's pretty and rich." One of the central themes of the play is thus discreetly announced—the conflict between Tim's view of communication as an ontological response cry expressing true feeling and Jack's view of communication as a commercial contract or conquest.

Friel has Tim expound his linguistic thesis in the opening act of the play, thereby establishing the conceptual coordinates for the subsequent unfolding of the plot. Tim argues that language operates on two levels—as *information* and as *conversation*. At the first and ultimately inferior level, words function as messengers transmitting information from a speaker to a listener. Language becomes a process of encoding and decoding messages. Where a common code exists messages can be exchanged, where not there is misunderstanding. Echoing the terms of Levi-Strauss, Tim explains that "all social behaviour, the entire social order, depends on communicational structures, on words mutually agreed on and mutually understood. Without that agreement, without that shared code, you have chaos." It is surely no coincidence that the example that Tim chooses to illustrate his point is the absence of a common code of *translation* when one person speaks only English and the other only German.

At the second but more fundamental level, language transcends its purely pragmatic function as a formal transmission of information and seeks a more personal and profound sharing of one's ontological experience: "You desire to share my experience—and because of that desire our exchange is immediately lifted out of the realm of mere exchange of basic messages and aspires to something higher, something much more important—*conversation* . . . a response cry!" Response cries bespeak the existential interiority of the heart's space. They are by definition "involuntary," Tim observes, in that they forgo all linguistic strategies of willful manipulation or commerce. But the difficulty is how to discriminate between genuine response cries which speak straight from the heart and the mere pretense at such speech. How is language to escape from the insincerity of role-playing (or as Wittgenstein would put it, the ploys of "language games")? Tim's inability to resolve this dilemma is not only the reason why he cannot complete his thesis or decide whom he truly loves; it is the very *raison d'être* for the play itself! It is the importance of being earnest all over again. Indeed Friel's debt to Wilde's comic genius is perhaps nowhere more evident than in *Communication Cord.*

**********

The entire action of the play may be seen as an experimental testing of Tim's linguistic hypothesis of restoring the modern positivistic model of language to its ontological origins. The plot unfolds accordingly as a farcical rewind of *Translations.*

Tim is not only a recast of Hugh but also of Manus, the schoolmaster's sincere and penurious son. He is, as Jack jibes, "worthy and penniless—all nobility and no nous." Just as Manus remained implacably opposed to Owen's translation project, so too Tim denounces Jack's abuse of language as a transmission of financial and erotic messages as "damned perfidious." Like Owen, Jack is a dealer in identities, mediating between the cunning locals (he recognizes his neighbor Nora Dan to be a "quintessential noble peasant—obsessed with curiosity, greed and envy") and the mercenary outsiders (Senator Donovan from Dublin and the German blow-in eager to purchase a property in the locality—Barney the Banks). Jack is at once adept in the communal game of *pietas*—as when, in mock-Heideggerean fashion, he goes to "the well for a bucket of the purest of pure spring water"—and a master of modern pragmatism. The *map* of translation is replaced here by the *watch* of time-keeping: the new symbol of progress! Appropriately, Jack can mastermind the plot by virtue of the expert timing of his watch, whereas Tim, whose watch keeps stopping, has no control whatsoever over all the comings and goings.

Other characters in the play may also be seen as comic reincarnations of the *dramatis personae* in *Translations.* Claire, Tim's former girlfriend and the one love of his heart, recalls both Sarah and Máire. She is described as "open and humorous" and is bravely determined to communicate her love for Tim, come what may. The German prospector of property recalls the Royal Engineers. And Nora Dan recalls her eponymous forebear who left the hedge school as soon as she learnt her name. The modern day Nora Dan, in a pastiche of the patrilinear nomenclature practiced in *Translations,* explains her double name to Tim as follows: "I get the Dan from my father—that's the queer way we have of naming people around here." Nora Dan is a peasant who, Friel tells us, "likes to present herself as a peasant." She is a stage Irishwoman who has perfected her stagecraft.

Lastly, Senator Donovan is presented as a sort of modern antitype of Jimmy Jack. He is cast as an "amateur antiquarian," a self-made man full of his own self-importance as both doctor and politician, who fatuously extols the "absolute verity" of the cottage. Donovan is a caricature of all that is sentimental and sententious in the modern bourgeois Republic. His speeches are reeled off like farcical travesties of Hugh's and Jimmy's *desiderium nostrorum*—their sacramental longing for older, quieter things. Arriving in Ballybeg he pretentiously muses:

> This silence, this peace, the restorative power of that landscape . . . this speaks to me, this whispers to me. . . And despite the market place, all the years of trafficking in politics and medicine, a small voice within me still knows the *responses* . . . This is the touchstone . . . the apotheosis.

Donovan's version of the response cry traduces Tim's genuine predication of this term. And his interpretation of love play with pretty women as another means of moving from word representation to wordless response is a further falsification of Tim's real meaning. "When you're as young and as beautiful as Madame Giroux," opines the lusty Senator, "language doesn't matter does it? Words are superfluous aren't they?" The radical difference between Tim's and Donovan's respective attitudes to language becomes clear in their dramatic exchanges. While Donovan pursues his pseudo-cultural cant about getting back "to the true centre" or spiritual renewal in the heart of rural Ireland, Tim confesses that he "hates all it represents." Similarly though Donovan tries to negotiate the sale of the cottage with Tim (mistaking him for the owner), Tim simply cannot make the cap of commercial proprietor fit. He cannot bring himself to conform to the language-game of mercantile deceit.

Donovan's misidentification of Tim, a symptom of his misuse of language, is multiplied in the countless mistaken identities of the other characters: Claire is mistaken of Ivette; Donovan for Dr. Bollacks; Barny the Banks for Jack and for a fictitious wife-beater; Nora Dan for a local scrambling champion, and so on. Friel seems to be suggesting that this confusion of each character with the other is a logical consequence of the historical translation, documented in *Translations,* of the native Irish language and culture into the contemporary Babel of the International European Community (Donovan commutes between Dublin and Brussels as an E.E.C. Senator). This mix-up of cultural and linguistic identities (Irish, English, German, French) epitomizes the radical absence of a shared code or context of communication which characterizes life in *Ballybeg* one hundred and fifty years after its translation from *Baile Beag.*

Donovan, while exploiting to the full the commercial conveniences of the modern multi-national society, still clings to the craven illusion that nothing has changed, that Romantic Ireland is alive and well in a restored Donegal cottage waiting to be purchased by the highest bidder. In other words, Donovan would have it both ways. He is hypocrisy incarnate, a symbol of the very *discontinuity* in

Irish cultural history which he refuses to acknowledge. But Donovan's charade of assumed *pietas* is finally scotched when, invoking the mythic shibboleth of Ireland as the "'woman with two cows," he actually chains himself to a restored cow harness in the cottage and is unable to extricate himself. The myth becomes literal. As his rantings become more desperate, the entire stage is plunged into darkness. All the characters lose their bearings and stagger about in farcical mimicry of the cultural-linguistic disorientation which has befallen them.

When the light returns the truth begins to dawn; the aliases and alibis are debunked and the artifices of the confounding language-games exposed. This enlightenment of consciousness is nowhere more evident than in the concluding love scene between Tim and Claire. Their masks removed and their real feelings made plain, the lovers move towards the most authentic form of language—the response cry of silence. As Tim explains: "Maybe the units of communication don't matter that much . . . We're conversing now but we're not exchanging units . . . I'm not too sure what I'm saying . . . Maybe the message doesn't matter at all then . . . Maybe silence is the perfect language." The structuralist model of communication as the circulation of word-units in the symbolic form of *woman* (Susan/Ivette/Claire) or *commodities* (Donovan, Barney, Jack and Nora Dan are all engaged in mercenary negotiations for the purchase of the cottage) is shown to be hopelessly inadequate. The employment of language for the exchange of women and property between the different individuals or tribes in the play (Irish, German, and French), does not produce either communication or community as Levi-Strauss's theory would have us believe. The ontological secrets of the heart's space cannot, Tim and Claire discover, be disclosed through the verbal exchange of informational units, but only through the "reverberations" occasioned by a genuine "response" of human feeling. Responding to Claire's genuine response cry—"Kiss me"—Time embraces her. As he does so, the lovers lean against the fragile upright beam of the cottage, causing it to collapse around them in a climactic flurry of apocalyptic chaos. The local tower of babel is demolished in one loving stroke. And even Jack, the consummate wizard of word-play, is compelled to a response cry—"O my God."

## CONCLUSION

What do Friel's plays say about language? More specifically, what do they tell us about their author's attitude or contribution to the native Irish tradition of verbal theatre? Are Friel's plays Trojan horses in the citadel of this tradition, contesting its constraints of story-telling from within and pointing towards the possibility of more immediate, non-verbal modes of expression? Are the apocalyptic endings to his language plays symptoms of a crisis of faith in the power of words? More simply, does Friel subscribe in the final analysis to a theatre of the Word or to a theatre of the Senses?

I think this formulation of the question is probably inadequate. Friel's work ultimately resists the facility of such an either-or alternativism. The conclusion to *The Communication Cord* is, for instance, disquietingly equivocal. The hint of some salvation through silence (recalling Heidegger's notion of a mystical "tolling of silence" at the heart of language) is counteracted by the literal unleashing of darkness and destruction. While the abandonment of speech spells loving communion for Tim and Claire, it spells the collapse of the community as a whole. Silence is a double-edged sword heralding *both* the beginning of love and the end of society. While the departure from language may well lead to love, it may equally well lead to violence. So that Friel's ontological optimism with regard to silence as the "perfect language" appears to go hand in glove with a pessimistic, or at least sceptical, appraisal of its socio-historical implications. The term "cord" itself conveys this double sense of a bond and an alarm signal.

Seen in conjunction with *Translations,* the ambiguity of Friel's conclusion becomes even more explicit. If *Translations* tended to mythologize language, *The Communication Cord* demythologizes it. While the former attempted to show how language once operated in terms of a cultural rootedness and centredness, the latter de-centres all easy assumptions about the retrieval of such lost, cultural origins. One sponsors the original fidelity of language to a timeless, ontological piety of *nature*, the other affirms the irreversibility of history as an alienation from the natural pre-history of words; and this very affirmation exposes the impotence of language to save a community from the corrosive effects of time, from the mixed blessings of Modern Progress.

Seamus Deane, one of the directors of Friel's *Field Day Theatre Company,* states this dilemma with admirable concision in his preface to *The Communication Cord.* "Nostalgia for the lost native culture—so potent and plaintive in *Translations,*" writes Deane,

> appears ludicrous and sham . . . Real communication has begun to disappear the moment you begin to isolate it as a problem and give degrees in it. Friel has presented us here with the vacuous world of a dying culture. The roof is coming in on our heads . . . There is little or no possibility of inwardness, of dwelling in rather than on history.

Situating this crisis of language in the more specific context of Irish cultural history, Deane adds:

Irish discourse, especially literary discourse, is ready invoke history
but reluctant to come to terms with it . . . So we manage to think
of our great writers as explorers of *nature,* as people who
successfully fled the historical nightmare and reintroduced us to the
daily nature we all share, yet this feeling is itself historically
determined. A colony always wants to escape from history. It longs
for its own authenticity, the element it had before history came to
disfigure it."

Friel's insistence that *Translations* and *The Communication Cord* be
considered "in tandem" suggests that their respective claims—the claims of nature
and history, of mythologization and demythologization, of silence and speech—are
perhaps *both* valid in some sense, serving as two supporting arches of a mutually
sustaining dialectic. The very tension created by their contrary approaches to
language is in itself creative. It has certainly proved conducive to some of Friel's
finest dramatic work.

But the implications of this dialectic extend even further, calling into
question the conventional notions of what "culture" actually means. Friel refuses
to accept the conventional policy of apartheid which see the cultural and the socio-
historical as entirely separate spheres of discourse. His language plays represent a
powerful evocation of the ways in which our cultural use of words determines our
society and is determined by it in turn. Friel regards culture, in F.S.L. Lyons'
phrase, as "everything from the furniture in men's kitchens to the furniture in their
minds." Hence *Field Day's* determination to foster a new dialectical rapport
between the timeless images of nature and the transient facts of history. Such a
dialectic, if successful, might not only project new possibilities for the future
development of Irish culture, but might also liberate the dramatic tradition of
story-telling from its more encrusted or stereotyped moulds. The fact that the six
directors of *Field Day* include both poets (Seamus Deane, Seamus Heaney, Tom
Paulin) and non-poets (Stephen Rea, a performer, and David Hammond, a
musician) may well be an indication of Friel's own desire, as dramatist, to reconcile
the respective resources of the verbal and non-verbal media of his art. As the
prefatory note to the *Communication Cord* intimates:

if a congealed idea of theatre can be broken then the audience
which experiences this break would be the more open to the
modification of other established forms. Almost everything which
we believe to be nature or native is in fact historical; more
precisely, is an historical fiction. If *Field Day* can breed a new

fiction of theatre, or of any other area, which is sufficiently successful to be believed in as though it were natural and an outgrowth of the past, then it will have succeeded. At the moment, it is six characters in search of a story that can be believed.

Friel, like Christy Mahon, is asking his audience to make his fiction true. He is asking that the promise of *Field Day* be made real by the power of a lie. Unlike Christy, however, and the Irish dramatic movement which created him, Friel holds out the possibility of a new kind of story-telling, one more cognizant of history and more attentive to those forms of expression which reach beyond the word.

# APPENDIX

The following is a list of key passages from George Steiner's essay "Understanding and Translation" (contained in *After Babel: Aspects of Language and Translation,* Oxford University Press, 1975, pp. 1-50) which served as a major critical and philosophical source for Friel's language plays.

1. "In certain civilizations there come epochs in which syntax stiffens, in which the available resources of live perception and restatement wither. Words seem to go dead under the weight of sanctified usage: the frequency and sclerotic forces of clichés, of unexamined similes, of worn tropes increases. Instead of acting as a living membrane, grammar and vocabulary become a barrier to new feeling. A civilization is imprisoned in a linguistic contour which no longer matches, or matches only at certain ritual, arbitrary points, the changing landscape of fact" (p. 21).

2. "We have histories of massacre and deception, but none of metaphor . . . Such figures (i.e. metaphors) are new mappings of the world, they reorganize our habitation of reality" (p. 23).

3. "No semantic form is timeless. When using a word we wake into resonance, as it were, its entire previous history. A text is embedded in specific historical time; it has what linguists call a diachronic structure. To read fully is to restore all that one can of the immediacies of value and intent in which speech actually occurs" (p. 24).

4. "The schematic model of translation is one in which a message from a source-language passes into a receptor-language via a transformational process. The barrier is the obvious fact that one language differs from the other, that an interpretative transfer sometimes, albeit misleadingly, described as encoding and

decoding, must occur so that the message "gets through." Exactly the same model—and this is what is rarely stressed—is operative *within a single language*" (p. 28).

5. "What material reality has history outside language, outside our interpretative belief in essentially linguistic records (silence knows no history)? Where worms, fires of London, or totalitarian regimes obliterate such records, our consciousness of past being comes on a blank space. We have no total history, no history which could be defined as objectively real because it contained the literal sum of past life. To remember Everything is a condition of madness. We remember culturally, as we do individually, by conventions of emphasis, foreshadowing, omission. The landscape composed by the past tense, the semantic organization of remembrance, is stylized and differently coded by different cultures" (p. 29).

6. "The metaphysics of the instant, this slamming of the doors on the long galleries of historical consciousness, is understandable. It has a fierce innocence. . . But it is an innocence as destructive of civilization as it is, by concomitant logic, destructive of literate speech. Without the true fiction of history, without the unbroken animation of a chosen past, we become flat shadows. Literature, whose genius stems from what Eluard called *le dur désir de durer*, has no chance of life outside constant translation within its own language . . . In short, the existence of art and literature, the reality of felt history in a community, depend on a never-ending, though very often unconscious, act of internal translation" (p. 30).

7. "Languages conceal and internalize more, perhaps, than they convey outwardly. Social classes, racial ghettoes speak at rather than to each other" (p. 32).

8. "When anti-thetical meanings are forced upon the same word (Orwell's newspeak), when the conceptual reach and valuation of a word can be uttered by political decree, language loses credibility" (p. 34).

9. "At any given time in a community and in the history of language, speech modulates across generations" (p 34).

10. "Eros and language mesh at every point. Intercourse and discourse, copula and copulation, are sub-classes of the dominant fact of communication. They arise from the life-need of the ego to reach out and comprehend, in the two vital senses of 'understanding' and 'containment,' another human being. Sex is a profoundly semantic act. Like language, it is subject to the shaping force of social convention, rules of proceeding, and accumulated precedent" (p. 38).

11. "Hence the argument of modern anthropology that the incest taboo, which appears to be primal to the organization of communal life, is inseparable from linguistic evolution. We can only prohibit that which we can name. Kinship systems, which are the coding and classification of sex for purposes of social

survival, are analogous with syntax. The seminal and semantic functions (is there, ultimately, an etymological link?) determine the genetic and social structure of human experience. Together they construe the grammar of being" (p. 39).

12. "Under extreme stress, men and women declare their absolute being to each other, only to discover that their respective experience of eros and language has set them desperately apart."

13. "Levi-Strauss's contention is that women and words are analogous media of exchange in the grammar of social life" (p. 45).

14. "It is not as 'translators' that women novelists and poets excel, but as declaimers of their own, long-stifled tongue" (p. 45).

15. "Any model of communication is at the same time a model of translation, of a vertical or horizontal transfer of significance. No two historical epochs, no two social classes, no two localities use words and syntax to signify exactly the same things, to send identical signals of valuation and inference. Neither do two human beings. Each person draws, deliberately or in immediate habit, on two sources of linguistic supply: the current vulgate corresponding to his level of literacy, and a private thesaurus. The latter is inextricably a part of his subconscious, of his memories so far as they may be verbalized, and of the singular, irreducibly specific ensemble of his somatic and psychological identity. Part of the answer to the notorious logical conundrum as to whether or not there can be a 'private language' is that aspects of every language-act are unique and individual . . . The concept of a normal or standard idiom is a statistically-based fiction (though it may have real existence in machine-translation). The language of a community, however uniform its social contour, is an inexhaustibly multiple aggregate of speech-atoms, of finally irreducible personal meanings . . . We speak to communicate. But also to conceal, to leave unspoken. The ability of human beings to misinform modulates through every wavelength from outright lying to silence" (p. 46).

16. "Thus a human being performs an act of translation, in the full sense of the word, when receiving a speech-message from any other human being. Time, distance, disparities in outlook or assumed reference, make this act more or less difficult. Where the difficulty is great enough the process passes from reflex to conscious technique. Intimacy, on the other hand, be it of hatred or of love, can be defined as confident, quasi-immediate translation . . . With intimacy the external vulgate and the private mass of language grow more and more concordant. Soon the private dimension penetrates and takes over the customary forms of public exchange . . . In old age the impulse towards translation wanes and the pointers of reference turn inward. The old listen less or principally to themselves. Their dictionary is, increasingly, one of private remembrance" (p. 47).

17. "Interlingual translation is . . . an access to an inquiry into language itself.

'Translation,' properly understood, is a special case of the arc of communication which every successful speech-act closes within a given language . . . The model 'sender to receiver' which represents any semiological and semantic process is ontologically equivalent to the model *'source-language to receptor-language'* used in the theory of translation. . . . In short, inside or between languages, human communication equals translation. A study of translation is a study of language" (p. 47).

# NOTES

1. *Complete Works of Oscar Wilde*. London: Collins, 1948, p.1023.
2. *Anglo-Irish Playwrights and Comic Tradition* by T. Kilroy, in *Crane Bag*, V.3, No. 2, 1979.
3. *Dialogue*, by Ciaran Carty, Arts Page, *Sunday Independent*, Oct. 24, 1982.
4. *Word and Flesh: A View of Theatre as Performance* by D. McKenna in *Crane Bag*, Vol. 6, No.1, 1982.
5. *Dublin Theatre Festival Guide: 1982*, p.24.
6. *The Man from God Knows Where*, Interview with Brian Friel by F. O'Toole, *In Dublin*, No. 165, Oct. 1982, p.21.
7. *Ibid.*, p.21.
8. *Ibid.*, p.22.
9. *Ibid.*, p.20.
10. *Ibid.*, p.21. See *The Crane Bag Book of Irish Studies*. Dublin: Blackwater Press, 1982, ed. R. Kearney and P. Hederman, pp.10-12.
11. *Ibid.*, p.23.
12. *Ibid.*, p.23.
13. "Poetically Man Dwells." In *Poetry, Language, Thought* by Martin Heidegger, Tr. A. Hofstadter. New York: Harper and Row, 1971, p.215.
14. "What Are Poets for?" *Ibid.*, p.134.
15. *The Man from God Knows Where, op cit.*, p.22.
16. *Ibid.*, p.22.
17. "Poetically Man Dwells." In *Poetry, Language, Thought, op. cit.*, p.22.
18. In part III of the *Essay*, entitled "Words of Language in General," Locke used his "historical, plain method" of empiricist rationalism in order to overcome "the artifice, fallacy . . . and cheat of words" (III, x) caused by the traditional notions of a natural or ontological language, and to replace it with a pragmatic interpretation of language based on the commonsense correlation of words with empirical sensations. "All words," Locke argued, "are taken from the operations of

sensible things" (III, i). He maintained that these operations were best appreciated by "those minds the study of mathematics has opened" (Locke, *Works*, Vol. VIII). Language can be exploited in the domination of the logos of Being by the logic of science, for "the making of *Species* and *Genera* is in order to general names" (III, vi). Locke wished to abolish the confusion and uncertainty spawned by mystical or metaphysical doctrines of language (e.g. Boehme's belief in the "signatures of things," the "language of nature . . . which is a secret, a mystery granted by the grace of God"). He promoted instead a *conventionalist* theory of naming which argued that there is no essential or intrinsic relationship between being and words, only an arbitrary rapport *imposed* by men for reasons of ease, order, efficacy and utility—what he called "the improvement of understanding." Rejecting all ontological models of naming in favor of a representational model, Locke insisted that "the same liberty also, that Adam had of affixing any new name to any Idea, the same has one still . . . But in communication with others, it is necessary, that we conform the ideas (i.e. common sensible ideas) we make the Vulgar Words of any language stand for, to their known proper signfications, or else to make known that new signification we apply to them" (IIII, v). "The signification of sounds" Locke affirms accordingly, "is not natural, but only imposed and arbitrary" (III, iv). Locke's exclusive emphasis on scientific objectivity compelled him to jettison the ancient doctrine that some etymological alliance could obtain between language and nature; he had no time for the etymologist's reverence for language as a remembrance of the hidden *origins* of meaning or community (See Hans Aarleff, *From Locke to Saussure, Essays on the Study of Language and Intellectual History*, Athlone, London, 1982, pp.66-69, 82-83). To Locke language was merely a tool for the attainment of certain and certifiable knowledge. Words were legitimate in so far as they were useful and useful in so far as they enabled men to "range (things) into sorts, in order to their naming, for the convenience of comprehensive signs . . . so that we may truly say, such a manner of sorting of things is the Workmanship of Men" (III, vi).

Speaking of how such Enlightenment positivism serves to reduce man's rich sense of temporal and historical being to a manageable "picture," William Spanos, the Heideggerean critic, talks appositely of "a flattened out, static and homogenous Euclidean space—a totalized and ontologically depthless system of referents (a *map*)—if the objectifying consciousness is positivistic . . . " (See *Deconstructive Criticism*, by V. Leitch. New York: Columbia University Press, 1983, p.74.)

19. *Anthropologie Structurale*. Paris: Plan, 1958; see also *Structuralism and Since*. New York: Oxford U.P., 1979, ed. John Sturrock.

20. *The Man from God Knows Where, op. cit.*, p. 23.

# BRIAN FRIEL'S USES OF LAUGHTER

## Kathleen Ferris

Although there are no happy endings in the plays of Brian Friel, there are many funny moments. A few of his plays, such as *The Mundy Scheme*, *Losers*, and *The Communication Cord*, provide outright belly laughs, but even these farcical works, which clearly belong to the domain of comedy, have their dark undersides, their satiric barbs. Most of Friel's dramas combine tragic and comic modes. Sometimes, in plays such as *Philadelphia, Here I Come!* and *Dancing at Lughnasa*, the mixture is of fairly equal measure; however, even those works which are predominately tragic, such as *Translations*, *The Freedom of the City*, *Volunteers*, and *Wonderful Tennessee*, also contain comic elements. Frequently laughter in Friel's theater is blended with an element of poignancy, for within the dark tradition of Irish comedy in which he writes, the more it hurts, the more we laugh.

Although critics have often mentioned comic elements in Friel's plays, they have tended to do so in passing, not focusing specifically on his use of comedy. My purpose then is to examine some of the plays mentioned above to see how Friel uses laughter, what ideas he conveys through humor, and how these plays fit into the Irish comic tradition. In order to observe his development as a dramatist, we will look at the plays in chronological order.

Friel's first stage success, *Philadelphia, Here I Come!* (1964), employs the innovative device of dividing the protagonist, Gareth O'Donnell into two characters, Public and Private. The play begins in an exuberant mood as Gar prepares to leave Ireland for America on the morrow. However, gradually, as the young man bids farewell to his friends and family, we learn the sad reasons for his leaving home. The situation allows Friel to introduce some of the major themes which will recur in variation throughout his later works: the failure of love and joy in Ireland; the lack of economic opportunity; the dependence upon alcohol and imagination to escape the hopelessness of existence; and the conflict between generations, the younger generation representing rebellion and sexual frustration, the older representing established orthodoxy and power. If none of these subjects seem appropriately funny for our investigation, we need to keep in mind that comedy depends upon the treatment of material, not upon the nature of the material in itself.[1] As W. Moelwyn Merchant has observed,

> within any situation loosely definable as 'comic' there exist possibilities of profound latent differences, of sardonic comment on human frailty, of ironic, even destructive wit, of compassionate involvement in the pathos of vulnerable human concerns, and finally of a recognition that the comic mask sometimes leers with a grimace dangerously near the tragic.[2]

Much of humour in *Philadelphia* depends upon the discrepancy between what Public Gar says and does and what Private Gar thinks. Through this device, Friel exploits the comic elements (and also the pathetic elements) inherent in the plot. Whereas Public Gar is deferential in his behavior with authority figures—his father, the elderly Canon Mick O'Byrne, his former schoolmaster Boyle, and Senator Doogan—in private Gar mocks his elders outrageously. For example, his nickname for his father, who exploits his son's labor in return for only a pittance of pay, and whose initials are S. B., is "Screwballs." He takes delight in being able to anticipate almost *verbatim* the ritualistic phrases which constitute most of his father's conversation with his companion, the Canon. He refers to Senator Doogan, who has successfully thwarted his plans to marry the Senator's daughter Kate, as the father of fourteen unborn illegitimate children.

Gar illustrates the principle which David Krause has noted in *The Profane Book of Irish Comedy*, ". . . the comic figure must escape from the oppressive world and mock sacred values". Krause's thesis, based upon Freud's essay *Jokes and Their Relation to the Unconscious*, is that Irish jokes represent rebellion against authority and hence provide liberation from its pressure. Private Gar's rebellious laughter directed against his elders is the means by which the young man redresses the imbalance of power in his society. This is a technique which we will see repeated in variation in many of Friel's plays. Like important Irish dramatists who came before him—J. M. Synge, Sean O'Casey, Brendan Behan—Friel's sympathies are with the underdog, the victim of oppression. Those who are politically or economically or psychologically powerless use the one weapon available to them, the power of laughter, to belittle those who control their lives, thus achieving a temporary victory over tyranny, which has many guises. The subversion of order is, as Krause reminds us, the essence of comedy: "Low comedy is the natural enemy of order. Indeed, wherever the instruments of order are most rigorously imposed, there knockabout comedy finds its most tempting targets for profanation".[3]

In *Philadelphia*, another source of humor, in this case of poignant humor, is Private Gar's ability to see through and expose the lies told by other characters. In the meeting between Gar and Master Boyle, the schoolmaster tells Gar that he too is thinking of going to the United States, that he has been offered "a big post in Boston, head of education in a reputable university there". Gar's reaction is "Poor bastard!"[4] Although lies and tall tales frequently provide the material of comedy (a device Friel uses much later in *Dancing at Lughnasa*), in this case Gar recognizes that his old friend is attempting to save face, to mask the hopelessness of his life. Boyle is the man who had loved Gar's mother and had lost her to an older and richer man, Gar's father. As a consequence, Boyle drinks to try to forget his unhappiness, and he is in danger of losing his position as schoolmaster. When taking leave of Gar, Boyle makes jokes insulting the younger man's intelligence, but Gar does not take offense because he recognizes that again the older man is masking his real feelings, his sadness over his pupil's departure. One role of Private Gar is to uncover the despair and pain that often lie behind false words.

A similar incident occurs when Gar says good-bye to his buddies, Ned, Tom and Joe. The young men reminisce over the good times they have had together, boasting about their wild sexual escapades with local women, especially those of one particular evening when they think Gar was not present. But Gar was there, and though his Public persona pretends to believe their lies, Private Gar recalls a different version of their story:

> We were there that night, Ned. And the girls' names were Gladys
> and Susan. And they sat on the rocks dangling their feet in the
> water. And we sat in the cave, peeping out at them.[5]

Gar's deflation of his friends' exaggerated account of their sexual prowess serves to underline not only the emptiness of their boasts, but also the lack of adventure and romance in Ireland, a culture where strong taboos forbid sexuality outside of marriage, an institution which many cannot afford. Thus the theme of sexual repression, which recurs in later plays by Friel, is a frequent source of laughter in Irish comedy, a source often intermingled with pathos.

When Gar looks at his friends, he recognizes how remote are the possibilities of his finding love and happiness in his native land. In Boyle, he sees the example of what his own life might become if he does not escape Ireland, where he too has lost his girl to a wealthier man, and where marriage is frequently arranged as a matter of financial convenience. Because the atmosphere in Ireland seems so inimical to romantic love, the only chance that Gar can see for a good life is through emigration. And the option is a painful one, he discovers, as he bids farewell, perhaps forever, to the people he loves. The movement in this play, as in so many of Friel's works, is downward, from optimism and joy to sorrow and despair.

The impossibility of love in modern Ireland is the theme of Friel's paired plays *Lovers* (1967), the first a tragedy ironically entitled *Winners* and the second a comedy called *Losers*. The winners, a young unmarried couple who have conceived a child, are spared a lifetime of unhappiness in a marriage that is clearly doomed when they accidentally drown while boating on a lake. The losers are a middle-aged couple who are spared none of the unhappiness of marriage, but whose misery inspires hilarity. These plays were very successful both in Dublin and on Broadway. In reviewing the latter piece for *The Times* of London, Ulick O'Connor wrote, "*Losers* is perhaps the funniest play to be seen on the Irish stage for many a year. At times the audience were reduced to that state of chaotic disruption which only high comedy can bring on."[6]

Part of the humor in *Losers* stems from the ludicrousness of an older couple's love-making. When Hanna, a factory-worker in her late forties falls in love with Andy, a "heavily built" man of fifty, a "solid, decent, reliable, slightly dull man," we are told that "this sudden injection of romance into a life that seemed to be rigidly and permanently patterned has transformed a very plain spinster into an *almost* attractive woman" (emphasis added). During their courtship, Andy confides to the audience, "By God, we were lively enough, too. Eh? I mean to say, people think that when you're . . . well, when you're over the forty mark, that you're passified. But aul' Hanna, by God, I'll say that for her, she was keen as a terrier in those days."[7] The sight of the "almost attractive" spinster throwing herself passionately on her rotund Andy is in itself amusing. A touch of poignancy is added to the situation if one realizes that for generations among the poorer people of Ireland, marriage had to be postponed until parents died, at which time the oldest son could inherit the land, or until a man could accumulate wealth enough to support a family, a feat which might require a good number of years.

The main element of comedy in the play *Losers* is the power struggle that develops between Andy and Hanna's mother, Mrs. Wilson, a widow who dominates her daughter's life. In this contest, poor Andy doesn't stand a chance. The old woman, frail and angelic-looking, has weapons against which Andy is helpless— her weak heart (feigned), her piety (false), and a loud bell with which she summons Hanna to her bedside. During the lovers' courtship, Mrs. Wilson clangs her bell whenever she hears prolonged periods of silence downstairs (presumably in order to protect her daughter's virginity). After the couple are married, the bell rings only during moments of conversation. Every evening the couple is summoned to join Mrs. Wilson and her friend Cissy in prayers offered up before a statue of Saint Philomena, a ritual against which Andy rebels, recognizing that the act of gathering them all around her bedside is part of Mrs. Wilson's exercise of control.

When Andy learns that the Pope has forbidden prayers to Saint Philomena because no evidence exists that such a saint ever lived, the husband believes that at last he has found the weapon to undermine Mrs. Wilson's dominance of their lives. His mistake is in visiting a pub before going home. When he returns late and in a drunken state, his belligerence offends Hanna and causes Mrs. Wilson to feign a heart attack, thus strengthening the old woman's hold on her daughter. Not only does Andy's comic rebellion fail, but from this time on, he is more hopelessly than ever under Mrs. Wilson's rule, being forced to join each evening in prayers to a new saint whose name the women will not tell him.

*Losers* illustrates perfectly the human tendency to laugh at that which is unhappy, the principle upon which Samuel Beckett based his comedies. Even though all of our sympathy goes out to Andy, a good fellow who has done nothing to merit his misery, even though we cheer him on in his rebellion against the tyranny of old age and false piety and feigned weakness, which stifle love and passion and all hope of happiness, yet we laugh at his defeat. In Irish comedy, laugher and defeat frequently go together.[8]

Friel's next play, *The Mundy Scheme* (1969), is concerned not with the struggle against power, but with the struggle for power. Set in Dublin, in the office of the Taoiseach, *The Mundy Scheme* satirizes greed and corruption in politics. The play succeeded in Dublin, but when Clive Barnes panned it in *The New York Times*, it folded on Broadway after four performances. One can only wonder whether a post-Watergate American audience might not be more appreciative of this comic rendition of the political world. Although some of the satire is aimed specifically at Irish culture, the larger issues which Friel addresses are certainly universal.

The central character in *The Mundy Scheme* is the Taoiseach, Francis Xavier Ryan, who has converted the drawing room of his home into an office because he is suffering from inner-ear trouble—i.e. because he lacks balance. This situation enables us to observe that in his private life, F. X., a bachelor, is still under the domination of his aged mother. Mrs. Ryan keeps control of her son by keeping his eardrops in her own pocket, and she keeps a sharp eye on any young woman who might prove a rival to her power. Though in public F. X. behaves abusively toward his mother, in private we see that he is very dependent upon her, another variation of the Public/Private split that Friel dramatized in *Philadelphia*. Initially the humor of the play depends upon the irony that this infantile man should be the leader of a nation. As the play progresses we see Ryan develop from a comic rogue to a comic villain, who betrays his best friend in order to satisfy his greed.

The central joke of the play is the scheme devised by a wealthy Irish-Texan named Mundy and the Irish Minister of External Affairs, Ryan's old friend Moloney, to save the floundering economy of Ireland. Just when it looks as if Ryan's government is about to collapse, Moloney returns from America with a plan that will rescue them all. Mundy Real Estate Incorporated will lease all the worthless bogland of western Ireland and convert it into cemeteries for the overcrowded cities of the industrial western nations (a scheme reminiscent of the one G. B. Shaw proposed in *John Bull's Other Island*, where the land would be used for golf courses). Cargoes of corpses from New York, London and Paris will be flown into Dublin in Irish-built caskets, then transported to outlying regions for burial or for cremation in facilities fueled by turf. Airports and highways will be built, the tourist industry will be improved, and jobs will be created for all. Laughable as we find the idea that Ireland, a nation "addicted to death," should become the burial ground of the world, theoretically the plan seems feasible.[9]

This comic situation provides Friel with the opportunity to warn his Irish audience of the dangers of excessive materialism and to taunt them for their failure to measure up to the lofty ideals for which so many patriots died (the play being subtitled *or, May We Write Your Epitaph Now, Mr. Emmet?*). It also enables him to inform a non-Irish audience of the problems facing a small nation emerging from centuries of British domination, of Ireland's difficulty in finding its proper role in the scheme of world politics. Further, he is able to subvert through laughter an old stereotype about the Irish, the belief expounded by Matthew Arnold (and used as a rationale for imperialist domination) that the Celtic people lack the organizational capability of governing themselves. What Friel demonstrates is that Irishmen can excel at flattery, at dishonesty, at duplicity, at demagoguery, at manipulation of the media, at corruption and treachery—at all the skills essential to govern. He also reveals the subtle parallels between the world of politics and the world of theatre: by playing a role, the public man persuades others to believe in the illusions he creates.

In the 1970s, Brian Friel turned his satiric pen from the venal politics of southern Ireland to the violent politics of the North. In reaction to the upheaval in his homeland, Friel wrote two protest plays which are among his most powerful works, both of which combine elements of comedy and tragedy. *The Freedom of the City* (1973) dramatizes the fact that people being shot down by British soldiers in the streets of Derry were not organized revolutionaries or armed terrorists, but poor working-class citizens who were demonstrating against the harsh and unjust conditions of their lives. As the curtain opens, the corpses of the three principals, Lily, Michael and Skinner, are sprawled on the stage, providing the audience with foreknowledge of the grim outcome of the drama. The action which we witness is a flashback to the period immediately before their deaths, from the time the three citizens wandered inadvertently into the Guildhall in Derry, trying to escape from the teargas that was used on the marchers. The drama is a comedy played against this tragic backdrop.

We laugh at the antics of the three as they find themselves within what Skinner calls the "holy of holies," the parlour of the Lord Mayor. [10] Their crime is transgression. Much of the humor is based upon their irreverence, their desecration of power. They dress in the Lord Mayor's robes, they drink his wine, Skinner uses his ceremonial sword to fence with an imaginary British army, and Lily uses his telephone to call the few acquaintances she knows who have a telephone, including her sister Eileen who lives in Brisbane, Australia. The humour here is in a vein similar to that of Sean O'Casey's in *The Plough and the Stars*, where the citizens of Dublin are looting in the streets while the revolutionaries prepare for the Easter Rebellion. Friel's three citizens also move in a carnival atmosphere where, for a brief time, the rule of law is suspended and the underclasses reign.

The opulence which they find in the center of government provides Friel with an opportunity to contrast the luxury of those in power with the stark poverty of these ordinary people. Michael is awestruck by the sight of riches such as he has never seen, real silver, leather covered books, and oak covered walls. The charwoman Lily is less impressed, declaring that if she lived here, she would paint those walls a nice pink which could be washed clean, and that she would replace the dark windows with bright panes. She notes that this room is as large as the two-roomed flat which she and her "captain" occupy with their eleven children, a home where there is no running water, "Except what's running down the walls. Haaaaa!" [11] In the condemned warehouse turned tenement house where she lives, one bathroom down the hall serves eight families. When Skinner, the more knowing of the three, encourages his companions in their transgressions, suggesting that they take a shower under the golden fish in the Lord Mayor's private bath, Lily finds his idea amusing and replies, oblivious as usual to the humor of her own words,

> D'you see if it was a Sunday I'd take a shower myself. Sunday's my day. We all have our days for bathing over at the granny's—that's the chairman's mother. She has us all up on a time-table on the

kitchen wall, and if you miss your night you lose your turn. [12]

The spontaneity and vitality of Lily and Skinner, and to a lesser extent of the more restrained Michael, serve as a stark contrast to the three murdered corpses that we see at the start and again at the end of the play. The enormity of the crime against them is brought home to the audience because we have witnessed the comic *élan vital* of these three innocent people.

Friel's other protest play, *Volunteers* (1975), is a masterpiece of gallows humor that belongs to the same genre as the prison plays of Brendan Behan. Whereas in *The Freedom of the City* the victims are relatively unaware of their danger, with the possible exception of Skinner, who seems to suspect what lies ahead, in *Volunteers* the spectre of death is visibly present in the skeleton of the Norseman, Leif, which has been unearthed at the archaeological site in Dublin. In this play, political prisoners who have volunteered to work as diggers in the excavation are aware that as soon as the dig is over, they will be returned to prison to face the wrath of their fellow prisoners for having cooperated with the enemy. The central character, Keeney, has been informed that within the prison a kangaroo court has convened, that the men have been judged guilty, and that the sentence is "capital." In a riot planned for Block C, accidents will occur. Since he himself persuaded the others to volunteer for this dig, he realizes that he will be the first target. Though he is terrified, Keeney, wearing "the public mask of the joker," deflects his fear with humor. [13]

The drama that we witness is the antic clowning of a man under a death sentence. He and his sidekick Pyne maintain a steady stream of verbal wit which serves to mitigate the pending disaster. Much of the emotional intensity of the play comes from nerves strung taut, from wits sharpened by danger, from energy produced by pure adrenaline. We recognize the connection between life and artistic creation as we watch Keeney extemporize brilliantly. From the moment he enters the stage, he is mocking his captors with exaggerated politeness, with jokes and limericks that are grotesquely funny and which establish his own mental and verbal superiority to his jailers. No Irish clown ever more completely reversed the stereotype of the stage Irishman. Whereas the dull-witted foreman, George, remains unaware of his inadvertent pun when he says, "you certainly pulled us out of a hole, Mr. Wilson," Keeney invents analogies of the excavation to a bomb crater, to a huge womb, to a prison. [14] His imagination is so vivid that he is able on occasion to cause his listeners to suspend their disbelief in his fantastic tales. For instance, his comic routine, backed by Pyne, elicits sympathy for the student worker, Desmond, who (according to Keeney) has had his stomach pumped for forty-five minutes because he had mistaken the cremated ashes of his Aunt Coco, which he had received in the mail, for instant coffee. Heaping one lie upon another, Keeney ends the story with, "But the really disquieting thing is this: Wilson says he *loved* the taste". [15] Shortly afterwards, when Des offers to make coffee for everyone, he is mystified by the chuckles of the prisoners.

Desmond is an idealistic young man who doesn't allow his ideals to interfere with his ambition. After learning that this is the last day of the dig, that the work will go unfinished, he makes an impassioned speech urging the prisoners to protest and promising them his full support. Keeney turns the young man's rashness against him in a practical joke. When Des returns, much subdued after an interview with his superiors, Keeney pretends to have acted upon Desmond's promise and to have implicated him in their rebellion, thereby exposing the falseness and shallowness of the young man's rhetoric.

Keeney uses humor not only to mask his own feelings, but also to unmask the seeming goodwill of his captors and to reveal the deep animosity toward the prisoners that lurks beneath the surface. Whereas Mr. Wilson is forthright in expressing his belief that they are "all bloody criminals," George the foreman says that the men have performed "a public service" and expresses the pious hope that perhaps "we expanded their horizons," indicating his desire to reform their misguided souls. [16] The ideologue Desmond treats the incarcerated men humanely, purchasing for them items such as cigarettes and newspapers. Eventually, however, Keeney's corrosive humor wears away the thin layer of Des's and George's goodwill, prompting them to reveal their underlying hostilities. In rage Des bursts forth, "Over the past five months, Keeney, I thought I had come to understand *you people* and maybe even to have a measure of sympathy with you. But by God I think now that hanging's too good for you" (emphasis added). [17] The more hypocritical George, who never directly expresses his anger to Keeney, confides to Butt, the most diligent of the workers, whom he expects to sympathize with his values, that he is sending in a negative report on Keeney, who has "No loyalty to the job". [18] This revelation, that George desires Keeney to be punished for his non-cooperation, prompts Butt to destroy the ancient jug which George has labored so lovingly to reassemble. One implication of this act is that things should not be valued over human life.

The underground setting of *Volunteers* emphasizes the stratification that exists in society whereby those below are oppressed by those above. These prisoners, whose precise political affiliation is never established, are part of the often forgotten substratum of society, whose frustrations and anger lead them into rebellion against authority, and whose rebellion is usually punished harshly. Friel carefully avoids endorsing the violence of extremists, and he makes the men victims not of the state, but of their own group. Nevertheless he indicts those who constitute the establishment—the Georges, the Mr. Wilsons and the Desmonds, and other respectable citizens of the world—who would willingly allow these men to be murdered because they believe political prisoners to be only "riff-raff," "only a parcel of shite" of which they are happy to be rid.[19] In unmasking the private hatred and prejudice that lurk beneath civilized behavior, Friel is excavating the underside of political violence.

In *Volunteers*, as in *The Freedom of the City*, Friel celebrates the heroic power of the comic spirit, the life force, which endures despite the tragic movement of life towards death, despite the forces at work within society to crush its energy. By stressing the wit and vitality of his victims, Friel emphasizes their value as human beings. The wild antics of the underground men, Keeney and Pyne, with their macabre jokes about Leif, the grinning dead man ("You're a persistent joker, too, aren't you?"), underline the endurance of the rebel spirit which through the ages has laughed in the face of death.[20] Together these protest plays form a paean to the spirit of resistance, a fact which probably accounts for why they have never received the popular acclaim they deserve.

After *Volunteers*, during the latter half of the 1970s, Friel avoided political issues in his plays and dealt with other, less incendiary Irish themes, such as the decline of the aristocracy and of the family. In the early 1980s, he wrote two more paired plays with political implications: *Translations* (1980), the first dramatic production of the then newly formed Field Day Theatre Company, and its companion piece, *The Communication Cord* (1982). The first, a powerful play set in rural Donegal in the 1830s, is a tragedy about language: language as a weapon in the imperialistic conquest of one culture by another, language as a tool for exploring complex ideas, language as a medium for understanding other individuals and cultures, language as a source of aesthetic pleasure. Friel also explores the limits of language, and the possibilities for its perversion. These latter, negative aspects of language are the themes which he explores again in a comic mode in *The Communication Cord* (1982).

Vivian Mercier's commentary on the Irish sense of the ludicrous seems to shed some light on Friel's dialectic method of writing:

> Behind the bards and the hagiographers, who endlessly strive to outdo each other in their accounts of heroic deeds and saintly miracles, there lurks the figure of the sceptic and/or parodist. Anyone who knows the contradictions of the Irish mind may come to suspect that the sceptical parodist is but the bard or the hagiographer himself in a different mood.[21]

Although Mercier was referring here to writers from the distant Irish past, we can see in the contemporary playwright Brian Friel a similar sense of the ludicrous, an awareness of the humor which lies beneath the serious, and conversely of the darkness which lurks behind the jest. As he explored the problems of lovers first in a tragic and then in a comic mode in the paired plays *Winners* and *Losers*, so in other paired plays (which are not billed together but which nevertheless reflect upon each other) he explores a variety of issues from contrasting points of view. This is the technique he employed not only in *Translations* and *The Communication Cord*, but also in *Philadelphia, Here I Come!* and *The Loves of Cass McGuire*, in *Dancing at Lughnasa* and *Wonderful Tennessee*, and most recently, in *Faith Healer* and *Molly Sweeney*. In some cases the dialectic is between the tragic and the comic, but it can also be between the past and the present.

On the surface, *The Communication Cord* seems like pure farce, having all the trappings of slapstick humor: pranks and pratfalls, disguised or mistaken identities, misunderstandings, blunders and deceptions. The plot is a variation of a pattern which T.G.A. Nelson traces back to the New Comedy of Menander, the pattern in which boy and girl overcome whatever obstacles stand in the way of their union, thus arriving at a happy ending which leads to renewal for the community.[22] At least that is what the audience is set up to expect. But in *The Communication Cord*, just as the setting misleads us to believe that we are in a rural Irish cottage and to expect another peasant play, so the plot proves to be more a parody of a genre than the genuine article.

Indeed, one might say that falsity is the overarching theme of the entire play. When Susan Donovan decides that her current boyfriend, Tim Gallagher, will not meet with her father's approval on his own merits, she plots with Tim and his friend Jack McNeilis, a young barrister, to deceive Senator Doctor Donovan into believing that Tim is owner and restorer of a peasant cottage in County Donegal. Susan thinks that because the Doctor fancies himself an antiquarian, he will appreciate a similar interest in Tim. Jack, whose parents are the real owners of the cottage, gives Tim access to the premises for an hour, after which he plans to use the place himself for an assignation with his French girlfriend, Evette. Unknown to either of the young men, the cottage is already occupied by Claire Harkin, a professor of English at the university where Tim teaches, who is there for the weekend at the invitation of Jack's mother. Claire, who has a romantic interest in Tim, plays jokes on the young man by leaving her underwear in conspicuous places about the cottage in an attempt to thwart Tim's courtship of Susan. Because he is attracted to Claire, Tim feels compelled to lie to Susan and her father about Claire's real identity. As the complications ensue, one lie is piled upon another until half the characters are pretending to be somebody other than the person they really are.

Senator Doctor Donovan is exactly the kind of pompous authority figure that Friel loves to make the butt of laughter. Taken in by Tim's lies, the Doctor admires every detail of the rustic cottage, especially the stocks for keeping the cow indoors. Before the play is over, "Dr. Bollocks," as the young men call him, is confined in these stocks and reduced to bestial absurdity. From this predicament, he is rescued by a "stage German," known as Barney the Banks, who like the "stage Irishman" of English and Anglo-Irish comedies about the Irish, provides many laughs because of his imperfect understanding of the English language.[23]

The uses and abuses of language are the target of much of Friel's satire. As the Doctor and Tim exchange platitudes about ancestral pieties and eternal verities associated with the rural Irish landscape and setting, Tim mouths clever but empty words, phrases he has borrowed from the glib lawyer Jack, who uttered them to him just a few minutes earlier.

Tim is another type that Friel loves to target as the object satire, the academic expert. Along with Dr. Dodds, the sociologist who comments upon the action in *The Freedom of the City*, and Dr. King, the professor of archaeology who directs the excavations but remains off-stage in *Volunteers*, Tim is an inept expert, an untenured junior lecturer in linguistics at the local university, where he is writing a dissertation on "Discourse Analysis with Particular Reference to Response Cries." In spite of his academic training, Tim's speech is awkward and ineffective. As his friend Jack observes, "For one who professes the English language, your vocabulary is damned limp".[24] Compared with the eloquence of Hugh, the hedge-school master in *Translations*, Professor Tim's speech is a sad commentary on the progress of language and learning over the course of the last century and a half.

Indeed, if the world portrayed in *The Communication Cord* is contrasted with the world portrayed in *Translations*, it is possible to interpret the latter play as a satire of the state of the world's decline, not only in terms of language, but also of love and of faith. The subject of Tim's ridiculous dissertation suggests that "God!" and "Christ!" and "Good Lord!" have become reduced to nothing more than response cries, meaningless expletives. In this debased world, love relationships are built upon lies and resemble a game of musical chairs: Jack exchanges Evette for Susan; Tim exchanges Susan for Claire; Evette leaves Jack for "Teddy" (her nickname for her old friend, Senator Doctor Donovan). As all of the lovers find their proper mates and it seems that the plot is at last happily resolved, Tim and Claire, in a passionate embrace, inadvertently lean against the upright which is supporting the sagging ceiling of the cottage. Then the upper floor comes crashing down upon them, the lamp dies, and the play ends in total darkness.

Because we are in the terrain of comedy, we laugh at this mishap, but the dark, apocalyptic ending of the play suggests a crumbling, disintegrating society, vaguely reminiscent of the ending of Shaw's *Heartbreak House*. At this point we begin to realize, if we have not done so earlier, that we are in that marginal world where comedy borders on tragedy, a terrain which David Krause describes thus:

> it is precisely that ironic interplay between the farcical and the serious . . . which . . . defines what is the comic mainstream of the Irish dramatic imagination. Farce often casts long and grotesque shadows into the territory of tragedy without moving over the line that separates the two genres. [25]

*The Communication Cord* has been called light-weight in comparison with the emotionally powerful tragedy *Translations*. However, if comedy really is directed at our minds rather than our emotions, then Friel has succeeded in giving his audience substance to ponder: is a society built upon false values, false words, and false authority doomed to collapse?

Friel's last really funny play, as of this writing, is his bittersweet drama, *Dancing at Lughnasa*. Here, as in *Philadelphia, Here I Come!*, he employs the tragicomic mode, the one with which he has succeeded best in pleasing audiences. In 1966 *Philadelphia* ran for 326 performances in New York, the longest running Irish play on Broadway to date, and in 1990 *Dancing at Lughnasa* won both the Tony Award and the New York Drama Critics Award for the best play of the season. In both of these popular works, Friel's point of departure is a poignant circumstance of Irish life, in *Philadelphia* the necessity for emigration, in *Dancing at Lughnasa* the scarcity of eligible men for Irish women.

Sexual frustration is a comic theme which Friel had exploited in several of the earlier plays that we have considered. In *Philadelphia*, Private Gar imagines having a conversation with his father about sex:

> I'm beginning to wonder, Screwballs—I suspect—I'm afraid . . . I think I'm a sex maniac! . . . But I'm not the only one, Screwballs; oh indeed I am not; all the boys around—some of them far worse than I am. . . . Why? Why do I think we're all s.ms.? Well, because none of us is married. Because we're never done boasting about the number of hot courts we know—and the point is we're all virgins. [26]

Likewise, Andy's sexual frustration in *Losers* and the prisoners' jokes about their sexual deprivation in *Volunteers* poke fun at men's need for women. But not until *Dancing at Lughnasa* does Friel look at the reverse side of the joke, the need of women for men. Wisely, he allows jokes about female frustration to be made by the women themselves, not by men about women. Even as we laugh, we recognize that the subject of our amusement is the pain of human loneliness.

*Dancing at Lughnasa* is a memory play, narrated by the young boy Michael many years later, after he himself is grown and all the other principals of the story are dead. The use of this retrospective point of view lends poignancy to the story of five aging, unmarried sisters who live in a rural area some distance from Ballybeg, a village in County Donegal. The eldest sister, Kate, supports the family through her job as schoolmistress at the village school. As head of the family, Kate is the authority figure in the play, in which role she receives less satiric treatment than Friel usually accords such characters, for he allows us glimpses of her gentler side. Nevertheless, as spokesperson for orthodoxy, for respectability, and for narrow conventional values, Kate's speeches have a dampening effect on the high spirits of her younger, more vivacious sisters. They also provide her sisters with the occasion for ridicule.

Chris, the youngest sister, is the mother of Michael, a boy of seven in the summer of 1936. This child, born out of wedlock, is in a sense the shared child of all of the women, who have no other outlet for their maternal instincts.

The boy's father, Gerry Evans, is a comic rogue. An itinerant Welsh salesman who drops in upon the family for occasional visits and then departs again, Gerry is a playboy and a liar, but Chris, a realist, rarely believes his lies, which only make her laugh. Much to Kate's chagrin, Gerry contributes nothing to the support of his son, but his jokes and fantasies provides laughter and joy to Chris, and vicariously through her to her sisters, who watch enviously as the pair dance together. As an artist, a dancer and a fabricator of tall tales, Gerry's role is to create illusions, to entertain, to give pleasure. He also represents the procreative life force, the source of life's most profound pleasure.

Maggie, the most comical of the sisters, makes jokes about the sad lack of men in her and her sisters' lives, declaring that her Wonderful Wild Woodbine cigarettes are the "Next best thing to a wonderful, wild man".[27] She teases Michael, invents games, asks the boy silly riddles, and sings suggestive songs. In spite of the hard life which the family shares, Maggie tries to keep up her own and her sisters' spirits through her comic antics. Her spirit of fun counters the killjoy effect of Kate, who tells her, "If you knew your prayers as well as you know the words of those aul pagan songs!"[28]

Another foil to Kate, with her narrow religiosity, is the sisters' only brother, Jack, the most ludicrous figure in the play. During the summer of 1936, Jack, a priest, has returned home after serving twenty-five years as chaplain in Ryanga, a leper colony in Uganda. His long absence from Ireland has caused him to forget many words of English (thus making him another variation of the traditional stage Irishman), and during his sojourn away from civilization, he has also acquired many strange and amusing manners. As the sisters become reacquainted with their brother, it becomes apparent to them that instead of his having Christianized the natives, Jack has been converted by them to paganism. Thus the contrast of Christian views to pagan provides both a source of laughter and also a subtle criticism of life-negating religion in "civilized" society.

Kate accurately foresees that the paganization of her brother portends disaster for them all. After the local priest and parishioners, who had earlier been ready to welcome Jack home as a hero, discover his apostasy, they turn their disapproval not only upon the errant priest, but also upon his family. As a result, in time Kate will lose her job at the local school, and the family will face destitution. But these sad events lie in the future, not in the relatively happy present of summer, 1936.

Jack is the wise fool of the play, who despite his bizarre dress, strange behavior and absent-minded ways, has learned wisdom from the primitive people among whom he lived, people who make no distinction between the religious and the secular, and whose religion is a joyous celebration of life. Because of his contact with another culture, Jack can discern similarities between the ritual sacrifice of the Mass, the ritual sacrifice of a fowl or goat in a Ryangan fertility ceremony, and the blood sacrifices of the Irish at the feast of Lughnasa, ancient Celtic ceremonies in honor of the fertility god Lugh, remnants of which still persist in the back hills of Ireland. However, the positive aspects of Jack's cultural broadmindedness are undercut by the death of Rose's pet rooster, which turns up bloody but uneaten, the victim, we suspect, not of a fox, but of Jack's pagan rituals. Friel does not allow his audience to forget the dark and violent side of primitivism.

The incongruence of primitive and civilized ways provides much of the humor of *Dancing at Lughnasa*. Based upon the customs of the Ryangans, Jack offers his sisters a practical but comical solution to their problem of celibacy. When Maggie jokingly asks Jack whether in Ryanga he could guarantee a man for each of them, he replies, "I couldn't promise four men but I should be able to get one husband for all of you."[29] Bizarre as the suggestion of polygamy seems to these women from western culture, it turns out to be not much different from the practical solution to which Gerry Evans had secretly resorted with Chris, dividing his time between her and a wife and three children back home, including another son named Michael. Friel's play explores the issue of cultural differences, showing that a practice which is normal and acceptable in one society is sinful and taboo in another. Compared with the painful deprivation of the five sisters who must live with no man, Ryangan polygamy seems a saner way of life.[30]

When Chris and Gerry dance together in *Dancing at Lughnasa*, we witness a celebration of the pagan spirit, the *joie de vivre* of which sex and dance are a vital part. When Maggie and Rose dance to music on the wireless, Agnes jokingly calls them, "A right pair of pagans, the two of you" (12).[31] This joyous spirit is repeatedly quelled by Kate, the repressed spinster, who opposes everything that smacks of paganism.

Ironically, Kate's rejection of paganism includes a rejection of her own cultural past. Her reaction to the story about the Sweeney boy from the back hills, who was terribly burnt in the bonfires of Lughnasa, is cruelly judgmental:

> they're savages! I know those people from the back hills! I've taught them! Savages—that's what they are! And what pagan practices they have are no concern of ours—none whatever! It's a sorry day to hear talk like that in a Christian home, a Catholic Home![32]

"Savages" is the epithet which the English applied to the Irish when they first entered Ireland, a stereotype which Friel is subverting here. The feast of Lughnasa which Kate denounces celebrates fertility and abundance, both of which are sadly lacking in the home of the Mundy sisters. By contrasting Kate's conventional orthodoxy with Jack's primitive belief in the oneness of nature and religion, Friel establishes how far the Irish have departed from their ancient roots. Paganism, primitivism, wildness, and savagery represent the life force which Kate's religion would repress. This play, with its contrasting themes of sexual vitality and sexual repression, brings to mind other dramas attacking puritanical elements of religion, such as J. M. Synge's *The Tinkers' Wedding* and the later pastoral plays of Sean O'Casey.

In Friel's portrayal of the world of Ballybeg in the 1930s, the forces of primitivism are not entirely dead. Bonfires are still being lit during Lughnasa, and pagan customs are still observed. Despite the best efforts of Kate, the vital spirit is still alive in the Mundy sisters, as we see during the ecstatic dance which they perform in Act One. As Maggie begins the uninhibited dance, she is joined in turn by each of her sisters, until even Kate succumbs to the wild beat of the Irish dance music: "With this too loud music, this pounding beat, this shouting—calling—singing, this parodic reel, there is a sense of order being consciously subverted."[33] As we have noted earlier, the subversion of order is the essence of the comic spirit.[34]

The vitality of these rural Irishwomen of sixty years ago contrasts sadly with the listless spirits of the six contemporary city folk in Friel's next play, *Wonderful Tennessee* (1993). Uncomfortable in their native Irish countryside, these three middle-aged couples, none of them very happily married, try in vain to create a festive, Dionysian atmosphere with wine and food, music and dance. The main character, Terry, has planned to take his wife and two other couples on an excursion to an island off the coast of Donegal, an island which he had visited when he was a child, a place associated with ancient penitential pilgrimages. But the impossibility of modern Irish men and women returning to ancient traditions becomes clear (to the audience if not to Terry) while the six people wait all night for the boat that never comes to ferry them to the island. Despite their best efforts to enjoy themselves while they wait, their jokes fall flat, their performances lack energy, their stories become more and more dismal and depressing. In this play, Friel creates a Beckett-like comedy of despair, but unlike Beckett, he places his characters in a realistic, not a surrealistic setting. Unrelieved by comic exaggeration, defeat is not funny. When juxtaposed to *Dancing at Lughnasa*, *Wonderful Tennessee* indicates the increasingly pessimistic view that the playwright seems to take toward the direction in which modern civilization is moving. In a world where ancient beliefs have lost their force, the couples in *Wonderful Tennessee* endure unfulfilled lives without joy and without hope of ever reaching the vital pagan Otherworld.

In surveying the dramatic *oeuvre* of Brian Friel, we have seen how over the last four decades, the playwright has used a wide variety of comic modes, devices, and techniques to make his audience laugh, sometimes mockingly, sometimes painfully. His plays, without being derivative or imitative, often bear kinship to works of other great Irish comedians who have preceded him—Shaw and Wilde, Synge and O'Casey, Behan and Beckett. Using his art to deflate and expose figures of pompous or oppressive authority, to mock those aspects of society which appear to him ludicrous or destructive, to subvert stereotypes harmful to the Irish people, Friel takes his place among the great social satirists of the stage. His works, though always entertaining and never specifically didactic, often aim at the amelioration of social ills. Friel began his career as a teacher, and as a dramatist he continues in that role. Through the use of laughter, he alerts his Irish audience to the shortcomings and pitfalls within their society, he educates his international audience about the complexity of the Irish past and the difficulties facing Ireland in the present, and he makes us all more alive to those universal pagan instincts, both vital and violent, that lurk beneath the veneer of civilization.

# NOTES

1. See T.G.A. Nelson's discussion of tragic and comic modes in *Comedy: An Introduction to Comedy in Literature, Drama, and Cinema*. Oxford: Oxford UP, 1990. 28-34.

2. W. Moelwyn Merchant. *Comedy*. London: Methuen & Co., 1972. 47.

3. David Krause. *The Profane Book of Irish Comedy*. Ithaca: Cornell UP,

1982. 30, 271-72.

4. Brian Friel. *Selected Plays*. Washington: Catholic University of America Press, 1986. 52.

5. *Ibid*. 73.

6. *The Times*, 22 July 1967, p.7.

7. Brian Friel. *Lovers*. Dublin: Gallery Books, 1984. 53.

8. Krause, Chapter 5.

9. Brian Friel. *The Mundy Scheme*. In *Crystal and Fox and The Mumdy Scheme*. New York: Farrar, Straus, & Giroux, 1970. 220.

10. *Selected Plays* 116.

11. *Ibid*. 137.

12. *Ibid*. 130.

13. Brian Friel. *Volunteers*. London: Faber and Faber, 1979. 18.

14. *Ibid*. 14.

15. *Ibid*. 27.

16. *Ibid*. 15, 16.

17. *Ibid*. 56.

18. *Ibid*. 63.

19. *Ibid*. 33, 70.

20. *Ibid*. 25.

21. Vivian Mercier. *The Irish Comic Tradition*. Oxford: Clarendon Press, 1962. 12

22. Nelson, 20.

23. Maureen Waters. *The Comic Irishman*. Albany: State University of New York Press, 1984. 3, 11, 23.

24. Brian Friel. *The Communication Cord*. Dublin. Gallery Books, 1989. 15.

25. Krause, 278.

26. *Selected Plays*, 51.

27. Brian Friel. *Dancing at Lughnasa*. New York: Dramatists Play Service, 1993. 32.

28. *Ibid*., 45.

29. *Ibid*., 75.

30. See Terence Brown's excellent discussion of polygamy in "'Have We a Context?': Self and Society in the Theatre of Brian Friel," in *The Achievement of Brian Friel*, ed. Alan Peacock. Gerrards Cross: Colin Smythe, 1993. 199-200.

31. *Dancing at Lughnasa*, 12.

32. *Ibid*., 26.

33. *Ibid*., 31.

34. See Krause, 271-72; Nelson, 33.

# HOMELESS WORDS: FIELD DAY AND THE POLITICS OF TRANSLATION

## W. B. Worthen

"[. . .] I did a new adaptation of *Antigone*, an attempt along the
lines we discussed, to see what we can do for the old plays and
what they can do for us.
> —Bertolt Brecht to Ferdinand Reyher, April
> 1948 ( *Letters* 448)

Throughout his career, Bertolt Brecht often returned to "old plays" to
explore, refine, and enlarge the scope of dialectical theater. What is perhaps
surprising is that this strategy—the translation of Western classics—has remained a
staple means of political critique in the theater, including theaters emerging from
colonial domination. This is surprising in part because translation so readily raises
questions of fidelity; translation can appear to locate resistant theater in a belated
relation to dominant or hegemonic culture. Yet while translation enacts a gesture
of fidelity, it also performs an act of appropriation, blurring a merely dualistic
politics, particularly when verbal translation is accompanied by the transformation
or hybridization of form. Translation draws our attention not only to the social
and political interfaces between literatures and languages, but also to how those
borders are configured, and to the cultural work that translating between or across
them claims to accomplish. As Walter Benjamin argues, it is precisely the otherness
of the source, the world constituted by its verbal identity, that resists and defeats

translation between languages: a similar disjunction occurs between any dramatic text and its reproduction in the divergent discourses of the stage. Indeed, this necessary betrayal is perhaps what makes translation an attractive gambit for playwrights engaged in cultural resistance. In works like Wole Soyinka's *The Bacchae of Euripides* and *Opera Wonyosi*; Carlos Morton's *The Miser of Mexico*; Athol Fugard, John Kani, and Winston Ntshona's *The Island*; or Aimé Cesaire's *A Tempest*, for example, the "classic" is both presented and represented, doubled in ways that foreground the original's position *as* classic, and also interrogate the work that translation can be made to do in refiguring the relation between the classic and contemporary culture. [1]

Such plays dramatize the rhetoricity of translation, a rhetoricity it shares with performance in the Brechtian mode. To Gayatri Spivak, this dialectical interplay between the rhetoricity of language—which works "in the silence between and around words"—and the "logic" of language (syntax, grammar) is what forms agents in the world, and agents of a world: "The jagged relationship between rhetoric and logic, condition and effect of knowing, is a relationship by which a world is made for the agent, so that the agent can act in an ethical way, a political way, a day-to-day way; so that the agent can be alive, in a human way, in the world" (181). The translator's task is to model and expose this *other* means of agency. Rather than using translation to transfer "bodies of meaning" (179), the translator engages a "staging of the agent," and attempts to "enter or direct that staging, as one directs a play, as an actor interprets a script" (181). Though Spivak is not really interested in performance, her elegant account of the "politics of translation" verges on the politics of theater, in refocusing the activity of theater away from the "faithful" reproduction of a text toward a more searching encounter with agency, with how agents—actors, characters, spectators—are produced at the interface between languages and between the languages of the text and the semiotics of the stage. This emphasis on the performative emerges more emphatically in Homi Bhabha's evocation of "the *agency* of foreignness" in translation, of translation as "the performative nature of cultural communication. It is language *in actu* (enunciation, positionality) rather than language *in situ* (*énoncé*, or propositionality). And the sign of translation continually tells, or 'tolls' the different times and spaces between cultural authority and its performative practices" (228). Bhabha's sense of "translation" marks out two modes of cultural transmission, the propositional and the positional, a dialectic resembling that between the domain of the text (emphasis on origin, authenticity) and the domain of performance (emphasis on expression, alterity). In their mutual sense of translation as an interrogation of agency, Spivak and Bhabha provide some leverage on the refractory problem of the postcolonial production of classic

Western drama as a strategy of resistance.[2] For if such "translations" are to engage political change—or, indeed, even fulfill the more inchoate agenda often associated with hybrid forms—they must engage the performative, positional, rhetorical dimension of their own cultural production.

Here, I want to consider the politics of theatrical "translation" in the work of the Field Day Theatre Company of Derry, Northern Ireland. From its inception in 1980, Field Day has been associated both with the difficult politics of nationalist/unionist struggle in Northern Ireland, and with the thematics of "translation" at the center of its most widely-known play, Brian Friel's *Translations*. In addition to two fine classical translations—Tom Paulin's *The Riot Act: A Version of Sophocles' Antigone* (1984) and Seamus Heaney's *The Cure at Troy: A Version of Sophocles' Philoctetes* (1990)—the company has also produced Friel's notable Irish setting of Anton Chekhov's *Three Sisters* (1981), Derek Mahon's 1984 adaptation of Molière's *School for Husbands* as *High Time*, and has staged English language plays like Athol Fugard's *Boesman and Lena* in a recognizably Irish *mise-en-scène*. Producing at the conjunction of colonial and postcolonial, of the Republic of Ireland and the United Kingdom, of Ireland north and south, of Protestant and Catholic, Field Day takes "translation" as its central image and instrument of political change.[3]

This commitment to origin and expression, proposition and position, logic and rhetoric, text and performance, haunts the translational politics of Field Day's theater, and inflects the kind of resistance its "translations" can perform. Seamus Heaney's desire "To be at home / In my own place and dwell within / Its proper name" ("Open Letter" 26) maps the topography of Field Day's cultural nationalism: Field Day not only takes the theme of language and naming as critical to the representation of personal and public identity in Northern Ireland; it sees "Irish" identity to be inextricably bound to the languages of Ireland (Gaelic, English, Irish English), languages defined largely in terms of their innate cultural authority, rather than as fungible vehicles of political agency. As a result, Field Day's politics of translation seem strangely divided. Its major works for the stage— *The Riot Act* and *Translations*—seem poised to use "translation" to frame questions of history and agency, while at the same time finding in "translation" a vehicle for the faithful enunciation of cultural mythology, the reiterative authority of the classic.

Tom Paulin's pamphlet, "A New Look at the Language Question," clarifies the strains animating Field Day's use of "translation." Paulin aims to legitimate Irish English as a recognized form of English, and as a literary, aesthetic, and political medium. Arguing that the "history of a language is often a story of possession and dispossession, territorial struggle and the establishment or imposition of a culture" (3), Paulin lays claim to Irish English as a necessary vehicle of cultural translation, a hybrid and supple language mediating between the various languages of "Ireland" that nevertheless claims the authority of native speech. Noting that "With the exception of Ulster, the English spoken in most parts of Ireland today is descended from the language of Cromwell's planters" (4), Paulin locates the authority of Irish English in the seminal imposition of English in Ireland in the seventeenth century:

> In England, the English language reached a peak of creative power during the Elizabethan and Jacobean periods when writers formed sentences by instinct or guesswork rather than by stated rule. In time it was felt that the language was overseeded and in need of more careful cultivation. Writers began to argue that the absence of a standard of "correct" English created an ugly and uncivilized linguistic climate, and Dryden remarked that he sometimes had to translate an idea into Latin before he could decide on the proper way of expressing it in English (4).

Paulin's history of the language locates the translational authority of Irish English in the mystical "creative vitality" of its Elizabethan and Jacobean ancestors, forging a romantic connection to a primitive and spontaneous language still unstraitened by the efforts of Dryden, Swift, Johnson, H. W. Fowler, or James Murray.

Rooting Irish English in Shakespearean soil proves critical to the political and aesthetic prerogatives that Paulin assigns to the language. While Standard English is taught in state schools in the North and Irish is taught in Catholic schools in the North and in state schools in the Republic, the native language of Northern Ireland—Irish *English*—has been reduced to the status of corrupt dialect, a language "in a state of near anarchy," in which "many words are literally homeless." Like its Elizabethan progenitor, Irish English words and phrases now live mainly "in the careless richness of speech" (11). On the one hand, what makes Irish English plausible as a "federal" language is its authenticity; it is legitimately the language of Ireland, a hybrid and local speech sharing the "creative vitality" characteristic home-grown dialects: "dialect is notable for its intimacy and for the bonds which it creates among speakers. Standard speech frequently gives way to dialect when people soothe or talk to small children, and sexual love, too, is often expressed through dialect words" (12). Yet at the same time, this "federal concept of Irish English" (15) requires that the language be recorded, institutionalized (in dictionaries, style guides, school support), and find literary expression if it is going to mediate between the equally "authentic" claims of its constitutive states or provinces:

Thus in Ireland there would exist three fully-fledged languages—Irish, Ulster Scots, and Irish English. Irish and Ulster Scots would be preserved and nourished, while Irish English would be a form of modern English which draws on Irish, the Yola and Fingallian dialects, Ulster Scots, Elizabethan English, Hiberno-English, British English and American English. A confident concept of Irish English would substantially increase the vocabulary and this would invigorate the written language. A language that lives lithely on the tongue ought to be capable of becoming the flexible written instrument of a complete cultural idea (15).

Although Irish English is not seen as a "dominant" language, the fact that it is to give expression to a "complete cultural idea" implies that Irish English will be the intermediate language framing, expressing, and federating that culture and its idea. [4] Irish English appears at once to mark the boundary between the different versions of culture engrained in Ireland's several languages, and at the same time to gesture toward the authentic, the indigenous, the original; as a political medium, Irish English appears committed at once to preservation and to change, to history and to adaptation. But what seems absent from Paulin's account of Irish English is a sense of its relation to *agency*, a sense that Irish English is more than a lexical departure from Standard English, but a rhetoric for constituting a world and its agents. To sidestep the interplay between language and agency is to reify language and politics as distinct spheres, and this rather wan "revolutionary effect" typifies Field Day's cultural politics. As F. C. McGrath reports, "Friel says: 'I think that the political problem of this island is going to be solved by language,' and that the 'linguistic overhaul' will 'lead to a cultural state, not a political one,' but 'out of that cultural state, the possibility of a political state follows'" ("Introducing" 147). Distinguishing language from political agency, Field Day participates in a familiar nationalist mythology, an effort to uncover "a common ground beneath political conflicts, whether between peasant and landlord, Catholic and Protestant, or class and class, which could then be seen as mere surface phenomena of Irish society. In such a way, Irish literature was to become a 'central institution or idea,' forming a 'social bond' to replace the historically evolved constitution that was thought to override and integrate social differences in England" (Lloyd 15). Much as the "creative vitality" of Irish English derives from its mystified Elizabethan inheritance, so political change will take place through a magical dissemination of the authentic power of words.

Paulin's *The Riot Act* dramatizes the strain inherent in a politics of translation, what Anthony Roche—in a fine article on four recent Irish

*Antigones*—describes as "the difficult balance between the claims of the status quo and the urge to revolution, between the need to build stable political structures and maintain tribal loyalties" (249-50). Roche derives this dialectic from the tragic arithmetic of *Antigone*, but it obviously reflects the politics of translation as well, where the act of molding contemporary strife to the "universal" template of the classic frames its own tensions between past and present, the "logic" of the classic and the "rhetoric" of its reproduction. Viewing translation as "an ambitious type of neoclassicism which helps to form conscience" (*Ireland and the English Crisis* 214-15), Paulin seems inclined to use translation to restate the authority of the source, rather than to interrogate the consequences of that authority in its reproduction in the present; he seems, that is, to regard translation in largely propositional terms. This tension is, for instance, visible in the critical reception of *The Riot Act*. When Keith Jeffrey asked why a writer, "apart from 'plot exhaustion,'" might attempt such a translation, the answer seemed plain: "in order to make the enduring truths of the original more accessible to modern audiences"; yet if translation is conceived merely as the reproduction of "enduring truths," the play necessarily appears as "surprisingly tentative in its application to Northern Ireland" (Murray 285-86).

Paulin's instigation in writing the play, his barbed encounter with Conor Cruise O'Brien's claim to the moral authority of the play and of Antigone herself, dramatizes the divided claims of *The Riot Act* and the divided politics of translation. In a 1968 Belfast lecture—reprinted in *The Listener*, and revised for inclusion in *States of Ireland* in 1972—O'Brien drew a comparison between *Antigone* and the events of Northern Ireland; Paulin's extensive review of O'Brien and *States of Ireland* appeared in the *Times Literary Supplement*, and was reprinted in his *Ireland and the English Crisis* in 1984.[5] In 1968, O'Brien compared Antigone to Civil Rights workers like Bernadette Devlin—"Antigone's action was one of non-violent civil disobedience, the breaking of a law which she considered to be contrary to a higher law" (*The Listener* 24 October 1968; qtd. *States* 156)— and argued that despite the fact that "Creon's authority, after all, was legitimate, even if he had abused it" (157), the moral force of Antigone's position outweighs the slightly paranoid rage for order characteristic of the world's Creons:

> At present every Creon thinks some other Creon is behind the
> Antigone that is plaguing him. The communists, thinks Creon, are
> behind the student activists at Columbia: the CIA, thinks Creon,
> are behind the Czech intellectuals. We should be safer without the
> trouble-maker from Thebes. And that which would be lost, if she
> could be eliminated, is quite intangible: no more, perhaps, than a

way of imagining and dramatising man's dignity. It is true that this way may express the essence of what man's dignity actually is. In losing it, man might gain peace at the price of his soul. (qtd. *States* 158)

Revising the essay for *States of Ireland,* O'Brien remarks that "Reading that essay now, three years afterwards, I find myself no longer in sympathy with the conclusion. Antigone is very fine on the stage, or in retrospect or a long way off, or even in real life for a single, splendid epiphany. But after four years of Antigone and her under-studies and all those funerals—more than a hundred dead at the time of writing—you begin to feel that Ismene's commonsense and feeling for the living may make the more needful, if less spectacular element in 'human dignity'" (*States* 159).

Paulin's shrewd review of O'Brien's "translation" of *Antigone* traces O'Brien's process of revision and revisits his application of *Antigone* to the political situation in Northern Ireland in the 1970s. Paulin points out that O'Brien silently omitted several passages from his original lecture; more important, he challenges O'Brien's reading of Antigone's wilful rebellion as a "severe distortion of the tragic conflict" which not only renders Creon "almost innocent," but seems finally to support "Creon's rule of law" (*Ireland and the English Crisis* 28).[6] Yet for all the energy of their argument, O'Brien and Paulin merely duplicate the play's tragic logic: state and individual, civil and moral law, are phrased as mutually exclusive, mutually destructive, and inevitably opposed. *Antigone* operates not to translate between conceptions of moral agency in the past and present, but to define them, as Paulin and O'Brien both interpret the play and lay claim to the moral and cultural authority it metonymically represents. In this sense, Paulin and O'Brien also share a fundamentally similar politics of translation, a struggle to find in *Antigone* an enduring vocabulary of political and moral strife. Each argues for the adequacy of his application of the play's unquestioned theme and structure to the situation in Northern Ireland; neither challenges Sophocles' framing of the issues *as* tragic, nor the means or consequences of applying this tragic paradigm to Northern Ireland. The cultural authority of the classic prevents Paulin and O'Brien from regarding it as *other,* as offering tropes of fictive agency (and stage acting) that must be articulated *against* the grain of contemporary attitudes and behavior for an act of "translation" fully to emerge; neither questions the translational politics of how—or why—they make the play perform.[7]

As an instance of Paulin's "ambitious type of neoclassicism," *The Riot Act* registers a similar tension between competing commitments to translation. For Paulin's achievement in *The Riot Act* is only superficially to "find a home and context for such lexical outcasts as 'screggy', 'sleg', 'pobby'" and other Irish Englishisms (Roche 225). Although Paulin's translation generally accepts the narrative and thematic constraints of *Antigone*, he uses performed language—speech-action, the mode of characterization in the theater—to specify the play's political application to the present. Despite its investment in the authenticity of origins, *The Riot Act* verges on performative translation when it specifies and locates the positionality of its performers, exposing the rhetoric that constructs them as agents. Character—the articulation of language in speech and action constitutive of a subject—lies on the border between text and performance; it is at once traced into the design of the text and something that emerges onstage as the effect of acting, not its cause. The "state" characters in particular—Creon, the Guard, and the Messenger—are given more specific, modern characterization, made to articulate their positionality in the play's performance in more evocatively modern terms. Paulin's Creon resembles both Ian Paisley and Douglas Hurd, but likening Creon to authoritarian figures in Northern politics is a version of "translation" that accomplishes little more than the scuffle with O'Brien: Paulin sides with Antigone over Creon in a situation still defined by Sophocles' paradigm.[8] Paulin's "translation" is most effective when language and political agency are foregrounded performatively, when spoken language articulates modern social relations in ways that challenge or elucidate those inscribed in *Antigone*, and explore the relationship between Sophocles' rhetoric and the rhetoric of the modern state.

Although the actors all speak Irish English in performance, *The Riot Act* foregrounds the politics of translation in performance when it registers spoken dialect as an aspect of class, notably in the scenes between Creon and the Guard.[9] The Guard speaks in prose, not in verse, and Paulin carefully discriminates between Creon's smooth public discourse and the Guard's speech habits ("'Sammy, you're a fool, you're a complete eejit,'" he says to himself 18), a discursive relationship made concrete in Creon's belittling treatment of him: "My good man, / pray tell me simply / what's on your tiny mind" (19). Speaking style translates Sophocles' rank differential into a class relation in Paulin's play, and this kind of translation is especially evident when speaking itself becomes a kind of performance, as when the Guard narrates Antigone's burial of Polynices' body. He describes the condition of Polynices' body ("Soft and pobby he was, and he smelt rotten") using a blend of working class ("wains" 25) and army ("corp" 26) slang. And he describes the way the sandstorm blew up to conceal the body from the observers: "It was then the wind blew up and suddenly—*troubl*e!—we were lost in this huge dust-storm and the entire place was obliter*a*ed" (26). The "propositional" force of this pronunciation (the Irish English alternative to the

Standard English "obl *i*terated") is evasive at best, but its "positional" force is clear: it opposes the Guard's social (and possibly national) identification to Creon's affiliations, in ways that also intersect with the various pronunciations—and identifications—of individual members of the audience.

In most respects, Paulin's play hews to the trace of its original: though the Irish English lexicon and the occasional anachronism suggest an application to contemporary Northern Ireland, the play maintains Sophocles' static stalemate between civil and moral authority as its framework of political commentary. Paulin's ambitious neoclassicism, like all neoclassicism, evades political critique by seeing history underwritten by unchanging mythic paradigms. As David Lloyd suggests of Seamus Heaney's poem "The Tollund Man," "This is effectively to re-duce history to myth, furnishing an aesthetic resolution to conflicts constituted in quite specific historical junctures by rendering disparate events as symbolic mo-ments expressive of an underlying continuity of identity" (27). And yet Paulin's tiny inscription of the performative into the text—"obliter *a*ted"—points sugges-tively toward the political work translation might accomplish. For to hear Irish English spoken in the play and used to characterize its parts, to hear the play not only in the accents of Derry and Ulster, but also in accents that display (as Creon and the Guard do) different modes and degrees of access to speech, could be to use Paulin's "federal concept of Irish English" to interrogate Sophocles' Thebes—that unified city state, with its hesitant chorus, its institutions of rank and privilege and citizenship—as a model for political and moral interpretation, to chart the limits of its paradigmatic authority in the present. [10] Paulin's emphasis on the Guard's pronunciation here dramatizes the ways that texts are specified by performance, used to establish identities, positionalities, meanings that are incommensurable with the internal dynamics of the text, that lie silently alongside the text as its rhetorical potential. Irish English, in this fleeting moment, becomes more than a vehicle for reproducing the cultural authority of the classic. It qualifies the classic and suggests the terms and limits of its application to modern con straints of action and behavior, meaning and agency. It implies, perhaps, what we can do for the old plays in addition to what they continue to do for—and to—us.

Theatrical performance can bring the performative dimension of translation into a special kind of focus, and plays and productions that claim to use translation to political purpose must use performance in this general way, to interrogate the relationship between the classical "origin" or "source" and the rhetoric of con-temporary agency. This relationship between source and agency lies at the heart of Field Day's most familiar work for the theater, Brian Friel's *Translations*. The political thematics of translation in the play have been well and amply explored, as has Friel's use of George Steiner's *After Babel* in conceptualizing translation in the play, and often in developing specific passages of dialogue.[11] But theatrical performance plays a significant role in modeling Steiner's sense of translation, and dramatizes the relation between origin and performance inscribed in Friel's play. Early in *After Babel*, Steiner suggests that the translator's activity—like the work of editors, critics, musicians, and actors—epitomizes the working of language itself: the translator is "*un interprète*—a life-giving performer" (28). The notion that actors translate or interpret (Steiner prefers the stronger force of the French term to its weaker English cognate) a text is a familiar one, and Steiner glosses it nicely in thinking about the role of Posthumus in Shakespeare's *Cymbeline*:

> The function of the actor is particularly graphic. Each time *Cymbeline* is staged, Posthumus's monologue becomes the object of manifold "edition." An actor can choose to deliver the words of the Folio in what is thought to have been the pronunciation of Elizabethan English. He can adopt a neutral, though in fact basically nineteenth-century solemn register and *vibrato* (the equivalent of a Victorian prize calf-binding). He may by control of caesura and vowel-pitch convey an impression of modernity. His— the producer's—choice of costume is an act of practical criticism. A Roman Posthumus represents a correction of Elizabethan habits of anachronism or symbolic contemporaneity—themselves a convention of feeling which we may not fully grasp. A Jacobean costume points to the location of the play in a unique corpus: it declares of *Cymbeline* that Shakespeare's authorship is the dominant fact. Modern dress production argues a trope of "eternal relevance"; whatever the singularities of Jacobean idiom, the "meaning" of Posthumus's outburst is to be enforced here and now. But there can also be, indeed there have been, presentations of *Cymbeline* in Augustan, Byronic, or Edwardian garb. Each embodies a specific commentary on the text, each realizes a particular mode of animation. (27-28)

Steiner's account of acting and costume reveals the channels of authority guiding his understanding of translation, and of performance as well. Steiner's actor is like an editor in that his creative, interpretive, translational agency is deeply hedged by the authority Steiner locates in the original, the text.[12] The actor is akin to the translator in bringing the classic text into the present, but the actor's alternatives are all defanged: performance transpires either in the dominant register of the author, or (much the same thing) in the transcendent register of the "universal."

Performance, that is, works mainly to translate the *authority* of the original into a new key, rather than to represent its construction of agents or a world. When Steiner then remarks "As every generation retranslates the classics, out of a vital compulsion for immediacy and precise echo, so every generation uses language to build its own resonant past" (30), we can see the force of the classic underlying Steiner's treatise on language. Steiner's vision of history is a history of continuity, not of rupture; of progress, not of revolution. His notion of translation, firmly committed to preserving the origin, loses the sense of confrontation and revision, the articulating of new positionalities relative to origins, relative to production and reception, characteristic of more resistant versions of performance-translation.

Though Field Day is sometimes identified as "the cultural wing of the Provisional IRA" by its opponents (Callaghan 45), its politics of translation, derived to an extent from Steiner's, are hardly revolutionary. Yet in plays like *Translations*, the performative possibility of translation seems to suggest an interrogation of the relationship between origin, authority, and political agency. Based on *After Babel*, on P. J. Dowling's *The Hedge Schools of Ireland* (1968), and on J. H. Andrews's *A Paper Landscape* (1975), Friel's play interprets the Ordnance Survey as a distinctive colonial project, one in which the Irish language and Irish identity are written off the map. [13] Though Friel generally collapses and reinvents his sources in the play, *Translations* nonetheless recalls Benedict Anderson's sense that the "three institutions of power which, although invented before the mid nineteenth century, changed their form and function as the colonized zones entered the age of mechanical reproduction" were the census, the map, and the museum, which "profoundly shaped the way in which the colonial state imagined its dominion—the nature of the human beings it ruled, the geography of its domain, and the legitimacy of its ancestry" (163-64). *Translations* stages an image of that past at the moment of its subjugation to the colonial order; it offers a "translation" of an absent text, an "origin" now available only in translation, a text that has been systematically obliterated.

Friel's meditation on the relation between origins and performance is largely conducted at the interface between the play's three language-realms—classical (Greek and Latin), colonized (Irish), and imperial (English)—and performance. The play's first moments bring these into conjunction, as Manus's efforts to get Sarah to speak (performed in Irish English) are counterpointed by Jimmy's reading from Homer, "' *Ton d'emeibet epeita thea glaukopis Athene*'" (384). Greek and Latin are spoken throughout the play, and—perhaps recalling Steiner's remarks on the "totality of Homer, the capacity of the *Iliad* and *Odyssey* to serve as repertoire for most of the principal postures of Western consciousness" (22)—imply an informing parallel between the two "heroic," lost cultures of Athens and Ireland. [14]

As Yolland remarks, "I heard Jimmy Jack and your father swapping stories about Apollo and Cuchulainn and Paris and Ferdia—as if they lived down the road" (416). The ironies of this relationship are pointed as well, especially in the play's final moments, where Jimmy's announcement of his engagement to Athene counterpoints Hugh's recollection of their (failed) march to the 1798 Belfast Rising, "Two young gallants with pikes across their shoulders and the *Aeneid* in their pockets" (445). Although Friel strikes few narrative parallels between nineteenth-century Ireland and the classical myths mentioned in the play, the constant equipoise between classical and Irish civilization articulates Steiner's vision of history, in which the present is continually regenerated on the template of its cultural past. Yet it also points out the relationship between the "classics" and empire: the Greek and Latin classics shared by the Irish and English characters in the play will retain their power to trope the present; Irish mythology will be lost with its language.

The nostalgic cultural nationalism of *Translations*—which Friel sharply qualifies in the companion play *The Communication Cord*—relies in part on Steiner's vision of "translation," in which the authority of the past, the "classic," the origin becomes the master trope of the present. But Friel's performance of the past in *Translations* suggests an alternative reading of the politics of translation, in which performance can expose or interrogate rather than merely reproduce classical authority. Owen's introduction of Captain Lancey at the end of Act 1 and his strategic misrepresentation of Lancey's remarks offers a paradigmatic set-piece of the politics of translation in the play. [15] This scene dramatizes, of course, the power of translation to deceive, but it is also critical to the play's anatomy of the politics of performance-translation. For beyond Owen's deception, several smaller misprisions take place that enlarge and clarify the relation between language and performance Friel claims in the play.

The first of these takes place entirely in "English":

HUGH: What about a drop, sir?
LANCEY: A what?
HUGH: Perhaps a modest refreshment? A little sampling of our
       *aqua vitae*? (405)

Though Hugh carefully addresses Lancey in English, he uses dialect locutions of Irish English ("a drop") that Lancey doesn't follow. Lancey's confusion foregrounds the fact that the play's principal spoken language, the language of performance, is Irish English, which becomes the medium through which all other languages—including "Standard English"—are represented. Throughout *Trans-*

*lations* (which is now performed throughout the English-speaking world), Friel troubles the "English" surface of the play, using Irish English in ways that keep its language "other" to audiences whose English isn't Irish. [16] When Bridget describes the effect of learning in English at the new national schools, for example—"every subject will be taught through English and everyone'll end up as cute as the Buncrana people" (396)—it's clear that some items appear in the lexicons of, say, British, American, and Irish English, but with different meanings in each case. Similarly, Irish English syntax also differs from other Englishes, as when Maire calls Owen over to examine her map of England, "Come here till you see" (437). Language is never neutral, least so when it translates. Such moments trouble the translational transparency of spoken English in the play—the performed discourse that provides the audience's access to "English" as well as to "Irish"—by forcing performers and audiences to negotiate an "English" which may or may not be an oddly estranged tongue. Although Lancey is the play's invading villain, *Translations* uses the complexity of performed speech to place its audiences—some of its audiences, some of the time—on the cusp of Lancey's position, engaging a familiar language that becomes occasionally remote and fugitive. (Indeed, if Paulin is right about the pace of change that Irish English is currently undergoing, it may be possible to imagine Irish audiences occasionally baffled by an odd word or turn of phrase).

The opacity of Irish English is only one of the opacities that Lancey (and certain audiences) must confront in the play. Lancey proceeds to speak "*as if he were addressing children—a shade too loudly and enunciating excessively,*" to which Jimmy replies:

> JIMMY: *Nonne Latine loquitur?*
> (HUGH holds up a restraining hand.)
> HUGH: James.
> LANCEY: (To JIMMY) I do not speak Gaelic, sir. (405)

It's an easy joke, yet it clarifies *Translations's* systematic negotiation between text and performance. For Lancey's faint familiarity with both Latin and Gaelic points to a more subtle negotiation the play has already demanded from its theater audience several times. Much as Lancey mistakes which language is being spoken, audiences may well not be immediately clear which language the performers' Irish English represents. Early in Act 1, Doalty describes how he has craftily moved the markers of the English surveyors, causing them to examine and disassemble their theodolite, and in telling the story, Doalty briefly acts it out: "*And immediately he speaks in gibberish—an imitation of two very agitated and confused sappers in rapid conversation.*" "That's the image of them!" Bridget replies (391). English represents "Irish," and gibberish represents "English"; later the surface of language is troubled in a more complex way:

> MANUS: Time enough. Class won't begin for another half-hour.
> YOLLAND: Sorry—sorry?
> OWEN: Can't you speak English? (411)

If we thought Manus was speaking English, only Yolland's "Sorry—sorry" alerts us to the fact that the actor's English represents "Irish," a language Yolland doesn't understand. The more interesting question concerns Owen's reply: though performed in English, does it represent "English" or "Irish"—which language is Owen using to Manus? A stage performance might decide this question, but it would do so by positioning the verbal statement within the nonverbal rhetoric of performance—gesture, intonation, expression, movement, and so on. Though Irish English is privileged as the performative language of the play, Friel consistently uses the performance to compromise its "federal" authority to represent others, other languages, other agencies, other cultures. As Yolland and Maire remind us in Act 2, when they speak the "same" sentences in uncomprehending dialogue, the most powerful acts of signification in the play take shape in deeds, not words: love, invasion, murder, flight.

*Translations* is interested in politics in a cultural sense; Friel's "position, as an artist, is that he must stand aside from the actual events of the conflagration in Derry or Northern Ireland generally, in order to describe the greater freedom of which the Irish psyche is capable" (Pine 106). This investment in the "fifth province" of art exemplifies Friel's particular brand of cultural nationalism, one that links his playwriting to Paulin's conception of a federal language. Indeed, Paulin's sense of the Elizabethan vitality of Irish English is perhaps glancingly evident in a short sequence in *Translations*:

> JIMMY: I came across this last night—this'll interest you—in book
>      Two of Virgil's *Georgics.*
> DOALTY: Be God, that's my territory alright.
> BRIDGET: You clown you. (392)

Doalty's clowning around reminds us of the Elizabethan sense of "clown" as a rustic, the kind of pastoral laborer epitomized and idealized in the *Georgics.* Staging a "lost" civilization in the accents of modern Irish English, Friel verges more delicately, perhaps more skeptically, on Paulin's romantic blurring of origin into identity. As Seamus Deane argues, Romantic views of language often enact the complex subordination of the subaltern. Taking "pleasure in the notion that Ireland is a culture enriched by the ambiguity of its relationship to an anachronistic and a modernised present" ("Heroic Styles" 45), to the extent that Irish English and Irish literature restores a kind of lost vitality to English language and literature, "Cultural nationalism is thus transformed into a species of literary unionism" (47). Yet although "translation" often marks the necessity to forge "a new speech, a new history or life story" that would give "some rational or coherent form" to the traumatic crises of oppression (Deane, Introduction 14), such translation also works to invent cultural or historical origins as an enabling fiction, a means to identity. Paulin takes the "federal concept of Irish English" to express a "complete cultural idea" because it retains the original "creative vitality" of Elizabethan English, and because it is therefore able to mediate between the other native languages of Ireland; translating *Antigone*, Paulin's *The Riot Act* tends to reenact rather than interrogate the authority of its classical original, by assuming that the "meanings" of *Antigone* can be translated into the discourse of the present. Friel's use of Irish English in *Translations* seems to suggest a more tentative agenda. Not only is Irish English shown to produce both Irish language and Irish history as an absence, but the radical instability operating between languages seems finally to undermine translation between them and between their competing versions of culture, agency, and identity. Yet at the same time—as Lancey's use of the "translated" map to guide a brutal military action demonstrates—Friel suggests that if translation fails to communicate "meanings," it is nonetheless instrumental in enacting relations of political and cultural authority. By foregrounding the performative limits of Irish English, *Translations* at once expresses nostalgia for the sense of identity authorized by the collocation of language and cultural origin, and foregrounds the rhetorical work that this sense of language performs in forming the myth of nations.

As Sara Sulieri remarks in her study of the British Raj, to attend to the relation between authorized and subversive, colonial and postcolonial, is to "attempt to break down the incipient schizophrenia of a critical discourse that seeks to represent domination and subordination as though the two were mutually exclusive terms" (4). Field Day's cultural nationalism is often conveyed through the metaphor and process of translation. Yet the politics of translation, especially in theater works like *The Riot Act* and *Translations*, is complicated by the provisional relationship that performance strikes with "origins." This tension between origin and enactment, and the different strategies of authorization each enables, marks the translational politics of Field Day's work, much as it marks the urgent contestation of claims to identity and claims to origin in Northern Ireland.

Seamus Heaney captures the situation at one moment in his play *The Cure at Troy*. Heaney's version of Sophocles' *Philoctetes* follows the outlines of the original relatively closely, but toward the end of the play, just before Philoctetes' encounter with Hercules, Heaney inserts an instructive chorus. Beginning with anachronistic images of "A hunger-striker's father" and a "police widow in veils," the Chorus continues:

> History says, *Don't hope*
> *On this side of the grave.*
> But then, once in a lifetime
> The longed-for tidal wave
> Of justice can rise up,
> And hope and history rhyme. (77)

Translation is a powerful instrument for resistant theaters like Field Day, not least in its ability to use performance to articulate a critique of how "translations" can help to form and maintain certain versions of agency, by imagining and producing the cultural categories of the past in new and striking ways. But this kind of translation is difficult to produce, precisely because it requires a confrontation with the classic and with our means of reproducing it and ourselves. Like performance, translation is engaged in a complex project of identification, an elaborate encoding of personal and cultural identity and history through the negotiation of alterity. To claim "translation" as a theatrical politics is to keep that alterity visible, to prevent translation from gathering the other uncritically into the authorizing narrative of the self, to see translation performing the difference between languages, cultures, agents, histories, mythologies. Whether hope and history can rhyme—or, indeed, whether they *should* rhyme—may well depend on how they come to speak in the same language.

# NOTES

I would like to thank Peggy Meacham and my colleague Mary Trotter for their shrewd readings of different versions of this essay.

1. This way of inhabiting a slippery interface marks a difference from what we might think of as avant-gardist experiments like Charles Marowitz's various Shakespearean collages, or from confrontations that assume an explicitly allegorical or thematic position relative to an *absent* original, such as Edward Bond's *Lear* or Howard Barker's *Seven Lears,* or Tom Stoppard's *Rosencrantz and Guildenstern Are*

*Dead.* Where avant-gardist adaptation is generally conceived as a reading, critique, restatement, or interpretation of the *play* in question, resistant translation tends to instrumentalize or reposition the text as part of a wider cultural or political critique. Though not a postcolonial work, a production of the Split Britches/Bloolips collaboration *Belle Reprieve* dramatizes this sense of resistant performance/translation; it both articulates a reading of the contours of sexual and gender identity in Williams's *A Streetcar Named Desire* and places *Streetcar* in a complex critical relation to contemporary culture, interrogating how dominant modes of aesthetic representation (realism) contribute to the oppressive politics of sexuality in contemporary America. The production "translates" *Streetcar* into the discourse of camp and cabaret in order to examine and reconfigure the kinds of positionality made available by modern and postmodern performance, in the theater and in culture at large.

2. Jatinder Verma suggests one version of such "translation" in connection with his production of Molière's *Tartuffe*: "The main features were (a) the play as 'borne across' to seventeenth century India; (b) transposed 'in form' to Indian popular theatre conventions; (c) presented 'as a gift from the West' by a French traveller, François Bernier, to the Emperor Aurangzeb in a 'translation' by the Emperor's Court Poet; (d) the deliberate use of Indian languages, which at times were directly 'translated' by one of the two story-tellers; (e) the direct quotation from Indian and European texts, either as parody (in the case of Shakespeare) or as a substitute for Molière's original text" (59). It should be noted that this production was an equivocal act of "resistance": Verma's "first all-Asian" cast play was produced at Britain's Royal National Theatre.

3. As Seamus Deane remarks, Field Day's theater works to stage "a political crisis produces a clash of loyalties that is analyzable but irresolvable. [. . .] the dramatic analysis centers on anxieties of naming, speaking and voice and the relation of these to place, identity , and self-realization" (Introduction 14-15). And Eamonn Hughes notes, Friel's Irish-English adaptation of *Three Sisters* was "part of the general process of translation and re-translation that Field Day are engaged in; by interpreting non-Irish material for Ireland they hope to provoke questions about the condition of Ireland, questions which would not arise from standard versions, questions, indeed, which the work of the company suggests have been rendered unaskable by the existence of standard versions, from which Field Day are trying to escape" (72). Similarly, their production of Fugard's *Boesman and Lena* "caused more of a controversy by apparently offering the conditions of South African apartheid as an analogy for the North of Ireland" (73). It should be noted, however, that the politics of gender and sexuality are not especially prominent in Field Day work.

4. The notion of linguistic federalism is inherently troubling—to think, for example, of Gloria Anzaldúa's brilliant meditation on the relationship between Chicano Spanish, Mexican Spanish, Spanish, and English is both to recognize the difficulty of Paulin's desire to legitimate all languages spoken in Ireland while according priority to any one (and indeed, to see the nativism still located in Irish English, with its Elizabethan tang): "So, if you want to really hurt me, talk badly about my language. Ethnic identity is twin skin to linguistic identity—I am my language. Until I can take pride in my language, I cannot take pride in myself. Until I can accept as legitimate Chicano Texas Spanish, Tex-Mex and all the other languages I speak, I cannot accept the legitimacy of myself. Until I am free to write bilingually and to switch codes without having always to translate, while I still have to speak English or Spanish when I would rather speak Spanglish, and as long as I have to accommodate the English speakers rather than having them accommodate me, my tongue will be illegitimate" (Anzaldúa 59).

5. I am indebted to Roche's fine article for background on Paulin, O'Brien, and *Antigone*; in addition to treating *The Riot Act*, Roche also treats Aidan Carl Mathews's Beckettian version of *Antigone* (1984), and Brendan Kennelly's translation of the play.

6. Paulin continues, "It is as though a future member of Creon's think-tank can be discerned hiding behind the unfortunate Ismene" (28). Paulin points out that O'Brien's revision omits "the statement, 'Without Antigone, we could attain a quieter, more realistic world. The Creons might respect one another's spheres of influence if the instability of idealism were to cease to present, inside their own dominions, a threat to law and order'" (*Ireland and the English Crisis* 27).

7. This debate anticipates the terms of another 1984 study, George Steiner's *Antigones*. At the conclusion of *Antigones*, Steiner attempts to locate the enduring utility of Greek myths. It might be argued that Greek drama articulates either "certain primary biological and social confrontations and self-perceptions in the history of man" that "endure as an animate legacy in collective remembrance and recognition." Or, one might "theorize on a humbler level," that the centrality of Greek literature at the origin of Western culture "is so immediate and fertile that Greek mythology has become a constant centre or pivot of reference for all subsequent poetic invention and philosophic allegory. The Greek myths are a shorthand whose economy generates unlimited variations but which does not, in itself, need to be reinvented." Or it might be that "the principal Greek myths are imprinted in the evolution of our language, and of our grammars in particular," to the extent that "we speak organic vestiges of myth when we speak. Hence the indwelling in our mentality and culture of Oedipus and of Helen, of Eros and of Thanatos, of Apollo and of Dionysus" (Steiner 300-301, 303). Though Steiner

works to circumscribe the importance of Greek narrative to Western culture, his dialectic of origin and adaptation remains clearly inclined toward the determining power of the origin.

8. As several critics have noted, Creon is first called "the big man" by the Chorus Leader (and echoed again in the Guard's line, "Where's the big noise? [24]), an allusion to Ian Paisley; the pallid platitudes of his opening speech ("Mr. Chairman, loyal citizens of Thebes, these recent months have indeed been a most distressing time for us all" 15) evoke, and occasionally quote, Douglas Hurd. "From the first introduction of Creon as 'the big man' (6), the audience is led to make parallels between ancient Thebes and modern Ireland. 'The big man' is a well-known appellation for Ian Paisley. Creon's first speech to the people relates him directly to the then new Secretary of State for Northern Ireland, Douglas Hurd. Creon echoes Hurd's early statements and even utters some of his own words: 'I have always held that one of the soundest maxims of good government is— *always listen to the very best advice. And in the coming months I shall be doing a very great deal of listening*' (7). Fintan O'Toole in the Dublin *Sunday Tribune* called this first speech 'a brilliant parody of a Northern Ireland Office political functionary'. In fact, of the ten reviews of the play which I read, only Keith Jeffrey, writing for the London *Times Literary Supplement*, mentions another possible model for Creon's abuse of power: Richard Nixon" (Harris 258).

9. Ismene, for instance, alludes to the "screggy, smelly crowd" who will "sleg us" (12); Creon refers to Antigone as "the sneaky, sleaked one" (30); the Chorus describes the air on a hot day making "a clemmed shimmer, like chains" (44); Tiresias upbraids the "thrawn and jaggy hates" that divide Creon's state (54).

10. Paulin subtitles *The Riot Act "A Version of Sophocles' Antigone"* much as he subtitles his *Seize the Fire "A Version of Aeschylus's Prometheus Bound."* In *Seize the Fire*, however, Paulin's interest in adapting plot and language to represent a modern political dictatorship outweighs his evident use of Irish English. Although the play has an occasional Irishism—"Dirty beasts they are" says Violence at the outset (1)—Paulin seems here much less interested in having his characters speak in a visually-represented Irish dialect than in lending Aeschylus' play a more specific and local political orbit: Zeus becomes a modern dictator, Prometheus a kind of subversive political prisoner, Oceanos a Polonian tool of the state, and so on. See also Paulin's poem, "Under Creon."

11. For extended discussion of Friel's use of Steiner, see Richard Kearney's listing of passages "which served as a major critical and philosophical source for Friel's language plays" (*Transitions* 158-60); Pine *passim*; McGrath, "Irish Babel" and "Language, Myth, and History"; Meissner; Smith.

12. The actor's performance is said first to be of the words of the Folio,

which is unlikely to be the case, strictly speaking; although a few experimental companies work with facsimile Folio texts of the plays (which Folio text?), most productions work with modern editions, themselves "translations" in Steiner's strong sense, attempts to work through the vagaries of Renaissance publishing practice and the historical differences between Shakespeare's language and our own to produce a text that claims "authenticity" even though little about it is clearly or unproblematically "authentic."

13. Friel and Andrews discussed the play under the auspices of the Interdisciplinary Seminar at St. Patrick's College, Maynooth in January 1983, and their remarks were reprinted in edited form in *The Crane Bag*.

14. Note that Steiner describes the "collation of the *Iliad* and the composition of the *Odyssey*" (22)—a distinction that perhaps informs Friel's choice of Greek quotations exclusively from the *Odyssey*.

15. The principal performative convention of *Translations* has, by this time in the play, become clear: the actors perform in English to the theater audience, which represents either "Irish" (when the Irish characters are speaking among themselves) or "English" (when the Irish characters converse with the English, or when the English speak among themselves). Greek and Latin are spoken according to the conventions of classical pronunciation, and are usually "translated" directly or indirectly by the dialogue between the characters. Owen (addressed as Roland by the English) introduces Captain Lancey, and Friel brilliantly stages the politics of translation in Owen's deft, ameliorating rendering of Lancey's speech.

16. For example, Owen on Bridget and Maire teasing him about his supposed Dublin wealth, "God Almighty, would you listen to them—taking a hand at me!" (402); "poteen" throughout, especially Owen teaching the pronunciation to Yolland (416); "footless drunk" (401); "Had he drink on him last night at the dance?" (432); I was going to fell him" (432); "You're missing the crack, boys!" and "You never saw crack like it in your life, boys" (434, 435).

# WORKS CITED

Anderson, Benedict. *Imagined Communities: Reflections on the Origin and Spread of Nationalism.* rev. ed. London and New York: Verso, 1991.

Andrews, J. H. *A Paper Landscape: The Ordnance Survey in Nineteenth-Century Ireland.* Oxford: Clarendon P, 1975.

Anzaldúa, Gloria. *Borderlands / La Frontera: The New Mestiza.* San Francisco: Aunt Lute Books, 1987.

Benjamin, Walter. "The Task of the Translator." *Illuminations.* Trans. Harry Zohn. New York: Schocken, 1969. 69-82.

Bhabha, Homi. "How newness enters the world: Postmodern space, postcolonial times and the trials of cultural translation." *The Location of Culture.* London and New York: Routledge, 1994. 212-35.

Brecht, Bertolt. *Letters 1913-1956.* Trans. Ralph Manheim. Ed. John Willett. London: Methuen, 1990.

Callaghan, Dympna. "An Interview with Seamus Deane—University College, Dublin, June 1993." *Social Text* 38 (spring 1994): 39-50.

Deane, Seamus. "Heroic Styles: the tradition of an idea." Field Day Theatre Company, *Ireland's Field Day* 43-58.

———. Introduction. Field Day Theatre Company, *Nationalism, Colonialism, and Literature* 3-19.

Field Day Theatre Company. *Ireland's Field Day.* London: Hutchinson, 1985.

———. *Nationalism, Colonialism, and Literature.* Minneapolis: U of Minnesota P, 1990.

Friel, Brian. *Translations. Selected Plays of Brian Friel.* Washington, D. C.: Catholic UP, 1986. 377-451.

———. John Andrews, and Kevin Barry. "*Translations* and *A Paper Landscape*: Between Fiction and History." *The Crane Bag* 7:2 (1983): 118-24.

Harris, Claudia. "The Martyr-Wish in Contemporary Irish Dramatic Literature." Kenneally 251-68.

Heaney, Seamus. *The Cure at Troy: A Version of Sophocles' Philoctetes.* New York: Farrar, Straus and Giroux, 1991.

———. "An Open Letter." Field Day Theatre Company, *Ireland's Field Day* 19-30.

Hughes, Eamonn. " 'To Define Your Dissent': The Plays and Polemics of the Field Day Theatre Company." *Theatre Research International* 15:1 (1990): 67-77.

Jeffrey, Keith. "In defence of decency." *Times Literary Supplement* 19 October 1984.

Joyce, James. *A Portrait of the Artist as a Young Man: Text, Criticism, and Notes.* Ed. Chester G. Anderson. New York and Harmondsworth: Penguin, 1977.

Kearney, Richard. *Transitions: Narratives in Modern Irish Culture.* Manchester: Manchester UP, 1988.

Kenneally, Michael, ed. *Cultural Contexts and Literary Idioms in Contemporary Irish Literature.* Totowa, N.J.: Barnes and Noble, 1988.

Lloyd, David. *Anomalous States: Irish Writing and the Post-Colonial Moment.* Durham: Duke UP, 1993.

McGrath, F. C. "Introducing Ireland's Field Day." *Éire-Ireland: A Journal of Irish Studies* 23:4 (1988): 145-55.

———. "Irish Babel: Brian Friel's *Translations* and George Steiner's *After Babel.*" *Comparative Drama* 23 (1989): 31-49.

———. "Language, Myth, and History in the Later Plays of Brian Friel." *Contemporary Literature* 30 (1989): 534-45.

Meissner, Collin. "Words Between Worlds: The Irish Language, the English Army, and the Violence of Translation in Brian Friel's *Translations.*" *Colby Quarterly* 28 (1992): 164-74.

Murray, Christopher. "The History Play Today." Kenneally 269-89.

O'Brien, Conor Cruise. *States of Ireland.* New York: Random House, 1972.

Paulin, Tom. *Ireland and the English Crisis.* Newcastle upon Tyne: Bloodaxe Books, 1984.

———. "A New Look at the Language Question." Field Day Theatre Company 1-18.

———. *The Riot Act: A Version of Sophocles' Antigone.* London and Boston: Faber and Faber, 1985.

———. *Seize the Fire: A Version of Aeschylus's Prometheus Bound.* London and Boston: Faber and Faber, 1990.

———. "Under Creon." *Liberty Tree.* London: Faber and Faber, 1983. 13.

Pine, Richard. *Brian Friel and Ireland's Drama.* London and New York: Routledge, 1990.

Roche, Anthony. "Ireland's *Antigones*: Tragedy North and South." Kenneally 221-50.

Smith, Robert S. "The Hermeneutic Motion in Brian Friel's *Translations.*" *Modern Drama* 34 (1991): 392-409.

Spivak, Gayatri Chakravorty. "The Politics of Translation." *Outside in the Teaching Machine.* New York and London: Routledge, 1993. 179-200.

Steiner, George. *After Babel: Aspects of Language and Translation.* 1975. 2nd. ed. Oxford and New York: Oxford UP, 1992.

———. *Antigones.* New York and London: Oxford UP, 1984.

Sulieri, Sara. *The Rhetoric of English India.* Chicago and London: U of Chicago P, 1992.

Verma, Jatinder. "Cultural Transformations." *Contemporary British Theatre.* Ed. Theodore Shank. London: Macmillan, 1994. 55-61.

# THE WOMAN AS NATION IN
# BRIAN FRIEL'S *TRANSLATIONS*

## Lauren Onkey

The idea of the defeated nation being reborn as a triumphant woman was central to a certain kind of Irish poem. . . . The irony was that few Irish poets were nationalists. By and large, they had eschewed the fervour and crudity of that ideal. But long after they had rejected the politics of Irish nationalism, they continued to deploy the emblems and enchantments of its culture. (Eavan Boland 13)

Irish political and literary discourse is filled with women who represent the long suffering and proud nation: Dark Rosaleen, the women of the Aisling poems, Queen Medbh, Cathleen ni Houlihan, "Mother Ireland," de Valera's "comely maidens at the crossroads" and even women in such recent work as Seamus Heaney's "Act of Union" and Paul Muldoon's "Aisling." David Cairns and Shaun Richards argue that such leaders of the Easter Rising as Patrick Pearse and Joseph Plunkett believed strongly in "Mother Ireland." Because their deaths raised the status of their work to "founding truths," the trope of the nation as woman took an even stronger hold after southern independence: "the notion of an Ireland, symbolically represented as 'woman,' whose destiny was to be independent and united, passed into the education and cultural formation of two generations of Irish men and women" ("Tropes and traps" 130).

In an early Field Day pamphlet, Richard Kearney reads the symbol of woman as nation as a somewhat benevolent response to colonial conquest:

> The more dispossessed the people became in reality the more they sought to repossess a sense of identity in the realm of ideality. Since the women of colonized Ireland had become, in James Connolly's words, the 'slaves of slaves,' they were, in a sociological sense at least, obvious candidates for compensatory elevation in the realm of myth and mystery. . . Woman became as sexually intangible as the ideal of national independence became politically intangible. Both entered the unreality of myth. ("Myth and Motherland" 76)

Kearney's analysis, which traces the change from the use of Fatherland imagery to represent Ireland to Motherland imagery, is a provocative and useful study of the origins of Ireland as woman. But he fails to acknowledge the flip side of the Irish "elevation" of woman into myth. While the nation's discourse revered woman, raising her to emblematic status, it simultaneously created a legal climate hostile to women's freedom. As Eavan Boland asserts, the poetic tradition of the nation as woman both alienated her and hindered her development as a poet; she believes that "Mother Ireland" affects attitudes towards real women: "Once the idea of a nation influences the perception of a woman then that woman is suddenly and inevitably simplified. She can no longer have complex feelings and aspirations. She becomes the passive projection of a national idea" (13). If we trace the history of this symbol, we will find moments where it has not only simplified women, but has served to justify their oppression. Women may have represented the "native purity" of the nation, but they were shut out of power in post-colonial Ireland.

In his study of the psychology of Indian colonialism, Ashis Nandy points out that "feminizing" the colonies is an important discursive strategy of colonialism. Colonial discourse constructed the colonized as weak, barbaric, romantic and incapable of governing themselves in order to justify its "civilizing" mission. In nineteenth century Irish colonial discourse, for example, the Celtic race was defined as the inferior counterpart—an "essentially feminine race," according to Ernest Renan—to the English Teutonic race. [1] In response, colonized peoples often develop an overly masculine political discourse as a method of asserting power during the transition to independence. As feminist critic Gerardine Meaney argues, "Anxiety about one's fitness for a (masculine) role of authority, deriving from a history of defeat or helplessness, is assuaged by the assumption of sexual dominance" (7). In Ireland "the assumption of sexual dominance" was bolstered by constitutional discourse, which legislated women out of power. Thus, keeping women out of power became an important component of post-colonial Irish identity.[2]

Legal control follows logically from the "elevation" of woman as nation. When a woman becomes a symbol for the essential qualities of the nation, she is then its property. Therefore the nation can police her behavior. As Meaney argues, women become "guarantors of their men's status, bearers of national honour and the scapegoats of national identity. They are not merely transformed into symbols of the nation, they become the territory over which power is exercised" (7). Woman as the sign of tradition is a trap; when the rhetoric of national identity rests on women's sexual morality, women are both the promise of that identity and, if they fall, the mark of its failure.[3] This is a characteristic problem of women negotiating a space for themselves in the political discourse of a new post-colonial nation; in order to win independence, they often abandon their own agenda to make alliances with nationalists, who then marginalize them.[4] Irish feminists, for example, put aside their fight for emancipation in order to join the larger nationalist forces for independence in 1915-16. Margaret Ward argues that the women's alliance with nationalists later worked against them: "Because the right of women to organize autonomously was never accepted by nationalists . . . women were left helpless when faced with a threat to their specific interests that did not engage the concern of nationalists" (252).[5] At best, nationalist discourse defines women's issues as "private" and therefore far less important than issues of "politics" or "nationhood." At worst, women's emancipation is actually constructed as a threat to the achievement of nationhood.[6]

Ironically, the provocative cultural criticism of the Field Day group has again subsumed the work and the "subject" of women under a "gender free" notion of Irish identity in literature, history and politics. Field Day sought to complicate and rethink ideas about the nation, literature, politics and culture partly in an effort to help rethink the Northern conflict. Their objective is "to contribute to the solution of the present crisis by producing analyses of the established opinions, myths and stereotypes which had become both a symptom and a cause of the current situation" (*Ireland's Field Day* vii). While I cannot determine their impact on ideas about Northern Ireland, Field Day's analyses have transformed Irish studies by emphasizing literature's relationship to history and culture, and by reading culture as a lived process, not a fixed set of characteristics. Most observers see Field Day as successful in the goals they laid out in 1980, lauding the company for bringing more sophisticated ideas about colonialism and nationalism to the theater and political discourse.

However, women's issues have never been included in Field Day's agenda.

Although in an early Field Day pamphlet Seamus Deane asserts that "Everything, including our politics and our literature, has to be rewritten—i.e., re-read. That will enable new writing, new politics, unblemished by Irishness, but securely Irish" ("Heroic Styles" 58), Field Day has not published pamphlets about women, produced plays by women, or studied nationalism, colonialism and Irish identity as they affect women. The massive *Field Day Anthology of Irish Writing* (1991) is the best illustration of the group's blind spot. The anthology is a crucial intervention in Irish literary history; it is the first anthology to attempt a comprehensive history of Irish writing that sets poetry, drama and fiction (in both English and Irish) in complicated and sometimes contradictory relationship to historical documents, political speeches, and critical essays. In the process, it foregrounds cultural debate over nationalism, the effects of colonization, and Irish identity. But it fails to consider women as part of the Irish experience not by degrading or dismissing their work, but by ignoring it; of over 300 writers included covering 1500 years, only 39 are women. There is also a complete absence of women, sexuality, or gender as categories of literary and political analysis or of historical discourse.[7] They have constructed a history of Irish literature which leaves women as simplified and idealized as "Mother Ireland."

Brian Friel's *Translations* resonates into the volatile symbolic and real history of women in Ireland, as well as the problematic history of Field Day's indifference to women's writing and politics. Perhaps because it was the first production of Field Day, or because it so directly dramatizes the colonial confrontation, *Translations* has been associated with the Field Day objectives and, almost unanimously, declared a successful revision of Irish cultural myths. George O'Brien's comments are typical: "[The first act] . . . does as much as anything in modern Irish theater to erase the stereotype of the Irish peasant—drunken, fighting, cohabiting with pigs, craven, superstitious . . . Friel believes that his peasants have minds and that they are alive to learning" (103).[8]

But, like the work of Field Day itself, critical analyses of *Translations* have rarely studied the play's women characters or the issues about women and colonialism that the play raises. The struggle seen as central in the play—the supplanting of the Irish language by English—is read, quite reasonably, as a struggle between men. The women in the play have little to do with the institutionalized control of language. Hugh and Manus run the hedge school, and, along with Jimmy Jack, are the masters of Greek and Latin. Lancey commands the "general triangulation which will embrace detailed hydrographic and topographic information" (719), and Yolland and Owen's task is "to see that the place-names on this map are . . . correct . . . standardized . . . . Where there's ambiguity . . .

Anglicized" (719). Although Sarah and Maire do not teach, master, or translate language, their actions ignite the more material, physical tragedy of the play, and reveal the sexual coding inherent in colonial conquest. Sexual transgression, not linguistic struggle, ultimately causes the violence of the play. When Maire acts on her desire—embracing and kissing Yolland at the dance, thereby stepping outside the bounds of the community—and when Sarah witnesses and reports the act, violence erupts in Baile Beag. The community rises up to assert control over the sexual life of its symbolic property and Yolland disappears.

*Translations* re-reads and rewrites the hoary trope of woman as nation, critiquing and questioning its use. The play reveals that Maire's role as a symbol for the colonized people of Baile Beag is a tragic burden to her. Friel complicates the use of this symbol further with Sarah, who simultaneously invites highly symbolic readings and destabilizes efforts to read a national identity on her. Yet Maire is generally ignored by critics and Sarah is read as an unambiguous national emblem. Because woman as nation is such a powerful and entrenched trope, and because critics seem almost trained to exclude women from discussions of the Irish colonial experience, critics have constructed a version of *Translations* with a much more simple view of women than the text reveals and, ironically, have applauded Friel for the creation.

From the opening of the play, Maire's desires are directed outside Baile Beag; she has begun to reject Ireland. Because she has a clear head about her economic future, she has gotten enough money to go to America. When Manus objects to her plan, she responds "There's ten below me to be raised and no man in the house. What do you suggest?" (708). She is also the only one of the hedgeschool students who is eager to replace Irish with English: "We should all be learning to speak English. That's what my mother says. That's what I say. That's what Dan O'Connell said last month in Ennis. He said the sooner we all learn to speak English the better" (713). She expresses no romanticism about Baile Beag, its past, or the Irish language, and the soldier's presence excites her. She and Manus are romantically involved and have talked of marriage, but she plans to leave him for America if he does not apply for a job at the national school: "You talk to me about getting married—with neither a roof over your head nor a sod of ground under your foot" (717). Maire seems disgusted by the people of Baile Beag; when Bridget panics over the sweet smell of the potato blight, she cries:

> Sweet smell! Sweet smell! Every year at this time somebody comes
> back with stories of the sweet smell. Sweet God, did the potatoes
> ever fail in Baile Beag? . . . Never. But we're always sniffing about
> for it, aren't we?—looking for disaster. The rents are going to go

up again—the harvest's going to be lost—the herring have gone
away for ever—there's going to be evictions. Honest to God, some
of you people aren't happy unless you're miserable and you'll not
be right content until you're dead! (709)

This restless dissatisfaction draws her outside of the community to Yolland; it is in
fact just after she rebuffs Manus about his job prospects that Yolland and Lancey
appear on stage. Besides being English, Yolland is of a better class—he has "a
gentleman's hands"—and he represents the escape she so desperately wants.

Although it would appear that Yolland and Maire have a love that transcends
the rules of their respective tribes (and that's of course what they think), their
mutual desire is partly based on misunderstanding one another as symbols.
Yolland is attracted to Maire because he wants to stay in Ireland and she embodies
its qualities; he is, as Owen says, a "committed Hibernophile" (720). While Maire
decries the character of the people of Baile Beag, Yolland reveres it: "I had moved
into a consciousness that wasn't striving nor agitated, but at its ease and with its
own conviction and assurance" (727). Their misunderstanding culminates in the
crucial scene of their embrace. If he could speak her language, Yolland says, he
"would tell you how I want to be here—to live here—always—with you" and that
he's "not going to leave here" to which she happily responds "Take me away with
you, George" (738), revealing her perception of him as representative of all that
lies outside Baile Beag. With their interchange Friel highlights the ways in which
misreading is the inevitable result of reading symbolically, without ambiguity,
based solely on myths and stereotypes.

Friel foreshadows the uproar and violence that Maire and Yolland's embrace
incites by evoking the legend of Diarmuid and Grania early in the play. In the first
scene, Jimmy Jack muses about the sexual attributes of his beloved Athene; Manus
dismisses the notion, asserting that "She was a goddess, Jimmy" (701). In response
Jimmy Jack alludes to Grania's legendary lasciviousness: "Sure isn't our own
Grania a class of a goddess. . . . And sure she can't get her fill of men" (701). His
comment defines Grania as sexually rapacious, and suggests that her story has an
important cultural significance. According to the legend collected and published
by Standish O'Grady, Fianna leader Finn Mac Cumhall wanted to marry the
much younger Grania, daughter of King Cormac; she, however, put a claim on
Diarmuid, one of Finn's soldiers, in order to escape marrying the old warrior: "'It
is a great marvel to me,' said Grainne, 'that it is not for Oisin that Finn asks me,
for it were fitter to give me such as he, than a man that is older than my father'"
(Cross & Harris 373). Diarmuid is forced to flee with her, and is therefore at war
with Finn, a war that divides the Fianna for many years; Finn finally kills

Diarmuid, but the Fianna remain divided. Finn still desires Grania and wins her, much to the disgust of the men around her: "when the Fianna saw Finn and Grainne coming towards them in that manner, they gave one shout of derision and mockery at her, so that Grainne bowed her head through shame" (420). Their union is required for the reconciliation of the Fianna against the threat of a foreign army. Grania's mistake, of course, is that the object of her sexual desire is not the same man that the community has chosen for her.

The legend of Diarmuid and Grania has been retold in many versions, but most paint Grania as lustful and therefore responsible for the country's division. Anthony Farrow writes, "Of all the characters in Irish mythology, Grania is the one proverbially associated with inconstancy: in 1897 Yeats called the legend 'the strangest of all tales of the fickleness of woman'" (10). Yeats and George Moore's 1901 dramatic version of the play, *Diarmuid and Grania*, emphasizes the active role of Grania and the powerlessness of Diarmuid. The play was a flop—it had only three performances—but quite controversial. A priest in the *Freeman's Journal* criticized the playwrights for dramatizing such a "sensual and immoral legend" (Cairns & Richards, *Writing Ireland* 73) because it did not uphold the virtues of Irish womanhood. Cairns and Richards argue that the public's response to this play contributed to the creation of the more acceptable and romantic nationalist legend of *Cathleen ni Houlihan*. "Thus Yeats learned that in contemporary Ireland some symbols and evocations had meaning which were unproblematically clear for his audiences—. . . confirmed when he saw . . . *Cathleen* go on to become a nationalist classic . . . [it] extolled the sacrifice of one of the people-nation for the sake of Ireland" (73). Cathleen is an acceptable symbol of the nation because she puts the nation above personal desire; in fact, national priorities are her own priorities. Grania does the opposite. She represents sexual license, a woman freely choosing her own alliances, which is clearly a problematic source of disorder in the community. In a subtle way, Maire's choice of Yolland represents something similar to the people of Baile Beag, and so therefore they must make a move to stop her.

Because Baile Beag sees her as its representative, she cannot be "taken" by Yolland (i.e., the British). After the lovers part, Yolland is presumably killed by the Donnelly twins. In *Transitions*, Kearney reads their transgression as a breaking of community "codes":

> According to the local code, Maire has been promised to Manus and this tacit tribal contract cannot be gainsaid or 'decoded' by an outsider—even in an act of love. . . . Whatever about transgressing the mythological boundaries between the human and the divine,

the real boundaries between one human code and another cannot
be ignored with impunity (140).

Kearney correctly identifies the impenetrable boundaries between them but he
does not explore what motivates those "tribal" codes. In Maire and Yolland's case,
crossing the boundaries is dangerous because it takes the form of a sexual
transgression across colonial lines. After all, Owen does not inspire violence for
befriending Yolland, nor Doalty for clearing a path to his door. Maire cannot act
freely on her desires because she functions as property and symbol of Baile Beag. If
Maire stands in for Ireland, then Yolland's emotional or sexual possession of her is
equated with possession of the country.

But Friel writes this policing of desire as tragedy for Maire, critiquing the
symbolic burden she must carry. Baile Beag's "election" of Maire to symbol
devastates both her and the town. The hedgeschool community registers the
enormity of the tragedy by standing outside the reprisal against Maire. The
characters are silent about Maire's moment with Yolland; the assumed violence
remains unspoken among them, and in the last scene Maire is treated with
kindness by Hugh and Jimmy Jack. The people in the hedge school do not look
down upon Maire, but they are aware of the magnitude of her problems; nothing
in their response to her hints that she has betrayed them. Jimmy Jack is the only
character to allude to Maire's relationship with Yolland when he announces his
plans to marry the goddess Athene—a goddess he compared earlier to Grania. He
explains to Maire the Greek concepts of *Endogamein*, to marry within the tribe,
and *Exogamein*, to marry outside the tribe; he warns: ". . . you don't cross those
borders casually—both sides get very angry. Now, the problem is this: Is Athene
sufficiently mortal or am I sufficiently godlike for the marriage to be acceptable to
her people and to my people? You think about that" (752). His is the penultimate
speech of the play and the last word on Maire's actions; his words are not a harsh
judgment of Maire, but a plea for her to accept that she has tried to do what
cannot be done. The response of the hedgeschool community suggests that
although the violence against Yolland and Maire may have been inevitable, it was
not deserved or necessary. The impending reprisals of Lancey's troops indicate that
policing Maire's desires will make life worse in Baile Beag.

The story of Maire and Yolland dramatizes the potential tragedy of reading
woman as symbol, and it raises the question of how to interpret the impact of
politics on individual characters. Friel's diaries reveal that he struggled with that
question while composing *Translations*:

One of the mistakes of the direction in which the play is presently pulling is the almost wholly *public* concern of the theme: how does this eradication of the Irish language and the substitution of English affect this particular *society*? How long can a *society* live without its tongue? Public questions; issues for politicians; and that's what is wrong with the play now. The play must concern itself only with the exploration of the dark and private places of individual souls. ("Extracts" 60)

Obviously, the play engages larger issues of language and culture, but Maire's story suggests that we must be careful not to abandon the idea that characters have motivations which may contradict or work against their prescribed public roles. Interpretations of Sarah, who hardly speaks yet whose actions are crucial, have erased any private motivations that she may have. She offers us no clear meaning: her silence, ambiguous age, and virtually sexless identity (a "waif") make her a fascinatingly open sign, a voiceless character able to be read differently by each director. The description of her in the play only provides details about her speech: "Sarah's speech defect is so bad that all her life she has been considered locally to be dumb and she has accepted this: when she wishes to communicate, she grunts and makes unintelligible nasal sounds. She has a waiflike appearance and could be any age from seventeen to thirty-five" (699). She has very little to say in the play, only her name a few times, the name of her village, "flowers," and Manus's name. In some stagings of the play Sarah is placed at the front of the stage through all of the hedgeschool scenes, standing as silent witness to the translations as she struggles with her own speech. [9]

Sarah's ambiguity suggests that there would be a range of critical interpretations of her, but critics have consistently confined the meaning of Sarah to a representation of the tongue-tied nation. This perhaps originates with Seamus Heaney's eloquent and influential review in the *Times Literary Supplement* only a month after the play premiered. He sees a direct link between Sarah and Cathleen Ni Houlihan as representatives of Ireland:

Towards the end of the play, however, when the English captain demands who she is, his command and strangeness scare her: 'My name . . . my name is . . .' is all she can manage. It is as if some symbolic figure of Ireland from an eighteenth-century vision poem, the one who once confidently called herself Cathleen Ni Houlihan, has been struck dumb by the shock of modernity. Friel's work, not just here but in his fourteen preceding plays, constitutes a powerful therapy, a set of imaginative exercises that give her the chance to know and say herself properly to herself again. (1199)

Heaney suggests that Sarah is shocked back into silence by the arrival of the British soldiers and the "modernity" they represent: the loss of the hedgeschool and the destruction of the Irish language. In his argument, Sarah's silence represents the silence of the nation itself; Friel's work, in turn, gives the nation the opportunity to "know" and "say" itself properly. By comparing Sarah to Cathleen, the woman who beckons her men to fight for her, Heaney reads Sarah as yet another female representation of the nation, without acknowledging the problems inherent in that myth. Heaney's quote has largely determined what little reading of Sarah has been done. The quote is repeated in many studies of the play, and seconded by other critics. [10] Ronald Bryden, for example, describes *Translations* as "a play about Ireland's present griefs—the griefs, Friel suggests, of a people struggling to say who they are. For the traditional symbol of Kathleen ni Houlihan, he substitutes the figure of the tongue-tied peasant girl Sarah, unable to name herself to herself" (Zach 86). Robert Smith points out that the Hebrew Sarah "was the mother of nations" and argues therefore that "Friel's Sarah stands for a people's loss of tongue and name" (399). According to these readings, Friel's creation of Sarah as nation is a mark of what makes Friel and Field Day successful in their perceptions of politics: Friel has taken a traditional symbol and given it new life. But if Sarah represents the suffering nation, then Friel would be reinforcing rather than reconstructing old myths and stereotypes. If we read Sarah as Heaney suggests, i.e., as national symbol—however weakened and silenced—then we subsume her possible range of meanings under the weight of the nation. In this reading Friel's critique of the "nation as woman" gets lost as the critic focuses on a supposedly more important, national issue: the loss of the Irish language.

Sarah's silences in a play about the control of language, and her crucial role in witnessing Maire and Yolland suggest connections between Sarah and Cathleen as "Ireland." For example, though not old, Sarah is unattractive like Cathleen, and her witness to and reporting of the kiss between Maire and Yolland inspire a rising of sorts in Baile Beag which leads men to their deaths. Also, Sarah's father is a well known singer in Baile Beag, strengthening her connections to the tradition of the folk. She embodies no modern or English qualities.

But her silence and pain can also be read as a private reaction to Manus's departure. Her words upon seeing Maire and Yolland—Manus' name—reflect the more personal nature of her response to what the Donnelly twins and others perceive as a public issue. Readings of Sarah, following Heaney, take as a given that she is "struck dumb by modernity" i.e., struck dumb by the larger, social events occurring in the play. But the play itself remains unclear on this point. [11] Manus is perhaps the first person to treat Sarah compassionately; he senses that she would be capable of speech if she tried. The opening scene of the play is Manus' diligent and ultimately successful attempt to get Sarah to speak her name, and it functions as a sort of hesitant love scene between the two. She presents him with flowers and is "embarrassed" by doing so, and he responds by kissing her on the head. Maire enters, and the stage directions underscore their intimacy: "Manus stands awkwardly, having been caught kissing Sarah and with the flowers almost formally at his chest" (703). She has fallen in love with Manus, and listens intently when he talks with Maire about their marriage plans. In the early scenes, she seems to be developing under his gentle coaxing; she identifies herself to Owen, for example, but her efforts at speech are directed at Manus: "Sarah, very elated, 'I said it Manus'" (717). He is her only route to language. Despite her troubles, Sarah has no difficulty finding words when she sees Maire and Yolland kissing outside the dance: "She stands shocked, staring at them. Her mouth works. Then almost to herself. 'Manus . . . Manus!'" (738).

In order to make a connection between Sarah and Cathleen, one would have to read this scene as Sarah's act of informing on Maire. Sarah's reporting of the love scene between Yolland and Maire reveals the enormity of Maire's transgression: she connects the private act between the lovers to the community, and thus acts as a loyal spy for the tribe, helping to police Maire's behavior. But Sarah reported Maire and Yolland's embrace only to Manus, and by telling others in Baile Beag, he has transformed her private shock into a public act of reporting. Richard Pine argues that Sarah has been betrayed by Manus, "by making public the mute secrets of her privacy. In the public world she is destroyed" (172). Sarah's story, like Maire's, can be read as the tragedy of reading someone's behavior nationally, as having relevance for the tribe only.

Sarah's report to Manus, as well as his reaction, takes place offstage. Such a moment is indicative of the ambiguity surrounding Friel's representation of Sarah. Her many silences and ambiguous gestures require that we must remain open to a range of explanations for her behavior, especially in a play about ambiguous translations and the problematics of language. Sarah's meaning is most ambiguous in the scene the morning after the dance, where we are left to interpret three gestures: Sarah's silence to Lancey, her shake of the head, and her smile. When she appears she is no longer willing to speak. The stage directions read, "Sarah, more waiflike than ever, is sitting very still on a stool, an open book across her knee. She is pretending to read but her eyes keep going up to the room upstairs" (739), i.e., the room where Manus is packing. Manus assumes that she feels badly for setting off the violence against Yolland; before he leaves, he tries to console her: "'There's nothing to stop you now—nothing in the wide world. It's all right—it's all right—you did no harm—you did no harm at all.' He stoops over her and kisses the top of her head—as if in absolution" (741). But after he leaves, Sarah remains remorseful: "I'm sorry . . . I'm sorry . . . I'm so sorry, Manus . . ." (741). Sarah may be sorry because of Yolland's murder, but it seems equally likely that she's upset about Manus's departure.

After Manus leaves, Sarah is confronted by Lancey, who has come to the school to announce the army's repercussions for Yolland's disappearance. He demands her identity:

> LANCEY: Who are you? Name!
> (Sarah's mouth opens and shuts, opens and shuts. Her face
> becomes contorted.)
> LANCEY: What's your name?
> (Again Sarah tries frantically.)
> OWEN: Go on Sarah, You can tell him.
> (But Sarah cannot. And she knows she cannot. She closes her
> mouth. Her head goes down.) (746).

If Sarah represents the nation's difficulty with speech, then she is either silent in defiance or fear of the colonizer. Given her struggle to say her name revealed in her contorted face and her "frantic" attempts at saying her name, defiance is implausible. Most critics explain her response as fear of the colonial authority, but I think such a reading ignores the source of Sarah's attempts at speech. [12] Her success at speech is new, and has only been motivated by Manus' encouragement; without Manus, she has lost her ability and inspiration to speak. Sarah herself seems to reject Lancey's impact on her to Owen. After Lancey leaves, Owen tries to encourage her, but she asserts that she will not be speaking again: "'It will [come back]. You're upset now. He frightened you. That's all's wrong.' (Again Sarah shakes her head, slowly, emphatically, and smiles at Owen. Then she leaves)" (747). That emphatic shake of the head tells Owen that Manus, not Lancey, has caused her speech defect to return.

And her smile? It could be nothing more than a simple gesture of farewell to Owen. But it may also be read as a refusal to be simplified. To read Sarah only as a symbol of Ireland shuts down rather than opens up meaning. Such a reading allows us to construct an argument about how colonization silences the native Irish language. But the play suggests that if in response to colonization Ireland deploys "woman" as the representative of violated nation, it risks exercising another kind of oppression. Critics' willingness to brush aside Sarah's ambiguity and follow

Heaney's reading of her says more about their comfort with this deployment of the woman as nation than Friel's characters. It seems that women are dealt with most easily when they can be "translated" into a national rhetoric, which thus avoids the critique of nationalism that feminism raises. Friel's depiction of Maire should keep us from evoking the symbol of woman as nation without also enumerating its problems for women in national and colonial rhetoric.

In the same review where Seamus Heaney establishes the connection between Sarah and Cathleen, he praises Friel's fresh look at old myths. He says that while Friel shows "a constant personal urgency upon the need we have to create enabling myths of ourselves," there is also "the danger we run if we too credulously trust to the sufficiency of these myths" (1199).[13] Woman as national symbol is not a sufficient myth, precisely because it has enabled the kind of political oppression against women that has occurred in Ireland—and elsewhere, for that matter. By evoking and questioning the usefulness of such symbols, *Translations* can function as a critique of the destructive pattern of the woman as nation. But it seems the comfort some have with this pattern can work to obscure or negate that potential for critique.

# NOTES

I would like to thank Stacy Alaimo, Rick Canning, Barry Faulk, Brady Harrison, Mary Hocks and Robert Nowatzki for their assistance and insight on this essay.

1. For a thorough discussion of the construction of the Irish as a feminized race, see chapter three of Cairns and Richards, *Writing Ireland:* "An essentially feminine race."

2. Although women had been instrumental in the revolution, de Valera's government instituted a series of discriminatory laws policing women once freedom was won. The now notorious 1937 constitution legislates women's bodies quite specifically: "In particular the state recognises that by her life within the home, woman gives to the State a support without which the common good cannot be achieved. The State shall, therefore, endeavour to ensure that mothers shall not be obliged by economic necessity to engage in labour to the neglect of their duties in the home." By using the term "woman" and "mother" interchangeably, the document defines women's role in the country as solely reproductive. Prohibitions on divorce and birth control information or devices furthered the project of the control of women's bodies.

3. The Attic Press's series of "LIP" pamphlets contain excellent discussions

about Irish feminism, nationalism and colonialism. Twelve pamphlets have recently been published as *A Dozen Lips*. Dublin: Attic, 1994.

4. While a direct comparison cannot be made, the extensive and challenging work done on women in colonial/post-colonial India can be a useful starting point for studying Irish women. See *Feminism and Nationalism in the Third World*. London: Zed Press, 1986; *Recasting Women: Essays in Indian Colonial History*, Kumkum Sangari and Sudish Vaid, eds. New Brunswick: Rutgers University Press, 1990; Ketu Katrak, "Indian Nationalism, Gandhian 'Satyagraha,' and Representations of Female Sexuality," and R. Radhakrishanan, "Nationalism, Gender and the Narrative of Identity" in *Nationalisms and Sexualities*. Andrew Parker, Mary Russo, Doris Sommer and Patricia Yaeger, eds. New York: Routledge, 1992.

5. Ward's *Unmanageable Revolutionaries* is first in-depth study of the Irish suffragette movement. See also Cliona Murphy, *The Women's Suffrage Movement and Irish Society in the Early Twentieth Century* (Philadelphia: Temple University Press, 1989).

6. For a discussion of the representation of women in nationalist discourse, see Elin Ap Hywel "Elise and the Great Queens of Ireland: 'Femininity' as constructed by Sinn Fein and the Abbey Theatre, 1901-1907" in *Gender and Irish Writing*, Toni O'Brien Johnson and David Cairns, eds. Philadelphia: Open University Press, 1991.

7. In addition, none of the 43 critical introductions was written by a woman and only one woman, Maria Edgeworth, is given the "major author treatment" of an entire section. The omissions are perhaps most glaring in the twentieth century: not a single woman dramatist is included in the period from 1930-1986; only three of the 37 contemporary poets are women; and in the fiction section covering 1965-1990, only 6 of the 27 writers are women. In response to the controversy which erupted after the anthology's publication, Field Day is putting together a fourth volume of women's writing, edited by several leading feminist scholars. For further discussion of the Anthology's representation of women writers, see "The Whole Bustle" Siobhan Kilfeather, *London Review of Books* (January 9, 1992, 20-21); Patricia L. Haberstroh's review of Volume III in *Eire-Ireland* (Summer 1992, 118-123); and Margaret MacCurtain's review of Volume I and Riana O'Dwyer's review of Volume III in *The Irish Literary Supplement* (Fall 1992 Vol. 11, No. 2, 4-7).

8. There are a few dissenting voices; Edna Longley faults the play for its romanticism, didacticism, and its limited view of identity and Irishness: "the 'language' here appears theoretic, chosen with *Crane Bag* already in mind . . . Hugh himself embodies the play's pervasive nostalgia for 'what has been lost': for

the hedgeschool era, for a land of saints and scholars, for Ballybeg as a kind of Eden . . . . the play is partly 'fossilised' because he explores the ethos of a particular community exclusively in relation to British dominion over the native Irish" (*Poetry in the Wars* 191). Sean Connolly's critique is similar, arguing that the play presents an overly nostalgic portrait of the Irish past, "a picture of Hibernophone culture, prior to the coming of the English, so unrealistic and idealised as to cast doubt, not only on his history, but also on his art" ("Dreaming history: Brian Friel's *Translations*," *Theatre Ireland,* no. 13, 1987, 42).

9. My reading of *Translations* is based on the original text and its stage directions rather than a particular production of the play. Sarah could be played in such a way as to amplify or downplay her potential as national symbol, especially in how directors and actors choose to interpret her gestures.

10. See, for example, Ulf Dantanus, *Brian Friel: A Study* (London: Faber & Faber, 1988); Wolfgang Zach, "Brian Friel's *Translations*: National and Universal Dimensions" (*Medieval and Modern Ireland.* Richard Wall, ed. Totowa: Barnes and Noble Books, 1988); and George O'Brien, *Brian Friel* (Boston: Twayne, 1990).

11. Richard Pine is the only critic who refutes this reading, though without direct reference to the play's critical reception: "It would be wrong . . . to regard Sarah Johnny Sally's muteness merely as a symbol of a people who had lost their tongue, especially in the midst of such loquacity. Her silence is a private question of identity, not a public issue" (148). Pine can make this argument because he relies so much on the split between public and private throughout Friel's work.

12. Robert Smith has written a persuasive, though I think overly-determined, reading of Sarah linking her to the description of the autistic child in George Steiner's *After Babel*: "'Surrounded by incomprehensible or hostile reality, the autistic child breaks off verbal contact. He seems to choose silence to shield his identity but even more, perhaps, to destroy his imagined enemy' . . . For this reason, Sarah withholds her name from Lancey, a visible enemy" (399). His reading again reduces the range of meanings Sarah can have by ignoring Manus's influence on her.

13. Cairns and Richards use much of Deane's "Heroic Styles" argument in their assertion of how "urgently the deconstruction of the trope of idealized woman as suffering Ireland is needed" ("Tropes and traps" 137), yet they never mention that the idealization of the feminine is absent from Deane's essay and Deane's work overall.

# WORKS CITED

Boland, Eavan. *A Kind of Scar: The Woman Poet in a National Tradition.* Dublin: Attic Press, 1989.

Cairns, David and Shaun Richards. *Writing Ireland: Colonialism, Nationalism and Culture.* Manchester: Manchester University Press, 1988.

———. "Tropes and traps: Aspects of 'Woman' and nationality in twentieth-century Irish drama," in *Gender and Irish Writing.* Philadelphia: Open University Press, 1991: 128-137.

Cross, Tom Peete and Clark Harris Slover, eds. *Ancient Irish Tales.* New York: Henry Holt, 1939.

Deane, Seamus. "Heroic Styles: the tradition of an idea," in *Ireland's Field Day.* London: Hutchinson & Co., 1985: 45-58.

Farrow, Anthony. "Introduction." *Diarmuid and Grania* by George Moore and William Butler Yeats. Chicago: DePaul University, 1974.

Friel, Brian. *Translations,* in *Irish Drama 1900-1980.* Coilin Owens and Joan Radner, eds. Washington: Catholic University Press, 1990.

Heaney, Seamus. Rev. of *Translations* by Brian Friel. *Times Literary Supplement.* 24 October 1980: 1199.

Kearney, Richard. *Transitions: Narratives in Modern Irish Culture.* Manchester: Manchester University Press, 1988.

———. "Myth and Motherland," in *Ireland's Field Day.* London: Hutchinson & Co., 1985: 61-80.

Longley, Edna. *Poetry in the Wars.* Newark: University of Delaware Press, 1987.

O'Brien, George. *Brian Friel.* Boston: Twayne Publishers, 1990.

Smith, Robert. "The Hermeneutic Motion in Brian Friel's *Translations." Modern Drama.* 34.3. December 1991: 392-499.

Ward, Margaret. *Unmanageable Revolutionaries.* London: Pluto, 1983.

Zach, Wolfgang. "Brian Friel's *Translations:* National and Universal Dimensions," in *Medieval and Modern Ireland.* Richard Wall, ed. Totowa: Barnes and Noble Books, 1988: 74-90.

# *VOLUNTEERS:* CODES OF POWER, MODES OF RESISTANCE

## George O'Brien

Reviewers' respectful treatment of *Translations* and the large critical literature the play has generated; the controversial but undoubtedly worthwhile challenge presented to contemporary Irish cultural debate by Field Day; the unprecedented international popularity of *Dancing at Lughnasa* have all contributed to the consolidation of Friel's reputation as the leading Irish dramatist of the day and one of the most highly regarded voices in the English-speaking theater. The extent of his success tends to obscure the fact that there were periods when Friel's work was absent from the international commercial stage, during which he wrote works which are as noteworthy as those on which his reputation is conventionally claimed to rest.

The most notable of these periods lasted from 1969 to 1979. In these ten years, Friel had seven plays produced. All were staged in Dublin, but only one received a London production and three had very brief New York runs. [1] Yet, international neglect notwithstanding, a case might readily be made that this period is the most important in Friel's development. Despite its one-dimensional character, *The Mundy Scheme* initiates the confrontation of public issues and historical and cultural themes in Friel's work. This confrontation underwrites both the contemporary concerns of *The Freedom of the City* and *Volunteers* and the ostensibly more detached historical perspectivism of *Translations* and *Making History*. Although the melodrama of *The Gentle Island* is uncharacteristic of Friel's dramatic imagination, the play consolidates the diagnosis of the family as a power structure sketched in earlier works. This diagnosis is further developed in *Living Quarters* and *Aristocrats*, the plots of which deal with the death of the father. For all the intimacy of their family setting, these plots are by no means devoid of political and cultural resonances. In addition, during this period Friel's formal experimentation also evolves to find its most daring embodiment in *Faith Healer*.

The plays of this transitional decade reveal the dramatist in the process of identifying himself in a more challenging and comprehensive manner with themes latent in his earlier work, in particular with questions of power and its various familial, political and cultural manifestations. Yet, as his work became more far-reaching, Friel's reputation declined. His plays on public themes did receive some international attention, but their controversial reception "cost him dear financially."[2] Dublin critics, though not uniformly hostile, tended to be impatient and unsympathetic. Notices sarcastically identifying him as "our Drama Laureate,"[3] and suggesting that "Brian Friel's dramatic graph has taken a distinct downward journey in recent years"[4] were not uncommon. And reviews of *Volunteers*—the seminal play of this period, in which many of the preoccupations of *The Freedom of the City* are extended in ways which anticipate the artistic, cultural and political concerns (particularly those pertaining to identity politics) of his later work—were such as to prompt the usually reticent playwright to criticise the critics.[5]

Dublin's negative reception of *Volunteers* is particularly telling. Artistically and thematically speaking, the play can hardly have taken reviewers unawares, since it combines elements of two controversial predecessors, *The Mundy Scheme* and *The Freedom of the City*. It is sharper in its satire than *The Mundy Scheme*, and more explicit in its representation of national issues. And it is more economical in its indictment of officialdom than *The Freedom of the City*, while making more dramatically articulate that play's sense of transgressive vitality, and the parlous but necessary freedom which it denotes. Like these two predecessors, *Volunteers* also concentrates on questions of trust, responsibility and integrity in the public domain. And, not only does it dramatize these questions in terms of the possession and preservation of the country's national heritage, like *The Freedom of the City* it draws on contemporary events for its dramatic context.

In addition, although the opening words of the text of *Volunteers* are somewhat general—"The present in Ireland, an archaeological site in the centre of the city"[6]—the issues addressed by the play can be linked to a very specific context.

This context is the Wood Quay controversy which gripped Dublin passionately, if intermittently, during the mid-1970's. The controversy arose when Dublin Corporation decided to build a modern office block on the site of Viking Dublin, despite unearthing in the process "one of the major European archaeological discoveries of the century"[7] containing Viking artifacts and architecture in unprecedented abundance.

The danger of elected officials destroying physical evidence of one of Dublin's oldest known communities understandably raised questions about the relationship of heritage to property, of representatives to their electorate, and of present to past.

Intense public debate ensued, articulated through marches and sit-ins in addition to court documents and column inches. In addition to the specific issue of the fate of Wood Quay, reaction also touched on more general concerns. It broached the difficulties in arriving at a consensus about the relevance and accessibility of a common cultural heritage, in agreeing on mutual interests within a shared inheritance, in establishing a reliable account of cultural tradition so that public discussion regarding it might be in a common language, and in character-izing the nature of the common ground a society requires as a basis for its cultural identity.[8] By dramatizing the evidently insecure status of the national heritage in contemporary socio-political conditions, the Wood Quay affair also contributed to the anxious investigation of Irish cultural identity which has been the main feature of recent intellectual life in Ireland.[9]

The various productions and publications of the Field Day Theatre Company, co-founded by Friel and the actor Stephen Rea in 1980, have also contributed to the re-examination of Irish cultural identity, with the playwright's own most important artistic contribution being *Translations*, Field Day's inaugural production. Yet *Volunteers* suggests that *Translations* is a continuation of an earlier line of development in Friel's thinking. Like his work for Field Day, the political superstructure of *Volunteers* is grounded in cultural actualities. However, reviewers of the play were obviously unable to see it as part of the overall trajectory of Friel's awareness of the problematic cultural iconography of Irishness. Moreover, there was very little effort to locate the work in a contemporary Dublin context. Instead, reviewers thought of the play as an inadequate treatment of internment,[10] consisting of "a deal of talk that may hold more symbolism about our present troubles in relation to our past troubles than I am able to riddle."[11]

Reviewers' distancing perspectives implicitly confined the play's relevance to Northern Ireland, and as such will be largely of interest to historians assessing Southern opinion-makers' handling of the civil unrest in Northern Ireland. The perspectives conveniently overlook the status of Dublin in the story of Smiler's arrest and maltreatment, a status which acts as a reminder that the power of the state to violate the moral and physical integrity of the individual is not confined to one specific jurisdiction or one particular set of social conditions. Yet, while

*Volunteers* is conscious of the socio-political environment of contemporary Ireland, it is also "much more than a straightforward representation of specific acts of political or social violence." [12]

Nevertheless, responding to the play as though it "seeks in the myth of Viking Ireland a clearer vision of contemporary Irish politics" [13] is to some extent understandable. The play's title seems to invite such a reading by using a term which is rich in resonances of armed opposition in Irish history. Volunteer as a synonym for resistance dates from 1782. The Unionists who opposed Home Rule in 1912 called themselves volunteers, as did the Nationalists who responded to them. The insurgents of the Easter Rising of 1916 called themselves volunteers. Members of the I.R.A. who fought in the Anglo-Irish war of 1919-1921 are remembered by the same term. The designation is currently used by armed militants on both sides of the sectarian divide in Northern Ireland.

Typically, however, Friel invokes a resonant term in order to problematize and subvert it. The dual perspective which results not only destabilizes the term's familiar connotations (in the case of "volunteers" those deriving from a rigid view of a complicated historical nexus). It also declines to substitute the putative reassurance of an alternative code for the one being undermined. Indeed, "there is hardly an element in *Volunteers* . . . that can be taken simply for what it appears to be." [14] The volunteers' behavior insists that there is nothing predictable or traditional about them. The inappropriateness of taking them at face value, or assuming that they can be identified in terms of prior narratives, is introduced at the outset when Wilson the warder describes them as "bloody trash . . . 'Political prisoners'—huh! In my book they're all bloody criminals" (14). Later, however, the finality of Wilson's confident powers of nomenclature is itself undermined as he angrily rejects the English examiner's judgment of his daughter's viola-playing.

The latter interlude's structural awkwardness is overridden by the fact that it ratifies the inescapable experiencing of contending verbal codes which pervades the play. It is not just the volunteers who are susceptible to the forked tongue of language. Not even the trash is what it seems. George, the site foreman, can agree with Wilson's application of the term while at the same time speaking in quite a different register about the work that he and Wilson have supervised: "All the same they performed a public service" (15). And if the site contains trash—"the remains of three centuries of waste" (37)—it also contains Leif's remains, the jug shards, and potentially numerous other items of comparable interest. Moreover, as Keeney, the volunteers' chief spokesperson for the uncertainty, playfulness and fluidity of language, points out, the site itself may be regarded in various ways:

it does look more like a bomb-crater—or maybe a huge womb—or, as one of these men has suggested, like a prison yard with the high walls and the watch-tower up there and the naughty prisoners trying to tunnel their way out to freedom ha-ha-ha (35).

Leif, the skeleton, may be "a casualty of language" (28), but in the world of the play that makes him the rule rather than the exception.

All such casualties are a consequence of the manner in which any social system encodes, and attempts to stabilize, its integrity. Language is a prototype of law and order. In *Volunteers*, encoding focuses on public activity, with the acts of individual characters implicitly and explicitly discriminating between center and margin, victim and perpetrator, building and burying. But discrimination's arbitrary character is conveyed not only by the views of George and Wilson, or by the peremptory termination of the dig, or by the institutional powers behind the scene. It is also articulated by the "capital" sentence passed on the volunteers by the "sort of kangaroo court" of their "fellow-internees" (52). The limitations of individual perspectives may be revealed by the duplicities of language (the behavior of Dessie, the workers' friend, is a revealing counterpoint to Wilson's experience). The repression of these duplicities, however, is what equips language with its institutional power, the application of which results in casualties. It may be that "*Volunteers . . .* does not lend itself to easy interpretation,"[15] but it clearly speaks of that preoccupation with the ethics of naming which has distinguished Friel's most important work.

As a result of the power exerted on them by both gaolers and comrades alike, the volunteers occupy an indeterminate position within the encoding and evaluating which give the world of the play ostensible definition. They embody the effects of those processes' fallible but ineluctable power. George unwittingly describes their being where two structural forces converge by noting, "they're nicely cornered" (15). Yet it is from such a position that the volunteers derive their identity, and from which the play's ethics of naming emerges. The uncertain and provisional nature of their status, circumscribed as it is by the unimaginative orthodoxies of their gaolers on the one hand and by the unsympathetic judgment of their comrades on the other, underwrites how the volunteers behave. What in objective terms is a terminal condition is turned into a field day[16] by those whose end is at hand. And if they are criminals, "outsiders in both dimensions of the present world with which they are confronted,"[17] victims of injustice and disrespect, "trapped between political, economic and social realities and received ideas,"[18] they also have the power to respond to their state. That power is embodied in their voluntarism. If the term volunteer does possess a "sacral edge"[19] how does the play articulate it? What's in a name?

The beginnings of an answer may be found in the relationship between the volunteers themselves. On one level, "there are as many differences as similarities among the internees."[20] But difference on this level also applies to the non-internees as well, George, Wilson and Des. Needless to say, Knox is different from Keeney, Butt from Pyne. But in the play's moments of maximum drama, the volunteers' differences are transcended. A collective sense of themselves comes into being. Solidarity replaces singularity, conveying not merely an awareness of interdependent, sympathetic brotherhood but an awareness of its power and structural significance. The name of such fellow-feeling apparently does not exist in the vocabularies of their keepers. Although George, Wilson and Des also effectively close ranks in turning against the volunteers, they have no collective sense of doing so and act in the name of institutional rather than fraternal interests. The cost in human terms of institutional affiliation, and related questions of responsibility and self-awareness, are among the matters uncovered by the volunteers' presence.

The volunteers' capacity to relate to each other in a manner marked by spontaneity and unselfishness has not been eliminated by either the authorities or their comrades, despite the probably fatal consequences of volunteering. This quality of relatedness, devoid of ego and hierarchy, is not merely the volunteers' reaction to unforeseen developments in their present circumstances. On the contrary, it seems that it may have been their expression of this very quality which led to their internment.

The little that is known about the volunteers' background also draws attention to solidarity and collective action. Official justification for their incarceration is, according to Keeney, short on detail regarding due legal process and related considerations (a deficiency which the physical force of imprisonment overrides):

> . . . we deliberately "offended against the state," or to be strictly accurate . . . they interned us because of "attitudes that might be inimical to public security" (55).

The elements of Orwellian double-think in the official phrases quoted here is immediately followed by a much more detailed account of the causes, circumstances and consequences of Smiler's arrest. In this account, a similar combination of the verbal and the physical is present, though now with the emphasis on the latter much more obviously disproportionate and explicit. The pretext for Smiler's arrest is his expression of solidarity with "one of his mates" (55), the result of which is, to say the least, the exact opposite of anything that the term solidarity connotes—"they whipped Smiler off to jail in Dublin and beat the tar out of him for twelve consecutive hours" (56). But the witlessness that afflicts Smiler as a result of his beating makes him so vulnerable that he, in turn, becomes an expressive occasion for the solidarity which he initiated, as reaction to his disappearance demonstrates.

Smiler's temporary escape is one of the means whereby expressions of mutual support impart dramatic structure to the play's development. But their impact is not merely dramaturgical. Solidarity may be all that the volunteers possess, but its dramatic salience ratifies its significance as a source of dissent, a principle of resistance, and a basis for radical choice. The spontaneous impetus to protect the missing Smiler rehearses some of those values. A more comprehensive enactment of what the volunteers' collective interdependence represents is provided by a more conclusively climactic moment, Butt's breaking of the jug.

The immediate pretext for Butt's action is George's judgment of Keeney: "I doubt very much if he's even loyal to what the rest of you stand for" (78). George's presumption to speak on behalf of the volunteers recapitulates his glossing of his "public service" comment mentioned above—"not that they'll see it that way" (15). The imposition of his interpretative will on who or what the volunteers are, either individually or collectively, illustrates the play's overall dynamic. It confirms George's place to be, in principle, on the side of the gaolers while at the same time, in practice, cueing Butt's vandalism.

The fact that it is the rather colorless and unassuming and even cooperative Butt who demolishes George's pride and joy is, in itself, a telling instance of the volunteers' continually and surprisingly irrepressible awareness of, and fidelity to, a sense of alternative, both as strategy and principle. The rather desperate freedom articulated in Butt's gesture is the spirit which animates the play, not only in a broadly thematic sense but by sparking its highly-developed projections of playfulness. It is manifested in the unpredictability of the volunteers' responses, from the unattributed laughter that irrupts in mocking counterpoint to the opening conversation between George and Wilson to the combination of stoicism and irony in Keeney's parting, "Good night, sweet prince" (88). It is present in the irreverent and contrary ways in which the volunteers treat each other. Keeney's improvisations embody this playfulness, so that the uncertainty which underlies his play-acting—"I'm sure of nothing now" (72)—is both masked and made productive.

Keeney obviously embodies dissident energy most fully, not only because of the magnitude and somewhat manic nature of his role, or because "he's the one persuaded us to volunteer for this job" (75). As "the latest in a line of fiction-specialists, impresarios, symbol-conscious commentators, obsessive role-players, protean spirits, anguished doubters, dreamers with an almost compulsive resourcefulness,"[21] his "anarchic" (57) disposition constitutes at once the most elusive and the most self-conscious representation of the volunteers' nonconformist spirit. This disposition authorises his "almost overwhelming sense of power and control, generosity and liberation" (57), and fuels his "antic imagination" (71).

The integrated interplay between moral and political categories in that "sense" to which Keeney refers characterizes the nature of volunteer energy. That drive prompts not only Keeney's and Pyne's antics but the sober, dedicated labor of Butt and Knox. The outward manifestation of the voluntarist spirit is the volunteers' tirelessness. Spirit (or principle) articulated as energy (or action) fuels the volunteers' oppositional *elán*, their "turbulent tendencies" (37). One of the exemplary products of their spiritedness is to create an alternative, internalized zone—or site (or, punningly, stage)—which derives from the material conditions of their work. Their presence not only facilitates a critique of the political dimension of law and order, it also calls into question the cultural politics of the "speculators" (44) whose designs on contemporary time and space exert the ultimate control over the site and everyone connected with it. The unprogrammatic and ostensibly motiveless nature of voluntarism implements its revisionist function by introducing a different, open-ended type of speculation. The "masque of anarchy"[22] which the free play of voluntarism creates is at least a temporary rebuttal of the ethos of closure and enclosure connoted by the play's hints of the interlinkage between society's various institutional powers. By disrupting borders erected by institutionalized discourses between the moral and the political, Friel—whose "main interest is in the way meanings maintain themselves or are fought for in a world bereft of consensus"[23]—revises the traditional, reflexive associations of "volunteers."

But the volunteers cannot be merely figures in a "masque."[24] They cannot believe themselves to be diverting spokesmen for the speculative novelty of an alternative ethos to the ones which confine them. Were they to have such a view of themselves, the masque would have no dramatic significance; it would be beside the point. And their presence could not authenticate the spirit of voluntarism.

The sheer variety of Keeney's performances suggest his tacit awareness, or perhaps his unacknowledged fear, of the impermanence and unreliability of his presence and of the verbal constructs which distinguish it. Even when he is being serious, as when dealing with Smiler's escape, his comrades express doubts about his reading of the situation. And Keeney's desire that Smiler attain a less ironic mode of freedom than the one current conditions permit, that he become some other kind of entity—"at least now he's not going to be a volunteer" (57)—has no effect on Smiler himself, as his voluntary return to the site demonstrates. Keeney's angry response to Smiler's return—"He's an imbecile!" (75)—is a vehement renunciation of the playacting which he is "always" (28) at. Yet for all the literalness and uncharacteristic conclusiveness of "imbecile," the genuine anger and distress which it expresses has no more effect on the way things turn out than any other of Keeney's verbal gestures.

An audience may perceive criteria for authenticity in *Volunteers* by appreciating Friel's ideas and by being aware of the play's larger cultural context. But if the volunteers are to be more than masquers they must confront the problem of arriving at convincing criteria of authenticity for themselves. They must find a means of acting *for*, in addition to all their reacting against. The socio-political ethos which voluntarism underwrites must consist of more than skits and sketches, delaying tactics and diversions. It must have some power to intervene in the world of George and Wilson.

Keeney's references to Hamlet suggest that he is aware of this problem. The question of Hamlet's madness acts at one level as the plausible refrain of somebody "just trying to keep sane" (31). At another level, by virtue of both its recurrence and its unpredictability, it is an economical illustration of the play's insistence on the protean nature of language.[25] Keeney's allusions to Hamlet also provides a fleeting intimation of his concern, expressed in the context of Smiler's disappearance, to find an appropriate course of action to offset the implications of Smiler's beating, the handling of the site, and the volunteers' fate at the hands of their fellow-prisoners. These implications lead to the not very surprising conclusion that there is something rotten in the state. Contemporary Ireland may be perceived as a prison, though as such it replicates and internalizes the discovery that "Viking Ireland, like Denmark is a prison,[26] with houses "really the size of a prison cell" (38). Like Hamlet, Keeney is almost unbearably conscious of being so confined that whatever he does ultimately contributes to the digging of his own grave. But although his tone more resembles that of the grave-diggers' in *Hamlet* than that of the prince himself, Keeney is clearly unable to reproduce the formers' mordant insouciance. Even at the level of utterance and inflection, Keeney's language refuses to be grounded.

Yet there seems to be no specific artistic need to refer to Hamlet to show that Keeney's reaction to the fate of imprisonment is not madness. And the tone of Keeney's references to Hamlet is sufficiently casual and unpredictable to prevent them from inflating either the range of Friel's themes or Keeney's own character. Hamlet exists in *Volunteers* as neither a character or a tragedy, but as a cultural icon, a touchstone. As with the term "volunteers," the name acts as a mediating entity. Keeney's use of it enables him both to conjure up and, with understandable skittishness, to deflect thoughts of his destiny. Acting as a gloss, a set of associations, an imaginative resource, a signifier whose deployment seems random but whose connotations are effectively evocative, Hamlet not only participates in the play's complex ethics of naming but locates it specifically in the cultural realm.

Yet, although the name does help to highlight the problematic intersection of freedom and uncertainty, subversiveness and imagination, which Keeney embodies and articulates, Hamlet does not supply the key to all hermeneutical mythologies in *Volunteers*. Its verbal power is a commentary on the actual power structure within the *mise-en-scene*, underlining Friel's awareness of the necessity that language find ultimate expression in action. Hamlet exists rather as a prototype of the kind of resource which cultural artifacts provide, and which exists within the world of the volunteers in the much more explicit, down-to-earth, non-verbal forms of the jug and Leif. By providing pretexts for different courses of action, arising out of conflicting value systems, Leif and the jug mediate authenticity for the volunteers and offer them a means of representing themselves which is not confined to language.

These courses of action are at odds with each other. But on the face of it, the fact that Leif and the jug are in conflict seems surprising. They both them both occupy a common ground both in a literal sense and as fragmented historical disjecta. They both have been donated to the contemporary world by the site, and hence are aspects of a common heritage. In their found state they combine a three-dimensional specificity and a welter of possibilities. Their on-site state mediates between past and present, knowledge and ignorance, story and history, respect and indifference. As material objects, they are susceptible to, but not participants in, either their original world of language or the world of language into which they have been reborn. They may be perceived as empty vessels, or as indeterminate signifiers and evocative touchstones similar to Hamlet (a name that belongs to both, or either, a text and a character) or to the volunteers themselves (who embody an outlook which is both vital and suppressed).

But neither the jug or Leif's remains are allowed to exist in the innocence of their material presence. They are not merely thing, or even image. Much more important, they are susceptible to language, and the power of language over them represses their common material actuality. Their emergence from the womb, or grave, of the dig inevitably ushers them into imprisoning discourses of status and value. The discriminations which these discourses articulate make Leif and the jug seem to belong to different worlds. Such a perception reproduces the destructive dialectic of outsiders and insiders, jailers and prisoners, conformists and non-conformists, which authorises the volunteers' fate.

Leif and the jug are not allowed to exist in their own right by Wilson and George and their institutional backers. They must either be appropriated or abandoned by them. The pieces of the jug become "priceless" (14) only when reassembled.[27] Leif, on the other hand, whose remains cannot be commodified, is finally entombed within a structure whose existence is a monument to the doctrine that time is money—hence the surprise closing of the site and the resultant consignment of the volunteers to their last end also. The different values assigned to the two objects not only denote the conflict of values which the play addresses, but denotes that conflict in action. Butt breaks the jug "*without taking his eyes off it*" (79), indicating the deliberateness of the action. Butt has already displayed his scholarly acumen in identifying the Danish ship (41), so there is no doubt that he fully conscious of what he is doing. Yet, as he inexpressively "*returns to his work*" (79), impervious to George's threats, he indicates also his detached awareness of the exemplary force of his action. Clearly the destruction of George's pride and joy is not merely wanton, inexplicable, and unpredictable. It also conveys how vulnerable are George's notions of wholeness and value. Smashed, the jug retains iconic power of a kind that George can only make occasions of restitution and "regret" (79).

Leif, too, has been found in pieces and has been subjected to efforts to restore him to wholeness. This is the aim of the stories which Keeney and Pyne invent about him, stories which install Leif in time, domesticate him, equip him talents and adventures. The elaborate embroidery of these fictions do indeed "keep up the protection of the myth" (62), the myth of survival which the stories sketch and the myth of redemption to which the activity of story-telling itself subscribes. Actively as Keeney and Pyne attempt to propagate these myths, they cannot disguise the truth of Leif and of their own efforts. With regard to the latter, a myth greater than any of the stories invented about Leif is the one mockingly intoned by Keeney in his role as lecturer (master not only of material, but of purpose):

> And of course the more practical our information about our ancestors, the more accurate our deductions about his attitudes, the way he thought, what his philosophy was—in other words the more comprehensive our definitions of him. (36)

As to the matter of the truth of Leif, whatever it might be, it cannot ignore facts such as "*A leather rope hangs loosely round the neck. There is a small round hole in the skull*" (27).

The obvious implication that Leif's life was taken from him, and that he can be viewed as, among other things, "a victim of his society" (28), is one which does not detain the volunteers very long. Their reluctance to view Leif as somebody who may have fallen foul of the powers that be may be the result of an understandable unwillingness to dwell on their own fate and to regard themselves as victims. But it is also an expression of a refusal to think of him in a definitive manner. Instead of restricting Leif's story to one exclusive account of violence and subjugation, various stories are supplied, the incomplete and indeterminate nature of which free Leif from the narrative of the noose and provide him with a full gamut of human experiences.

By such means, Leif becomes a touchstone not so much of whatever policies and principles the volunteers espouse, but of the spirit that animates them. Leif becomes humanised by sharing in that spirit, unlike the jug which has been artificially transposed from the plane of its human context to that of priceless treasure. The audience is invited to compare the violence which breaks the jug to that which buries Leif. In covering Leif with the tarpaulin, Keeney carries out an understated ritual of interment. The fact that George undoes the gesture in the play's final action merely underscores the differences between the two value systems juxtaposed by *Volunteers*, and provides yet one more instance of why the two systems are inevitably in conflict. But that gesture of George's does not efface Keeney's commitment to treating Leif with dignity, which in this case simply amounts to treating him as one might any human remains. Eloquent in its silence, this act of solidarity with Leif is Keeney's least studied, least obviously performed, moment in the play. Its wordlessness and deliberateness also act as an effective complement to the jug-breaking episode.

Yet, although the spirit of the volunteers realizes itself in action, nothing changes. In ways which suggest subtle variations on structures of predetermined action in both *The Freedom of the City* and *Living Quarters*, the volunteers seem, to a greater or lesser extent, to be going through the motions of a script already written and completed by the authorities. The extent to which this seems to be so is lesser in the cases of Knox and Butt, absorbed as they are in the physical detail of work. It seems greater in the case of Pyne, and particularly, Keeney, who attempt to live with the awareness that their epitaphs have been written. The volunteers are powerless: that is their ultimate claim on our attention. The ethos of their name has been annulled. Their actions attain significance because of their resonances and their symbolic potential, rather than by virtue of directly affecting the course of events.

Yet the volunteers are also the center of the play, a position whose significance is ratified in the climactic but unavailing episodes of the jug being broken and the burial of Leif. The impact of those episodes on the world in which the play is set is negligible, so that the episodes seem reduced to merely symbolic gestures. By the time these episodes take place, however, the audience can be in no doubt that their focus—in contrast to that of George and Wilson—is the volunteers. The audience is placed in a position to redeem the symbolic nature of the volunteers' actions. Thus, Leif and the jug are offered as cultural artifacts whose presence resembles that of Hamlet for Keeney. They exist as icons of community, touchstones of a common humanity, amulets of belonging, images with which to be entrusted, condensed and inaccessible narratives of time and chance in which we are all uncomprehendingly participate. Leif and the jug are a means of mediating the possibilities of the volunteers' spirit and energy, and as such are a means of circumventing, however temporarily and inconclusively, society's overdetermining structural authorities.

At the beginning of Act III of *The Playboy of the Western World*, there's speculation concerning the whereabouts of Old Mahon. A "slightly drunk" Jimmy opines that if the body was found:

> They'd say it was an old Dane, maybe, was drowned in the
> flood . . . Did you never hear tell of the skulls they have in the city
> of Dublin, ranged out like blue jugs in a cabin of Connaught?[28]

These remarks, in addition to their ironical effect in the immediate context of the play, provide an arresting historical and cultural dimension to the play's plot. Yet this dimension, if applied in a schematic manner, will distort the main impetus and interest of *The Playboy*'s plot. Indeed, the plot may be regarded as a grotesque and elaborate pun on what Jimmy describes. But Jimmy's remark is neither gratuitous nor irrelevant. It calls to mind Walter Benjamin's remark: " The true picture of the past flits by. The past can be seized only as an image which flashes up at the instant when it can be recognized and is never seen again.[29]

In *Volunteers*, Friel seems to use this image-laden conception of how the past may be effectively apprehended as a basis for the symbolic actions of Butt and Keeney. In their different ways, these characters seize upon the irretrievability of the past as its reality, and use this acceptance of the past's integrity as a means of expressing their own. Another Benjamin remark seems apposite here: "In every era the attempt must be made anew to wrest tradition away from a conformism that is about to overpower it.[30] The reality of that attempt is represented in *Volunteers*. And while it may be argued that, ultimately, it is the very richness of the play's thematic resonances which vitiates its dramatic impact, its enactment of the conflicts between the voluntary and the mercenary, the spirit and the letter, potential and repression—conflicts which may be broadly identified by the names culture and politics—make this a central work in the Friel canon.

As the volunteers demonstrate, identity is formed at the intersection of these conflicting powers. And such is the force of these powers, represented here in terms of the authority of the moment and the obligations to the past, that they both engender and destabilize identity. As in Friel plays as different from one another in form and setting as *Philadelphia, Here I Come!*, *Faith Healer*, and *Making History*, *Volunteers* represents identity as an impotent potentiating of uncertainty, a known condition of difference, beyond ego and affiliation. What is valuable about this condition is not so much anything intrinsic to it; rather it's the ability and the willingness to bear it. Leif perhaps possessed the wherewithal. Keeney also may have what's required. In making such claims, however, we must be tentative, in order that uncertainty have its full play, in order to recognize the reality of the indeterminate. By declining to be prescriptive either in cultural terms (by presuming to state without contradiction how Leif met his end) or in political terms (by agreeing that the volunteers deserve to meet their end), we are introduced to the possibility of resisting identity-imposing forces. Our responses are thereby aligned with the vision of resistance which *Volunteers* is both too honest to deny and too sober to valorise.

# NOTES

1. The plays and their years of their premieres are *The Mundy Scheme* (1969), *The Gentle Island* (1971), *The Freedom of the City* (1973), *Volunteers* (1975), *Living Quarters* (1977), *Aristocrats* (1979) and *Faith Healer* (1979), which opened on Broadway. Other plays to receive New York productions were *The Mundy Scheme* (1970) and *The Freedom of the City* (1974); the latter was also staged in London in 1973. *Faith Healer* and *Aristocrats* subsequently received successful London productions, and the London production of *Aristocrats* played Off-Broadway.

2. Seamus Deane, "Introduction," *Brian Friel: Selected Plays* (Washington, D.C.: Catholic University of America Press, 1986): 19. Deane's point pertains basically to the New York reception of *The Freedom of the City*. See Clive Barnes' review, "*The Freedom of the City* about the Irish," *The New York Times*, 18 February, 1974, p. 32. For an example of the reaction this review provoked, see William Kennedy, "*Freedom of the City*. Clive Barnes is wrong about Brian Friel," in his *Riding the Yellow Trolley* (New York: Viking, 1991): 237-240. See also Sean

Cronin, "Storm over Friel play on Broadway," *The Irish Times*, 4 March, 1974, p. 13.

3. Mary Manning, "The Freedom of the City," *Hibernia* 37 (3-17 March, 1973): 28.

4. Michael Sheridan, "Little Life in *Living Quarters*," *The Irish Press*, 25 March, 1977, p. 7.

5. Fachtna O'Kelly, "Can critics kill a play?" *The Irish Press*, 28 March, 1975, p. 9, contains comments by Friel on the state of play-reviewing and the status of the theater implicit in that state. A corrective to the typical reaction of Dublin reviewers to *Volunteers* is provided by Seamus Heaney's review of the play: "Digging Deeper," *Times Literary Supplement*, 23 March, 1975, p. 306. Reprinted in Heaney, *Preoccupations: Selected Prose 1968-1978* (London: Faber and Faber, 1980): 214-216.

6. Brian Friel, *Volunteers* ([London: Faber and Faber, 1979]; Oldcastle: Gallery, 1989): further citations from the latter edition will be made parenthetically in the text.

7. Thomas Feral Heffernan, *Wood Quay* (Austin: University of Texas Press, 1988): 1. A sense of this significance occurs in *Volunteers* when Des exclaims: "a site the like of which this country has never seen before!" (44)

8. The struggle with such issues may be perceived, on the one hand, in the protracted litigation which arose from such an apparently straightforward matter as whether the Wood Quay site could be termed a public monument within in the meaning of the National Monuments Act (1930), which states: "the expression 'national monument' means a monument or remains of a monument the preservation of which is a matter of national importance by reason of the historical, architectural, traditional, artistic, or archaeological interest attaching thereto" (cited in Heffernan, *op. cit.*: 69). At another level, the struggle may be inferred from the tensions articulated in Thomas Kinsella's poem, "Night Conference, Wood Quay: 6 June 1979." Thomas Kinsella, *From Centre City* (Oxford: Oxford University Press, 1994): 25. An earlier version of the poem appears in Heffernan, *op. cit.*: 113.

9. The range of this debate embraces such works as Terence Brown, *Ireland's Literature* (Dublin: Lilliput, 1988); Edna Longley, *Poetry in the Wars* (Newcastle-upon-Tyne: Bloodaxe, 1986) and *The Living Stream* (Newcastle-upon-Tyne: Bloodaxe, 1994); Seamus Deane, Seamus Heaney, Richard Kearney, Declan Kiberd, Tom Paulin, *Ireland's Field Day* (Notre Dame, Ind.: Notre Dame University Press, 1986); Richard Kearney, *Transitions* (Dublin: Wolfhound, 1987) and Richard Kearney, ed. *Across the Frontiers*; W.J. McCormack, *The Battle of the Books* (Dublin: Lilliput, 1986); and Fintan O'Toole, *A Mass for Jesse James*

(Dublin: Raven Arts, 1990) and *Black Hole, Green Card* (Dublin: New Island, 1994). Most of these works contain essays written over a period of years prior to their publication in book form. The most important sites of cultural debate in the 1970's are the periodicals *Atlantis* (1970-1974) and *The Crane Bag* (1977-1985).

10. Cited in Heaney, *op. cit.*

11. Seamus Kelly, "*Volunteers* by Brian Friel at the Abbey," *The Irish Times*, 6 March, 1975, p. 11.

12. Richard Pine, *Brian Friel and Ireland's Drama* (London: Routledge, 1990): 192.

13. Ulf Dantanus, *Brian Friel: A Study* (London: Faber and Faber, 1988): 153.

14. Ruth Neil, "Digging into History: A Reading of Brian Friel's *Volunteers* and Seamus Heaney's "Viking Dublin: Trial Pieces," *Irish University Review*: 38.

15. Dantanus, *op. cit.*: 160.

16. It is interesting to trace the lineage and development of "field day" as an imaginative construct throughout Friel's work, and the operation of its energy and ethos is such diverse plays as *Philadelphia, Here I Come!*, *Lovers: Winners and Losers*, *Crystal and Fox*, in addition to its more explicit elaboration in *The Freedom of the City* and *Volunteers*.

17. Neil, *op. cit.*, 37.

18. Heaney, *op. cit.*, 215.

19. Heaney, *op. cit.*, 214.

20. Dantanus, *op. cit.*, 158.

21. Elmer Andrews, "The Fifth Province," in Alan Peacock (ed.), *The Achievement of Brian Friel* (Gerrard's Cross: Colin Smythe, 1993): 39. This "line" includes Private Gar *(Philadelphia, Here I Come!)*, Cass McGuire, Fox (*Crystal and Fox*), Shane (*The Gentle Island*), and Skinner (*The Freedom of the City*). The line continues beyond *Volunteers*.

22. Heaney, *op. cit.*: 215.

23. Andrews, *op. cit.*: 41.

24. Masque is being used in the sense intended by Heaney's pun on Shelley, "The Mask of Anarchy," a sense whereby "mere anarchy"—so to speak—is given form. In the strict, generic, sense of the term, *Volunteers* is obviously not a masque, for all the silence of its critical moments.

25. Private mantra, mnemonic of identity and abjectness, *non sequitur* in an environment where violence has supplanted reason, Keeney's use of Hamlet extends the dramatic effect of Gar O'Donnell's repetition (in *Philadelphia, Here I Come!*) of the phrase from Burke's *Reflections on the Revolution in France*.

26. Heaney, *op. cit.*: 215.

27. This ascription of value to the jug seems to contradict the claim that "the jug . . . can be seen as typical of the whole play. It avoids safe and clear-cut definitions and conclusions." Dantanus, *op.cit.*: 159.

28. J.M. Synge, *The Playboy of the Western World*. In Ann Saddlemyer (ed.), *J.M. Synge. Collected Works*. 4 Vols. (London: Oxford University Press, 1968). IV, p. 133. The opening line of the same quotation occurs in Seamus Heaney's poem, "Viking Dublin: Trial Pieces," a poem which also has an interesting gloss on "Hamlet the Dane." Seamus Heaney, "Viking Trial Pieces," *North* (London: Faber, 1975): 21-24. *Volunteers* is dedicated to Seamus Heaney.

29. Walter Benjamin, "Theses on the Philosophy of History," in Hannah Arendt (ed.), *Illuminations* (New York: Schocken Books, 1969): 255.

30. Benjamin, *op. cit.*: 255.

# "LIKE WALKING THROUGH MADAME TUSSAUD'S":[1] THE CATHOLIC ASCENDANCY AND PLACE IN BRIAN FRIEL'S *ARISTOCRATS*

## Garland Kimmer

*"It was a tall, ugly house of three stories high, its walls faced with weather-beaten slates, its windows staring, narrow, and vacant. Round the house ran an area, in which grew some laurustinas and holly bushes among ash heaps, and nettles, and broken bottles."* [2]

The question of how to deal with an Anglo-Irish Ascendancy has been posed in Irish culture for almost four centuries and has figured prominently in Anglo-Irish literature since the beginning of the nineteenth century. Of the contemporary writers who still portray the Ascendancy in their works, Brian Friel most eloquently explores the impact which the Ascendancy had and continues to have on the development of both class and individual identity in a divided Ireland. Following in the footsteps of writers as varied as Maria Edgeworth, E. Æ. Somerville and Martin Ross, Augusta Gregory, W. B. Yeats, and James Joyce, Friel questions what role these political and social elites had on both the communities around them and the individuals in those communities. More importantly, however, he probes the issue further by considering the impact that communities and changing times have on a seemingly anachronistic aristocracy. Like many of the chief figures of the Irish Literary Renaissance, Friel places a heavy burden upon the role of the Ascendancy in shaping Irish identity and self-understanding. Unlike his predecessors, Friel looks most closely at the minority members of Ascendancy – the Roman Catholics who attained social and political power in the wake of the Penal Laws' repeal during the latter half of the nineteenth century. Through the current social and economic dislocation of the Catholic Ascendancy remnants, Friel has been able to examine the mythologies we fabricate to situate ourselves more comfortably in a rapidly shifting world and does this without reverting to a Yeatsian litany for past grandeur. *Aristocrats* (1979) remains his most poignant consideration of the perils inherent in the rise and fall of this "Roman Catholic aristocracy" with its continual reconfiguration of historical narratives and its brilliant redeployment of traditional Irish understandings of place (*Aristocrats* 281).

Friel's significance to the contemporary Irish literary scene cannot be overstated. Richard Pine even suggests that "contemporary Irish drama begins in 1964 in *Philadelphia, Here I Come!*, with Gareth O'Donnell's bewilderment: 'I don't know. I—I—I don't know'" (1). What Friel brings to Irish drama is the understanding that the individual is more than the sum of the masks that he or she wears, that the individual also incorporates communal histories which often surface as localized myths. By splitting Gar O'Donnell into public and private selves, like Beckett before him Friel begins to "address the interior and exterior worlds, to maintain a private conversation while conducting a public address" (Pine 2). Even in this initial seminal play, however, Friel realizes that the individual identity he is seeking cannot simply be divided into two elements. His task is richer, more complex: to consider and reconstruct all of the diverse elements and to achieve the whole person, not merely the sum of the parts. As Irish drama, Friel's work could not remain a simple search for personal completion and self-understanding. He must consider local, national, and political components of individual identity and memory. In other words, Friel's drama becomes accessible to a larger public than Beckett's because his plays thrive on understanding and developing characters as part of a community. Even if Beckett's landscapes are admitted to be distinctively Irish, they maintain an otherworldly, isolated atmosphere which Friel's drama does not.[3] When Gar O'Donnell expresses confusion about his identity and turns toward the New World, he is forsaking the traditions and elements which define his identity. When he moves beyond that small world, he can be no more certain who he is than Beckett's Didi and Gogo are of their individual identity.

In much the same ways as Wilde and Synge created stories to provide their characters with depth and a version of the past, Friel's characters inevitably have a story, possibly several different *versions* of a story, to explain their present straits. This storytelling tendency in the plays leads Seamus Deane to conclude that "it is not surprising that his [Friel's] drama evolves, with increasing sureness, towards an analysis of the behaviour of language itself and, particularly, by the ways in which that behaviour, so ostensibly in the power of the individual is fundamentally dictated by historical circumstances" (*Selected Plays* 13). While *Translations* overtly illustrates the relationship between language and history that Deane seeks to isolate, it is *Aristocrats* which examines how an individual responds when the past overshadows the present, reducing accepted facts into personal myths. This play ultimately comes closest to bringing about the unification of public and private personae that were separated in *Philadelphia, Here I Come!* by foregrounding the fabrications which prop up both individual and social identity. *Aristocrats* has been generally ignored by Friel's commentators, presumably because it lacks *Translations'* overt political message, *Volunteers'* concentration on the IRA, or *Philadelphia, Here I Come!*'s wrenching schizophrenia. While *Aristocrats* may appear at first glance to be little more than a gentle consideration of a hapless nobility's passing, closer consideration reveals it to be a painful excavation of how the O'Donnell family has contributed and will continue to contribute to the imaginative life of the Ballybeg community.[4] Almost tragically, Friel unearths the myths of public life which are the buried skeletons marking the heart of this contradiction.

The plight of Ballybeg, or more aptly Baile Beg (small town) as we learn in *Translations*, is simultaneously the plight of modern Ireland and the rest of the world, frantically attempting to cope with the present in light of its past. Admittedly, Ballybeg's past is perhaps more checkered or more interesting than that of many places because of its Irishness, yet the dilemmas facing Friel's characters are universal. Again, it is Pine who provides the salient summation: "Friel becomes the Irish Chekhov because for him the world is not Ireland writ large but Ireland is the world writ small" (3). Perhaps it is this Chekhovian element in Friel's drama that allows him to shift so seamlessly between the past and the present, to concentrate on understanding present identity as a response to past actions or even past stature.

In order for Friel to accomplish this task, he creates a world which is simultaneously an acutely accurate portrayal of small town life and also a metaphor for the larger world. Deane suggests, "Ballybeg, which occurs so often in his plays as a standard setting, has fused within it the socially depressed and politically dislocated world of Derry and the haunting attraction of the lonely landscapes and traditional mores of rural Donegal" (12). The town itself would be located in the far northwest of the Republic. Donegal is attached to the rest of the Republic by a narrow isthmus in the south, while its largest border is with Derry. The border with Derry is both physical and psychological, serving to inhibit both economic and cultural traffic with Donegal's closest neighbor. Because of this isolation, Donegal becomes an ideal site for Friel's plays. He has the freedom to create a world that draws on aspects of both northern and southern Irish experiences and history in a way that he could not by following O'Casey's example and setting his plays in the heart of Dublin. Like Tolkien, C. S. Lewis, or Faulkner who all attempted to create entire worlds within their works, Friel has learned that in order to populate a town he has to consider the ghosts of the past as well as the people of the present. The "Ballybeg" plays range from the 1830s to the present, yet even those set in the present evoke the past at every turn.

The other element that Friel has discovered in populating his imagined Ireland, in Ballybeg and beyond, is the need to work with diverse social elements. *Volunteers* deals with local men who agree to work for the IRA, while the church appears prominently in *Dancing at Lughnasa* and takes on the unfortunate legacy of imperial power in the process. *Freedom of the City* considers the role of terrorists in modern society, and *Philadelphia, Here I Come!* deals with the predominantly Catholic middle and lower classes. The predecessors of *Aristocrats*' contemporary Ballybeg residents show up in *Translations* in the hedge school and Ordinance Survey teams of the 1830s. When all of these elements are considered, the most significant missing piece of society appears to be the former "ruling elite" or Ascendancy who so heavily influenced Irish policy and society during the eighteenth and nineteenth centuries. Like Chekhov's *Three Sisters*, *Aristocrats* succeeds at portraying the final days of a "noble family," yet unlike Chekhov Friel does not hand the social identity and responsibility on to a middle class "usurper." Instead, the O'Donnell family finds themselves "fortuitously freed into a future that catches them somewhat unawares but nevertheless willing to make a go of it," presumably by remaining an imaginative if not an economic force within the Ballybeg community (O'Brien 77).

Before considering the importance of the O'Donnells' demise and subsequent self-understanding, I would first like to briefly consider the cultural identity and significance of the Ascendancy in Ireland. In describing the members of the Ascendancy, we may ultimately do no better than Brendan Behan's definition: "a Protestant with a horse." A more complete definition would, however, suggest that the Ascendancy (or the Anglo-Irish) is a term that developed between the seventeenth and nineteenth centuries to describe the Protestant landlords and landowners in Ireland. Mark Bence-Jones breaks down the origins of the nineteenth century Ascendancy as follows:

The Protestant majority of the Ascendancy was not, as many would imagine, descended exclusively from English land-grabbers who came over with Cromwell and Presbyterian Lowland Scots who settled in Ulster under James I. Though the families of English and Scots settler stock together constituted the largest group in the Ascendancy, they nevertheless did not amount to more than 60 per cent of the total; and of their number, only about 10 per cent were of Cromwellian origin. The rest of the settler families were established in Ireland at different periods from the sixteenth century onwards ... Rather less than forty percent of the Ascendancy families were of old Celtic-Irish or Anglo-Norman stock; but this minority included some of the most important. The Duke of Leinster, Ireland's premier peer, and Marquess of Ormonde were the head, respectively of two historic Anglo-Norman families, the Fitzgeralds or Geraldines and their traditional rivals the Butlers. (14)

While many of these landowners and landlords chose to manage their estates through managers and become absentee landlords, others, especially among the Anglo-Norman families built homes on their lands and became integral parts of the communities around their homes. These homes have become known as "Big Houses" over time, since they are not truly castles yet represent the strongholds of the landed aristocracy. Coole Park and Lissadell are two of the more famous Big Houses immortalized in Anglo-Irish writings, and both were acquired by Protestant families during the eighteenth century. Appropriately, the former now survives only in verse, having been destroyed in 1941 after a contractor purchased it for the value of its stone.

Since the Ascendancy has so far been exclusively defined in terms of Protestantism, the pressing question becomes "what about the Catholic noble families?" After the Battle of the Boyne in 1691, most Catholic nobles were forced to flee Ireland in what became known as the Flight of the Wild Geese. After this point, the governmental affairs became increasingly handled by the Westminster Parliament and the members of the Protestant Ascendancy within Ireland. Even though Ireland maintained its own Parliament until the Act of Union in 1800, the Penal Laws went into effect during the eighteenth century. These laws forbade Irish Catholics from owning businesses and property above a certain value (including horses), holding their own schools, conducting Mass, and using primogeniture to insure that large estates remained intact. As a consequence, many Catholic families were forced to either convert to Protestantism, leave the country, or resort to subterfuge to maintain their ancestral homes. Terence De Vere White notes that by the beginning of the nineteenth century, "some Catholics—very few—managed to keep their heads up socially, but their number was insignificant" (17).

Catholics began to officially have political and social possibilities within the upper echelon again in 1829, through the act of Emancipation. With the final repeal of the Penal Laws (the process began in 1778), the Protestant Ascendancy began to gradually fade from public prominence, and "Catholic landowners took their place alongside their Protestant neighbours in Parliament, on the Bench of magistrates and on the Grand Jury which managed the affairs of the country" (Bence-Jones 13). Bence-Jones goes on to say, "The nineteenth-century Ascendancy included Catholics as well as Protestants: in County Kerry in 1879, the Queen's representative—known in Ireland as Her Majesty's Lieutenant, the equivalent English title of Lord Lieutenant being held only by the Viceroy—was the Catholic Earl of Kenmare; while out of sixteen Deputy-Lieutenants of that county, four were Catholics, including the grandson and the nephew of Daniel O'Connell" (14). Still, among the Irish landowners of the late nineteenth century, Catholics were on the whole poorer than their Protestant counterparts.

Almost coincident with the return of social prospects for Catholic families, the heyday of the Ascendancy was coming to an end. As late as the 1870s, it was still possible to think of the Ascendancy as the ruling class. The leading landowners of each county met every so often on the Grand Jury and settled all matters of local government. At the same time "the Ascendancy of the late 1870s hunted and generally enjoyed life,[5] not only was its political power being challenged, but the long period of agricultural depression which was to cause its economic collapse was already beginning" (Bence-Jones 19). Over the next century, the members of the Ascendancy shifted from roles of political leadership to an almost ghostly segment of the middle class. One observer suggests that "the sober Dublin Protestant who drives in his well-kept car to his office, minding his business, keeping out of controversies, hoping that his children will not form fatal attachments to Catholics . . . this quietly dressed, quietly speaking, bourgeois, whose social circle is usually small, has nothing whatever to do with the Anglo-Irish whom fancy depicts" (White 41). Most of the current members of the Ascendancy are middle-class. Their only visible differences from their middle-class, Catholic counterparts might be their accents and a certain quietness, both of which are disappearing as fewer children are educated in England.

Over the last century, the real impact of the Ascendancy and their Big Houses has been their effect on the Irish imagination, especially the literary imagination. I have already briefly mentioned the significance of Coole Park to W. B. Yeats, a place which could spark the impulse to suggest that "we were the last Romantics." Yeats's appreciation of the Ascendancy and their Big Houses was primarily due to the throwback to an earlier era that their lifestyle of leisure and hunting suggested. He did not really consider the members of the Protestant middle class to be members of the Ascendancy, only those who had money, land, and leisure:

> I meditate upon a swallow's flight,
> Upon an aged woman and her house,
> A sycamore and lime tree lost in night
> Although that western cloud is luminous,
> Great works constructed there in nature's spite
> For scholars and for poets after us,
> Thoughts long knitted into a single thought,
> A dance-like glory that those walls begot. (Yeats, 242-243, ll. 1-8)

What he finds in the houses and the people is the ability to inspire imagination. For himself, the result is artistic creation. For others, the effects of these houses vary substantially.

The idea of the Big House and its Ascendant residents has appeared a number of times in Friel's work. The first notable exploration of this social element occurs in the short story "Foundry House," an early treatment of elements which later reappear in *Aristocrats*. The story tells of the return of Joe Brennan and his family, a wife and nine children, to his family's old home, "the gate lodge to Foundry House" (52), and of Joe coming to terms with his memories in light of the present circumstances. The Hogan family, who live in Foundry House, are "supposed to be one of the best Catholic families in the North of Ireland" (52); however, the Hogans no longer possess the same grandeur and authority that they once did. Interestingly, the Hogans appear to have no trouble accepting their current status.

Joe, on the other hand, cannot come to terms with the difference between his memories of Foundry House and its present state. When his children want to play games near the big house, making no distinction between the estate's grounds and the small yard belonging to their cottage, Joe warns the children that "the old man, he'll soon scatter you! ... Or he'll put the big dog on you. God help you then!" (54). Knowing nothing of the past, the children can see the present for what it is and reply, "But there is no old man. Only the old woman and the maid. And there is no dog, either' (54). Joe cannot see the present without remembering the past, cannot accept that the Hogan fortunes have declined:

> No Mr. Bernard! Mr. Bernard always had been, Joe thought to
> himself, and always would be—a large, stern-faced man with a long
> white beard and a heavy step and a walking stick, the same ever
> since he remembered him. And beside him the Great Dane, who
> copied his master as best he could in expression and gait—a dour,
> sullen animal as big as a calf and as savage as a tiger, according to
> the men in the foundry. (54)

While he senses that the family line has ended when he discusses the fact that both children, Claire and Declan, have entered the church and that the house is literally falling apart, Joe refuses to reconcile this knowledge with his almost idyllic vision of the family: "Everything they could want in the world, anything that money could buy, and they turned their backs on it all. Strange, Joe thought. Strange. But right, because they were the Hogans" (55). Those final words, "because they were the Hogans," are the key to Joe's inability to reconcile his childhood and his adult experiences at Foundry House. He cannot or will not see beyond the mystique of the family name and the family house to understand, as the family seems to, that they are people whose time has past and whose cares are in another world.

Part of the reason that Joe cannot escape the mystique is that he has no real, first-hand experience of the family other than playing with Declan when they were children. He relies heavily on hearsay, as in the description of Mr. Bernard's dog, or his own fanciful renderings of what life must have been like inside Foundry House. We learn that "Joe had never been inside Foundry House, had never spoken to Mr. Bernard, and had not seen Declan since his ordination" (57). All of these elements suggest that the family has assumed such a large place in his imagination because of their "otherness" and distance from the rest of their Catholic neighbours. As the owners of the Foundry, they have both a material prosperity and a position of influence that their fellow parishioners do not. Consequently, they become the objects of childish imagination: simultaneously sublime and terrible. More than objects of the imagination, the Hogans become such a fixed, deific entity for Joe that he believes them to be timeless. The family and Foundry House become like gods to him rather than people capable of aging who must cut corners to make ends meet.

Consequently, when Joe is invited to the house to play a recording of Claire for the rest of the family, he cannot hide his discomfort at coming face to face with these larger than life figures who have populated his imagination for three and a half decades:

> And now, as he stood before the hall door and the evil face on the

leering knocker, the only introductory remark his mind would
supply him was one from his childhood: "My daddy says here are
the keys to the workshop and that he put out the fire in the office
before he left." He was still struggling to suppress this senseless
memory when Father Declan opened the door. (57)

By knocking on the door and entering Foundry House, Joe must admit to himself
how the Hogans have fallen, though he still cannot bring himself to admit to his
family what he experienced. In this case, his silence speaks louder than any words
he could supply in suggesting the importance of the Big House and the
Ascendancy to his imagination. Entering Foundry House and witnessing Mr.
Hogan's collapse caused a complete dismantling of his childhood preconceptions
and all the imagined terror and grandeur that went with them. Foundry House
stood for the kind of life he did not possess and could only aspire to. Witnessing
the final decline of the Hogan family left him with an emptiness that he could not
express, even to his own family.

Like "Foundry House," *Aristocrats* chronicles the demise of the "Catholic
Aristocracy" and is set in the northern portion of Ireland, this time in the border
town of Ballybeg, Co. Donegal. The play occurs during the mid-1970s at the
decaying O'Donnell family seat of Ballybeg Hall, which is described as structurally
crumbling throughout the play. While the play ostensibly chronicles a generational
shift and the demise of a family home in much the same manner as "Foundry
House" or Chekhov's *Three Sisters*, it more importantly suggests the way in which
a family has lost touch with its actual, factual history and replaced it with a
personal mythology that inflates the family's influence and significance. By
focusing on the upper class family rather than Ballybeg's other residents, it further
suggests the necessity of the O'Donnells doing so in light of the precarious social
and political position that the Catholic gentry has occupied in Irish society.

The O'Donnell family is clearly anomalous from any number of angles: the
abusively domineering father, the mother who committed suicide, the probably
gay only son, an alcoholic middle daughter, a manic depressive youngest daughter
who is marrying a much older man just to get out of the house, and an oldest
daughter who has been forced to leave her illegitimate son in an orphanage to
maintain family pretensions.[6] The most important anomaly of the play, however,
appears to be the O'Donnell family's status as one of the very few Catholic big
house families. Tom Hoffnung, an American sociologist, explains this seemingly
trivial note to Eamon, the townsperson who married into the O'Donnells and who
consistently presents the most sensible viewpoints throughout the play:

*Tom*: Well, when we talk about the big house in this country, we usually mean the Protestant big house with its Anglo-Irish tradition and culture; and the distinction is properly made between that tradition and culture and what we might call the native Irish tradition and culture which is Roman Catholic.

*Eamon*: With reservations—yes. So?

*Tom*: So what I'm researching is the life and life-style of the Roman Catholic big house—by no means as thick on the ground but still there; what we might call a Roman Catholic aristocracy—for want of a better term. (281)

In addition to explaining his research topic to Eamon, Tom outlines the essential problem that the O'Donnell family has faced for at least four generations: the failure to fit comfortably into any of Irish society's accepted niches and the subsequent inability to actively participate in the Ballybeg community.

The one given that we can take from this play is that the family is not middle class, or at least is not perceived as such by the people in the village or themselves, so any real political influence the family might have attained would have waned rapidly after the establishment of the Irish free state. Of course, the family also does not belong to the ruling Anglo-Irish Ascendancy, so they could not have participated in that liminal society. Tom further alludes to the O'Donnells' social incongruity when he says:

And the task I've set myself is to explore its [the Roman Catholic aristocracy's] political, cultural, and economic influence on both the ascendancy ruling class and on the native peasant tradition. Over the past one hundred and fifty years—in fact since Catholic emancipation—what political clout did they wield, what economic contribution did they make to the status of their coreligionists, what cultural effect did they have on local peasantry? (281)

This series of questions introduces the idea into the play that perhaps the O'Donnells could not belong to either social group cohesively, existing in the middle ground between Irish and Anglo-Irish societies and accepted by neither. If the Anglo-Irish society led a precarious existence between English and Irish cultures, then the experiences of families like the O'Donnells must have been doubly so. After rising above their peasant roots to become landowners, they would have been effectively barred from polite Anglo-Irish society because of their religion.

They are equally cut off from the lower class culture of Ballybeg by their material success. When the village boys, including Willie Diver, ape Casimir on his return from school, they amply demonstrate the distance that the villagers place between themselves and the O'Donnells. Eamon assumes a greater significance in the play when we realize that he is the only lower class character who participates in the family decisions or who becomes part of the family. In this role, he takes on the burden of representing the most common understanding of Irish culture, the social classes whose ancestors would have spoken Irish just over a century ago. Eamon alludes to the way that the Irish lower classes perceived the Catholic gentry and the way that the gentry perceived the peasants by asking Tom, "and what conclusions have you reached?" (281). When Tom replies that he has found none, Eamon offers

> Let's see can we help the Professor. What were the questions again? What political clout did they wield? *(Considers. Then sadly shakes his head.)* What economic help were they to their co-religionists? *(Considers. Then sadly shakes his head.)* What cultural effects did they have on the local peasantry? Alice? *(Considers. Then sadly shakes his head.)* We agree, I'm afraid. Sorry, Professor. Bogus thesis. (281)

Eamon is simultaneously being rude, humourous, and accurate. His statements suggest that the Catholic gentry were not generally well regarded by the lower class citizens of Ballybeg. Perhaps this sentiment arises out of envy for material prosperity, but a stronger possibility mentioned within the play is the suggestion that the O'Donnell family name was coincident with the criminal justice system in Co. Donegal. The family effectively moved up the social ladder by acting as the legal representatives and executors of English imperial policy in Ireland, which would alienate them from the peasants living, and occasionally starving, around them.

Still, it does not seem, as Marilyn Throne suggests, that Friel can find no usefulness in the play's aristocracy (196). That claim is effectively answered by Eamon's vehement defense of the big house in the play's final scene. Instead, Friel offers the O'Donnell family as uniquely representative of Irish dilemmas. Robbed of social prestige and political power over the course of a few generations, the O'Donnells become an allegory of the Irish situation of the eighteenth and nineteenth centuries. Because of their rather unique social standing they cannot look to Ballybeg for any kind of solution. As in Chekhov's *Three Sisters*, they must look to the cities to save them. Significantly, however, they cannot or will not look to Dublin as a source of employment or even of hope. The family has always turned to England for its inspiration and standing. As the Catholic gentry, the only real social status that they can consider a possibility is to possess equal standing with the Anglo-Irish Ascendancy. The obvious way to achieve this status is to emphasize their English ties rather than their Irish ones. Anna, the sister who is never seen, demonstrates the family's desire to emphasize their Englishness by her choice of names in the convent: Sister John Henry. Rather than selecting any of the number of Irish religious figures like Colmcille, Patrick, or Aidan, she chooses a nineteenth century English cardinal who reputedly had ties to the family.

Anna's namesake illustrates a trend that is present in all of the relics of a greater past mentioned in connection with Ballybeg Hall. All of the prominent persons who have been associated with household items are literary figures, presumably showing both the family's taste and patronage of the arts. Even a cursory glance at the list of names put forward, however, reveals that all of them are either English Catholics or Anglo-Irish Protestants: the Gerard Manley Hopkins tea stain, the G. K. Chesterton footstool, Daniel O'Connell's boot marks on the chaise longue, the George Moore candlestick, the Tom Moore book, the Bible given to Justice O'Connell by Hilaire Belloc, and Casimir's memory of Yeats's "cold, cold eyes" (267). These memories and keepsakes become even more significant when they are revealed to be merely figments of the family's collectively overactive imagination. Then, they become a way of marking time and place for the family, personal landmarks that delineate the topography of their home and establish a cultural niche that they have been lacking. The social strata that they are aiming at through these people are, however, unusual. By using English Catholics like John Henry Newman and Gerard Manley Hopkins and Anglo-Irish authors like Yeats, the O'Donnells create their own cultural tradition that is just outside of the English mainstream. They do not seek to become part of the dominant Anglican society, but seek to remain on the fringes with literary figures from social segments that reside outside polite society. Alice's residence in London highlights this idea even more clearly. The fact that she does not participate in English society in any way, remaining in their tiny apartment alone while Eamon works, suggests her reluctance to let go of a cultivated tradition that defined her as not part of English culture. While the family does establish itself within their own eyes as being part of the aristocratic tradition by supporting these artists, their patronage appears odd because the only thing that the artists visibly received from Ballybeg Hall was physical pain. The O'Donnells, on the other hand, could situate themselves above the local peasants and almost equal with the ascendancy landlords by virtue of their association with the same people. In other words, the stories about their furnishings gave them a sense of history relating to specific social niche.

The idea of place and the primacy of landscape have always been significant parts of Irish literature, but the coming of the British plantations and landlords and their subsequent renaming of Irish places that Friel captured so poignantly in *Translations* have reemphasized its importance. Speaking of this issue, Seamus Heaney suggests that "it is true, indeed, that we have talked much more about it in this country because of the peculiar fractures in our history, north and south, and because of the way possession of the land and possession of different languages have rendered the question particularly urgent" (136). There is an Irish literary tradition known as *dinnseanchas* that applies to tales and poems which describe the origin of a specific place name. Heaney has suggested that the *Tain Bo Cualigne* is full of incidental *dinnseanchas* when it relates how many of the geographical features between Connacht and Ulster got their names (131). Twentieth century Irish poets have rediscovered the significance of this genre and employed it to create a chiefly literary sense of place in Ireland.

More culturally significant, or at least more legally binding, than even its presence in poetry are the findings of the Irish High Court on Circuit. In 1983, the court settled a right-of-way case that documented the existence of a path supposedly traversed by Maeve and her armies. In the final ruling, the right-of-way was upheld because according to local tradition it had existed "from time immemorial" (Ferguson 451-52). The centenary celebration of the town of Ardee further demonstrates the ongoing presence of the *Tain* in everday life. Arthur Gribben suggests that

> the saga continues to have relevance for Ardee people. They perceive it to be theirs because the most famous combat scene of *TBC*—the fight between Cuchulain and Ferdia—happened in their small corner of Ireland. At Ardee, it is the very name of the place—*Ath Fhirdia*, the Ford of Ferdia—which bespeaks *TBC*. In celebrating the town's centenary, Ardee people proudly proclaimed the combat scene as their very own, enhancing in their eyes the small town's importance in the larger scheme of things (287).

Considering the tremendous significance of landscape and sense of place in Irish drama from Edward Martyn's *The Heather Field* to the present, it seems odd that no Irish dramatist has previously considered the necessity for creating this kind of *dinnseanchas* within a dramatic work. While Beckett comes close to doing so in *Waiting for Godot*, Friel is truly the first to situate this distinctively Irish tradition inside of an equally traditional family drama, *Aristocrats*, and use it to examine Irish attitudes toward class and identity.

In *Passing the Time at Ballymenone*, the noted ethonographer, Henry Glassie, suggests that "history's primary connections are made in space" (200). The connections established in County Louth are much like those Glassie encountered in the Ulster community of Ballymenone. He goes on to say that "space joins past events to each other, and it unifies past and present in two ways: progessively and mythically" (201). The progressive demarcation is a way of linking the past to the present by emphasizing changes, presumably for the better, in the landscape. Mythic demarcation is permanent, irrevocably branding the landscape with a name derived from some event or story. Connection to the live force of mythic events stems from involvement in place. The town of Ardee and the winner of the lawsuit essentially become part of their environment, adding to the myth of the *Tain* by preserving its places. Anyone can claim responsibility for progress, but the mythic past lies beyond human intention:

> It is served when people who are part of the environment, people like Master Corrigan and Michael Boyle—unlike Mrs. Owens and Mr. Flanagan—people who are "native," tell the inchoate tale of place. When Hugh Patrick Owens begins the story of the Ford with his own genealogy, he merges with the Arney and the battle as part of this locale. He is naturally responsible for his story. He is to be believed (Glassie 201).

This mythic sense of place is the one which dominates *Aristocrats*. A sense of place joins those who made, defined, and inhabited the land with those who remake it. In place, the person is actively part of history. The O'Donnell family has merged these literary figures with their imagined rememberings to create local myths about the significance of the family and to enhance their local standing. More importantly, creating these stories is the only way that the current generation can claim Ballybeg Hall as their own and, due to economic realities, take an active role in maintaining the family history.

Like the Irish families during the Penal Laws, the O'Donnells are being gradually dispossessed of their land. While Ballybeg Hall will probably not be taken over by Protestant planters, it will not continue to belong to the family. Therefore, like the native Irish of preceding generations, they have to come up with some way to make the premises and the furniture most certainly their own. The family then falls back into a rather common understanding of Irish landscape: the world above and the world within. While in more traditional Irish tales these two arenas would have been divided into the realm of humans and the realm of faeries, Friel metaphorically accomplishes the same thing by establishing the family's reality and the rest of the world's perception of that reality. The latter viewpoint is generally offered by Tom and Eamon, though only occasionally. Eamon is the gifted seer or poet in the play, capable of discerning both modes of reality and expressing them to the audience.

Like the Irish *dinnseanchas*, the stories the O'Donnells weave are always based on items in the household and attach some historical significance to their own possessions. Not even Willie Diver will continue to rent the estate's boggy land indefinitely, so the O'Donnells are being pushed off their land and into strange parts. Creating tales to go with the house's furnishings is the only way that the children can keep their heritage with them, even if it is a fictional heritage. This fictional heritage, however, possesses a political element. Edward Said discusses anti-imperialist literary creation by suggesting that the first step is to distinguish the native from the colonial master. In *Aristocrats*, the master is simultaneously the British and the native Irish traditions which simultaneously oppress the O'Donnells. The second part of Said's development scheme seems to fit the play more closely:

> Before this [development of a native literature] can be done, however, there is a pressing need for the recovery of the land, that, because of the presence of the colonizing outsider, is recoverable at first only through the imagination. . . . For the native, the history of his or her colonial servitude is inaugurated by the loss to an outsider of the local place, whose concrete geographical identity must thereafter be searched for and somehow restored (75-76).

The O'Donnells sit on the verge of such an event, as they prepare to shut the doors of Ballybeg Hall forever behind them. The stories act as myth and fix the house and its contents in their memories.

The connection between this imaginative life and Irish culture is further strengthened by the croquet scene in Act II. Willie's reluctance to throw himself into an imaginary game of croquet soon gives way to an exuberant attempt at victory, and he loses himself in the imaginative fiction of the afternoon. That this tendency seems particularly suited to the Irish lower classes is emphasized by Eamon's and Willie's exchange:

> *Willie:* Never had a mallet in my hand before! Never stood on a croquet court before! Bloody good, eh?

*Eamon*: 'Terrific'. *(He gives one of Casimir's grins.)* A real insider now, Willie.

*Willie*: Give us a slug of something there—I'm as dry as a lime-kiln. What's in that?

> *(Eamon hands him an empty wine bottle.)*

*Eamon*: Here.

*Willie*: Jaysus, that's empty!

*Eamon*: Imagine it's full. Use your peasant talent for fantasy, man.

The entire scene demonstrates the need to retreat into fantasy in order to survive and possibly even to understand the real truth. Eamon seems hostile to Willie in the above lines; however, it is difficult to ascertain whether his anger is over becoming like the O'Donnell children or because he does not sustain his imagination off the croquet court. The crucial element in this scene, however, is the fundamental connection established between the townspeople and the O'Donnell family in this game. Both employ their "peasant talent for fantasy."

Marilyn Throne is quite correct when she asserts that this aristocratic family has moved from the public sphere of influence into new roles as private citizens, just as Chekhov's Prozorov family did (196). Unlike the Russian family, Friel's characters can never be said to be divorced from public life. Although distanced from life in Ballybeg, the O'Donnells have always been models for the Ballybeg community, either consciously or unconsciously. The former sort of modeling is illustrated in Willie's description of the village boys "acting the maggot, you know, imitating" Casimir when he was home on holidays from boarding school (260). The latter more interesting form of modeling does not occur until the play's close when the children are discussing what is to become of the house. All are resigned to letting the house go, except for Eamon. Having been raised in the village by a grandmother who worshipped the life in the big house, Eamon does not belong to its lifestyle yet is the only one fully capable of understanding its significance to the village. Where Joe Hogan in "Foundry House" remains silent to his family about his experiences, Eamon gives utterance to his emotions:

> Sorry . . . sorry . . . sorry again . . . Seems to be a day of public contrition. What the hell is it but crumbling masonry. Sorry. *(Short laugh.)* Don't you know that all that fawning and forelock-touching and Paddy and shabby and greasy peasant in the Irish character finds a house like this irresistible? That's why we were ideal for colonizing. Something in us needs this . . . aspiration. Don't despise us—we're only hedgehogs, Judith. Sorry. (318-319)

Like Americans going to movies in the 1930s, the Irish peasants can use the big house as a way to live vicariously, to be a part of a wider world. They aspire to be part of that world, but cannot because of class and colonial practice.

The O'Donnell house is significant because it is as close as the Irish Catholics can get to participating in an English culture. Like Friel's statement about English literature, they can read that tradition but cannot fully interact with it. Like the O'Donnells, the Irish must come to terms with their own understanding of place and imagination to create a history. Unlike the O'Donnells, Friel suggests that turning away from Ireland and its land and people will ultimately be destructive. The overwhelming fact that confronts the audience at the end of the play is that all of the children are going to leave the house, the land, and each other. What the play asks us to understand is why they needed to create these myths of their own station in life and how that affects the Irish citizens around them.

The Irish Catholic members of the Ascendancy become something more than a minor historical footnote in the hands of Brian Friel. He skillfully uses them to indicate the manner in which everyone, both Irish and citizen of the world, constructs myths to guard and protect their past. More significantly, Friel uses the Catholic aristocracy to illustrate how we interact with historical "facts" and "myths" through the creation of our own fictions. Like the O'Donnells and their collection of literary victims, tying a story to a location gives both the place and the storyteller an active role.

# NOTES

1. *Aristocrats*, p. 274.

2. The quote is taken from Somerville's and Ross's *The Irish R. M.* (p. 8) and seems an uniquely appropriate depiction of the O'Donnell house in *Aristocrats*.

3. Maxwell suggests that "despite the skeletal topography, a vanished—or banished—knowledge of district, of parish, flutters in the details of Hamm's memories . . . in the intimately idiomatic tone of Estragon's 'We're not from these parts,' Vladimir's 'Are you from these parts?'" (191).

4. See Marilyn Throne's "The Disintegration of Authority: A Study of the Fathers in Five Plays of Brian Friel" or F. C. McGrath's "Brian Friel and the Politics of the Anglo-Irish Language" for more traditionally Chekhovian analyses of *Aristocrats*.

5. The first chapter of Mark Bence-Jones's *Twilight of the Ascendancy* paints an eloquent portrait of the Irish hunting estates at the close of the nineteenth century. They were renowned throughout the world and even provided two all too

brief holidays for Austria's Empress Elizabeth, the most glamorous huntswoman of Europe in the late 1800s.

6. After seeing his fundamental inaccuracies involving the rest of the family history, I can see no reason to trust his statements regarding Helga and the boys. The unnecessary reference to homosexuality in the conversation with Eamon (p. 310), his father's suggestion that there is something odd about him, and his fear of being found out a second time all point to his lying about the family.

# WORKS CITED

Bence-Jones, Mark. *Twilight of the Ascendancy*. London: Constable, 1987.

Donoghue, Denis. "The Problems of Being Irish." *Times Literary Supplement*, 17 Mar. 1972: 291-92.

Ferguson, K. 1984. Gerard Carroll and James Carroll v James Sheridan and Raymond Sheehan. *Irish Law Reports Monthly* 4: 451-461.

Friel, Brian. *Selected Plays of Brian Friel*. London: Faber and Faber, 1984.

———. "Foundry House" in *The Saucer of Larks*. Garden City, NY: Doubleday, 1962.

Glassie, Henry. *Passing the Time in Ballymenone*. Philadelphia: Univ. of Penn. Press, 1982.

Gribben, Arthur. "Tain Bo Cuailnge: A Place on the Map, A Place in the Mind." *Western Folklore* 49 (July 1990): 227-291.

Heaney, Seamus. *Preoccupations: Selected Prose, 1968 - 1978*. London: Faber & Faber, 1980.

O'Brien, George. *Brian Friel*. Boston: Twayne Publishers, 1990.

Pine, Richard. *Brian Friel and Ireland's Drama*. New York : Routledge, 1990.

Said, Edward. "Yeats and Decolonization." *Nationalism, Colonialism, and Literature*. Minneapolis, MN: Univ. of Minnesota Press, 1990.

Somerville, Edith Æ. and Martin Ross. *The Irish R. M.* New York: Penguin, 1984.

Throne, Marilyn. "The Social Value of the Privileged Class: A Comparison of Shaw's *Heartbreak House* and Friel's *Aristocrats*." *Colby Library Quarterly*, 24.4 (Dec. 1988): 187-196.

White, Terence De Vere. *The Anglo-Irish*. London: Gollancz, 1972.

Yeats, W. B. *The Poems*. Ed. Richard Finneran. New York: Macmillan, 1983.

# BRIAN FRIEL'S *FAITH HEALER*

## Declan Kiberd

*Faith Healer* by Brian Friel may well be the finest play to come out of Ireland since J.M. Synge's *Playboy of the Western World*. It is also, without a doubt, one of the most derivative works of art to be produced in Ireland this century—and this gives rise to a question. How can a play which is indebted so heavily to a number of previous works be nevertheless a work of profound and scintillating originality? And how can a play consisting of four separate monologues by characters who never openly confront each other be a fully *dramatic* work, in any real sense of that word?

We should first consider Friel's debts. *Faith Healer* might be called an intergeneric work where the forms of novel and drama meet, for it is a kind of dramatised novel. The idea of four contradictory monologues may have come to Friel from a reading of William Faulkner's most famous novel *The Sound and the Fury*. The method is identical, even down to the detail of having one of the monologues narrated by a witness of unstable mind, in Faulkner the lunatic Benjy, in Friel the shattered and suicidal Grace Hardy. This attempt to take an outstanding device of the modern novel, and redeploy it in the dramatic form is a characteristic modernist strategy, for modernism loves to mix genres—one thinks of Eliot's fusion of drama and poetry, Joyce's use of drama in the middle of *Ulysses*, Flann O'Brien's crazy blend of cowboy tale and Celtic lore in *At Swim-Two-Birds*. Although Faulkner's novel and Friel's play both challenge the audience to judge for itself the inconsistencies between the various monologues there is one crucial difference. The novel can be reread, the play cannot be rerun to some point of contention. To that extent, the dramatic form is even more baffling and unsettling in its effect on its audience.

Friel's other debt is even more striking. *Faith Healer is* clearly a remoulding of the legend of Deirdre of the Sorrows, a tale which has been dramatised by many leading Irish writers from George Russell to W. B. Yeats, from J. M. Synge to James Stephens. The idea of a well-brought-up girl, destined for a noble calling in the north of Ireland, but spirited away to Scotland by an attractive but feckless man, to the great dismay of an elderly guardian—that, in a nutshell, is the plot of both Friel's and Synge's plays. In Scotland, the lovers live well enough for many years, supported by their manager Teddy, who discharges the same role in *Faith Healer* as that played by Naisi's brothers, Ainnle and Ardan, in Synge's play. Ultimately, however, their nomadic and rootless life is felt to be increasingly hollow and stressful. With some foreboding, they decide to return to Ireland, but in their nervousness and apprehensiveness, each lover attributes the decision to the other. Their worst fears are realized on arrival in Ireland. As Francis Hardy says: "there was no sense of homecoming"[1] or as Synge's Naisi says, looking at the shabby rooms and open grave, which the King offers by way of greeting: "And that'll be our home in Emain."[2] Earlier, he gloomily remarks that "it's little we want with state or rich rooms or curtains, when we're used to the ferns only, and cold streams and they making a stir"[3]—a sentence which could just as aptly describe the raw, open-air life of Francis, Grace and Teddy camping out by the fields and streams of Scotland.

One of the great themes of Synge's play and of the original Gaelic legend is Deirdre's love of place. Before her final departure from Scotland, she lists the names of all the abandoned places with tender care. So it is with her laments for Glen Ruadh, Glen Laid, the Woods of Cuan and so on in Synge's play. In one of his less well-known essays on "The People of the Glens," Synge had remarked on the "curiously melodious names" to be found in Wicklow—Aughavanna, Glenmalure, Annamoe[4]—and he built lilting lists of the names into his Wicklow plays. Friel self-consciously builds on the ancient Gaelic tradition in those passages where Francis and Grace recite the Scottish place-names, as the Faith Healer says, "just for the mesmerism, the sedation, of the incantation."[5] This is an ancient Gaelic device redeployed by Seamus Heaney, for example in poems such as "The Tollund Man":

> Something of his sad freedom
> As he rode the tumbril
> Should come to me, driving,

Saying the names
Tollund, Grabaulle, Nebelgard,
Watching the pointing hands of country people,
Not knowing their tongue. [6]

What is revealing in Friel's play, however, is the fact that Grace fouls up the order of her husband's incantation. She omits his third line from the list and, at the end of her monologue, is so distraught that she cannot get beyond the opening lines:

Aberarder, Kinlochbervie,
Aberayron, Kinlochbervie
Invergordon, Kinlochbervie . . . in Sutherland, in
the north of Scotland. . . . [7]

She trails off helplessly and this linguistic failure is the sure sign of her imminent collapse.

In *Faith Healer,* as in the Deirdre legend, the lovers return to Ireland with the premonition that it will be a return to disaster and even death for the hero. And this is what happens. Only at the very end does Friel depart radically from Synge's plot. Whereas Synge's Deirdre dies soon after Naisi in the romantic medieval versions, Friel follows the more hard-edged Old Irish rendition by having her live on for a year in misery, before her eventual suicide.

Wherein, it might therefore be asked, does the originality of *Faith Healer* lie? One could answer by saying that the notion of the artist as inspired con-man is one of Friel's innermost themes and that all those debts to previous works and authors raise the whole question of the artist as con-man in our minds. So the play turns out to be about itself, since it, like its central character, veers between conmanship and brilliant innovation. The artist is like the Faith Healer, a man who never knows for certain whether he has been successful in bringing off an effect, a broker in risk who must stand before the audience nightly with no assurance that his magic will rub off on others yet again. Moreover, like the Faith Healer, the artist knows that if he gives free rein to his own self-doubts, the gift may desert him. Too anxious a self-scrutiny may kill the very gift which the analysis is supposed to illuminate. This is a truth even more obvious to the manager Teddy than it is to the healer himself. In his contrast between two performing dogs, Teddy illustrates for us the sense in which the artist has to be a con-man; one dog, sensitive and resourceful, could switch on the fire, pull the curtains and leave the master's slippers by the chair, but in front of an audience she went to pieces. The other dog hadn't the brains to learn his own name, but could perform to perfection on the bagpipes for any given audience. Teddy also cites the case of the brainless Miss Mulatto who could talk to one hundred and twenty pigeons in different languages, yet never know how she did it—she just made sounds. This leads Teddy to conclude that artists must not only have talent and ambition, but that they must also have no critical self-consciousness about their gift:

> They know they have something fantastic, sure, they're not that stupid. But what it is they have, how they do it, how it works, what that sensational talent is, what it all means—believe me, they don't know and they don't care and even if they did care they haven't the brains to analyse it. [8]

So the first audience the artist must con is himself. He must still those impulses to self-doubt and self-questioning which erupt in him from time to time. "Francis Hardy, Faith Healer, One Night Only"[9] says the tattered poster. Hardy knows that that "one night only" suggests the touch of the charlatan, the poseur who will not stay around to face the consequences of his own claims or the critical response to his performance. At times, he sees himself possessed of an awesome gift; on other occasions, a mere trickster—but there were moments, he still insists, when the gift *did* work.

When Francis Hardy talks about his gift, he sounds remarkably like Seamus Heaney discussing his involvement with poetry. "How did I get involved? As a young man I chanced to flirt with it and it possessed me. No, no, no, no, no,—that's rhetoric." [10] This seems close to Heaney's quotation, that a young man dabbles in verses and finds they are his life—a remark that becomes even more interesting when Heaney himself points out that it was Patrick Kavanagh who originally made it.[11] Francis Hardy claims, more humbly, that he did it because he found that he *could* do it. Heaney's account of poetry as a gift for divination is very close indeed to Francis Hardy's view of his gift. According to Heaney, divining is a gift for being in touch with what is there, hidden but real—"a gift for mediating between the latent resource and the community that wants it current and released." [12] The water diviner resembles the poet in his function of making contact with what lies hidden. To an artist like Friel that contact may be made with further possibilities lying hidden and dormant in previous works of literature such as the Deirdre legend; but if he becomes too self-conscious about those debts, he will never create anything original, because he will have no basis on which to build. So he must ruthlessly and mindlessly assimilate whatever resources from the past may be turned to use. Heaney compares this mindless wisdom to that of a somnambulist and sees one of the great pleasures of poetry in that somnambulist process of search and surrender, like the water diviner who moves forward with eyes closed, following only the hint and tug of the wooden stick. A process as unself-conscious as this is an exercise in high risk but to become self-analytical would be the greatest risk of all.

The artist can seldom, if ever, be his own critic. "A poem always has elements of accident about it, which can be made the subject of inquest afterwards," commented Heaney in a radio talk, "but there is always a risk in conducting your own inquest. You might begin to believe in the coroner in yourself, rather than put your trust in the man in you who is capable of accident."[13] It is precisely that ailment which afflicts the Faith Healer in his final days, as he comes to believe even more in the coroner of certainties than in the creator of risks. His first monologue is far too self-analytical for his own good as an artist:

> Was it all change?—or skill?—or illusion?—or delusion? Precisely what power did I possess? Could I summon it? When and how? Was I its servant? Did it reside in my ability to invest someone with faith in me or did I evoke from him a healing faith in himself? Could my healing be effected without faith? But faith in what?—in me?—in the possibility?—faith in faith? And is the power diminishing? You're beginning to masquerade, aren't you? You're becoming a husk, aren't you? . . . [14]

By Hardy's second soliloquy we realize that he is in fact speaking from the dead—a device appropriate enough for a man who is indeed his own coroner. Moreover, it is clear that he has returned to Ireland and to Donegal deliberately to seek out this death, because he can no longer bear the high-risk tensions of life as an artist, the uncertainty of a life spent hovering between mastery and humiliation, the uncertainty which is the true source of his mastery just as it is the inevitable prelude to his failure.

Hardy steps before us out of the darkness and into a ray of light at the beginning of the play, and recedes into the black at the end. This light/dark strategy is identical to that employed by Beckett in many dramas. Beckett explains it as a metaphysics of risk:

> If life and death did not present themselves to us, there would be no inscrutability. If there were only darkness, all would be clear. It is because there is not only darkness but also light that our situation becomes inexplicable. Take Augustine's doctrine of grace given and grace withheld . . . in the classical drama, such problems

do not arise. The destiny of Racine's *Phedre is* sealed from the beginning: she will proceed into the dark. As she goes, she herself will be illuminated. At the beginning of the play she has partial illumination and at the end she has complete illumination, but there has been no question but that she moves towards the dark. That is the play. Within this notion, clarity is possible, but for us who are neither Greek nor Jansenist there is no such clarity. The question would also be removed if we believed in the contrary—total salvation. But where we have both dark and light we also have the inexplicable. The key word in my plays is "perhaps."[15]

Beckett's plays are poignant satires on those still foolish enough to seek for signs and certainties—on critics—and a celebration of the random and chancy—of artists. Friel takes up where Beckett leaves off and in *Faith Healer* he depicts that lust for certainty as the last infirmity of the bourgeois mind. This is pictured most satirically in Grace's account of the fearful symmetry of her family home, with its Japanese gardens, straight avenues and ordered poplars. This haven of order she abandons for a life of risk which will lead finally to her self-destruction. Her sedate solicitor-father is merely an extreme example of that rage for order which dominates most of the characters in the play. The patients who come to Hardy's performances come in search of certainty even more than a cure. In a perverse kind of way, they come to be cured of uncertainty even more than to be cured of disease. Francis Hardy understands this well:

> . . . by coming to me they exposed, publicly acknowledged, their desperation. And even though they told themselves they were here because of the remote possibility of a cure, they knew in their hearts they had come not to be cured but for the confirmation that they were incurable; not in hope but for the elimination of hope; for the removal of that final, impossible change—that's why they came—to seal their anguish, for the content of a finality.
>
> And they knew that I knew. And so they defied me to endow them with hopelessness. But I couldn't do even that for them . . . Because occasionally, just occasionally, the miracle would happen.[16]

In the end, the healer felt that it would have been a kindness not to go near them, not to unsettle them with hope. Yet he knows, too, that it is the function of art to terrify and unsettle a community, to insult even more than to flatter it, to be unlike its idea of itself. The community may hate the artist for the cruel and sharp light which he throws on reality, but it knows also that his is a necessary insult, a necessary evil. The healer recalls evenings when he could sense that there were hundreds of people holding their breath in the locality, "waiting in the half-light." They were people poised between the certainty of darkness and the certainty of light, anxiously waiting to see what would happen to those audacious enough to attend the healer's meeting, intrepid legates on behalf of those too timid to look into the artist's face and handiwork. "And sometimes I got the impression, too, that if we hadn't come to them, they would have sought us out." [17] So the community assaults and finally slays the artist, whose ministry it nevertheless finds essential to its well-being.

The healer can sense the poignancy of those people's search for certainty, precisely because he can feel that yearning so deeply in himself. If safe, settled folk can feel that need, then how much more will he whose life is lived on a knife-edge of risk and somnambulist groping. At the end, the broker in risk runs out of courage and decides to cash his chips in return for a racing certainty. So, in his last days, as his con-man's courage dissolves, he lacerates himself with self-doubt and deliberately seeks out a spectacular failure that will kindly put an end to his own slender surviving hope. What he has tried and failed to do for others, he hopes now to achieve for himself—the elimination of hope. As he walks towards the drunken men in the bleak morning light, he knows that nothing will happen except his own death and finds a strange consolation in that knowledge:

> And as I moved across that yard towards them and offered myself to them, then for the first time I had a simple and genuine sense of homecoming. Then for the first time there was no atrophying terror, and the maddening questions were silent.
> At long last I was renouncing chance. [18]

But for the artist *that is* the only mortal sin, and Hardy must ultimately be judged as an artist, for that is the only word which his wife can find to descnbe her dead lover to the doctor:

> "He was an artist," I said—quickly, casually—but with complete conviction—just the way he might have said it. Wasn't that curious? Because the thought had never occurred to me before. And then because *I* said it and the doctor wrote it down I knew it was true. [19]

The thought strikes her almost by *accident.* Unlike her husband, who turns out in the end to be just like her orderly father, she has the courage to submit herself to chance. For her the accidental betokens a higher truth, for which she will die, rather than return to the world of bourgeois certainties which drove her mother mad. In the final scenario of his career, Hardy renounced change—and, in doing so, he degraded himself from the status of artist to that of mere performer. The artist always keeps his eye remorselessly on his subject, whereas the performer is always watching his audience. The artist risks the displeasure of his audience as he maintains a congenial relationship with his subject, whereas the performer risks the betrayal of his subject as he seeks a congenial relationship with his audience.

All through his career, up until this final night, Francis Hardy has been an artist, humble in the service of that mystery which has chosen to reveal itself through him, humble even to the point of believing that the world of family happiness and personal fulfillment is well lost for art. At the outset, he was so incorruptible that he resisted all the efforts of his manager to degrade his healing artistry to the level of mere performance, and so he resisted the use of background music. He scrupulously avoided stagey or theatrical effects, as on the night when in serene silence he cured ten in the village of Llanbethian. The garish Teddy is still amazed to recall that "there was no shouting or cheering or dancing with joy" and "hardly a word was spoken."[20] He admires the professionalism of a healer to whom the only final reality was his work. But, as his confidence waned, Hardy began to rely on the fake support of background music and surrendered to the view of himself as a mere performer. On his last night, the erstwhile professional declines into an amateur magician and prostitutes his art in a cheap publicity stunt. Seeing the bent finger of a Donegal farmer, he feels certain that he can cure it and so he seeks his own fate. Up to now, he has gathered the audience, great or small, around himself, but now he goes in search of the audience's approval and esteem. He seeks the certainty of public acclaim and sees the corruption of his art into a gaudy ad-man's dream. Up to now, he had wisely allowed his gift to possess him, but now he falsely tries to possess his gift. It is, of course, unnecessary to elaborate on the appropriateness of Friel's attack on art-as-mere-entertainment in what is his most complex and under-rated play.

If Friel had chosen to leave things at that, this would be a deft and subtle play about art and artistic illusion, but he extends these perceptions brilliantly to show how they apply also in life. If excessive self-scrutiny can destroy an artist, the playwright shows that it can also destroy anyone. The most moving element of the play is the strange, inconclusive but very deep relationship between Francis Hardy and his wife. It is a coupling that is full of cruelty—his cruelty to her in the momentous labour of childbirth; her vicious mockery of him when his charisma fails; their joint harshness to Teddy whom they abandon for days on end; their neglect of parents whom they have left behind in Ireland. It is a relationship which, like most deep loves, has awkward zones of emptiness and inscrutability where little is shared or understood. In a perverse way, Grace resented Hardy his moments of mastery, when he would stand (she says) "looking past you out of his completion, out of that private power, out of that certainty that was available only to him. God, how I resented that privacy . . . And then, for him, I didn't exist . . . But before a performance this exclusion—no, it wasn't an exclusion, it was an evasion—this evasion was absolute: he obliterated me."[21] It is, nevertheless, a relationship as beautiful as it is baffling, full in some respects, empty in others, but, above all, clumsy and inconsistent. When it is good it is good by accident, but when the intention to make it good is too overt, then it inevitably fails. Francis and Grace were aware of the rich potential of their love, but as often as not they are baffled when a tender impulse is misconstrued. Like the artist's attitude to his secret art, theirs is a relationship of fluctuations, which neither can hope fully to control; and Friel seems to be hinting that all good couplings must stay that way. If they become self-analytical in the attempt to remove imperfections or uncertainties, then they may also remove that element of risk which is the ultimate sign of love. To love someone is to risk hurting or even losing that person, but if such risks are not run, there can be no real relationship, no sense of something freely given despite its potential cost. In general, it seems to be true that most people only begin to analyze relationships when they start to go wrong—the glossy magazines are filled with news of famous couples splitting up just two months after they had analyzed and explained their happiness to some nosey reporter. In its handling of this theme, *Faith Healer* is remarkably similar to *Philadelphia, Here I Come!* which showed how a young man's conscious attempt to clarify his bond with his father failed. In Friel's earlier play, the memory which Gar O'Donnell strove to make his father share with him just would not overlap with the old man's recollection, but in the very effort at remembrance that goal is reached (without Gar's fully realizing it) when the youth tells the Canon "there's an affinity between old Screwballs and me."[22] For some strange reason, Gar still feels the need to define and analyze that affinity, when he should have been content enough to have sensed it.

Both dramas make great play with the distortion of memory, the most obvious being that nobody in *Faith Healer* can summon the courage to describe the murder in Ballybeg, just as nobody in *Philadelphia* could accurately recall the momentous events of the past or face the fact that Gar is about to emigrate. Both plays focus on the importance of names as a sign of that distorted memory— Francis Hardy, F.H., Faith Healer, if you are a believer in fate. To name something is to exercise a power over it, much as Hardy intones the list of those small village communities over which he has exercised his power. He remembers them clearly, but not the surnames or placenames of his own wife's origin: "Grace Dodsworth from Scarborough—or was it Knaresborough? I don't remember,"[23] as if to suggest my earlier point that *this* is one relationship which he can never hope to control completely. As if to confirm this loss of control, the healer's second soliloquy becomes stuck in a groove with the endless repetition of Kinlochbervie, the place in Scotland where Grace bore and lost their baby. That emotional scar is too deep to allow him to continue the recital. If by naming something we show our power over it, by misnaming it we may be showing its power over us. Grace thinks at first that Hardy constantly changed her surname in order to humiliate her, that he called her mistress instead of wife to upset her, that he said she was from Yorkshire or Kerry or London or Scarborough instead of Ulster to deprive her of an identity. But he told the theatre audience that he *honestly* couldn't remember where she came from. Because he is a lifelong healer of audiences, one assumes that it is part of his nature to be more honest with large audiences than with private individuals—his distrust of phony background music testifies to that. The real reason why he unknowingly represses or distorts the details of Grace's background is that he feels a deep guilt over the sufferings which he has inflicted on her and her parents. He tries to displace or remould an emotion, the better to cope with it; and so he never once mentions the loss of the baby in Kinlochbervie, or his own callous behaviour there, but simply pretends that Kinlochbervie was the place in which he happened to be when news of his mother's death arrived. By remoulding an emotion that might otherwise control him, he can begin to control it, and this is why Grace rightly calls him an *artist,* with a compulsion to adjust and refashion everything around him. She denounces him for this gift and bluntly opines that she would have been far happier if he had never had this capacity to remould twisted fingers or unsatisfactory lives. She sees that those he cured were not real to him as persons but as fictions, extensions of himself that came into being only because of him.

Nevertheless, by the end of her soliloquy, Grace is pleading to be reinstated as one of Hardy's fictions. Recognising that she needs Hardy in order to sustain her own illusion of being, she concedes that the distortions of the artist, however frustrating on a superficial level, are in the deepest sense necessary. By naming him "an artist," she establishes him as such, thereby reshaping and remoulding his character from quackdoctor to master artist—she engages in the very process for which she had earlier denounced him. Implicit in this is Wittgenstein's idea that the limits of my language are the limits of my world, that a thing only begins to exist when it is named as such. Of course, we cannot be sure of all the facts in Grace's own testimony, for her sentences are fragmented and she is verging on nervous breakdown. She is quite wrong to say that in his artist's egotism Hardy saw all successful cures as fictions that worked—extensions of himself—and forgot the failures. He was, in fact, haunted by his failures with clients even more than he was haunted by his failures in life. He could breathe life into others, but not into his own child, and so he suppressed all memory of the dead child and deliberately re-cast his own auto-biography in more flattering terms. Thus, Grace's sufferings when her father fails to recognize his returned vagabond daughter are recast in the myth as Hardy's own pain at not being recognized by his father, because this makes him feel better, more sinned against than sinning. By reshaping past events into a less accusing pattern, Hardy can save himself for his art, that art which has been the cause of sufferings in others which he must pretend to have been his own. This is yet another version of history as science fiction, of past events being remodelled in terms of a utopian future. Hence, Teddy is probably right to assert that Hardy, in his weird private way, almost certainly felt and understood the plight of the grimy stillborn infant whose tragedy he had caused but refused to witness.

Teddy's soliloquy initially promises to clarify some of the discrepancies between earlier accounts, if only because he is an apparent outsider to the relationship, an objective professional manager. "Personally, in the privacy of your heart, you may love them or you may hate them," he says, "but that has nothing to do with it. Your client has his job to do. You have your job to do" [24]. Moreover, Francis Hardy has already hinted at unsuspected depths in Teddy, a man who was outwardly a romantic optimist but may secretly have been more realistic about their prospects. Sure enough, at the start of his talk, he does clarify one problem, as to who exactly chose the theme music. Grace chose a song which was a hit when she married Francis, but the couple soon forgot that and blamed Teddy's twisted mind for the selection. Thus they too create those necessary fictions which allow them to survive with a modicum of self-respect.

On a more serious level, it emerges from Teddy's account that Grace has also been lying to herself about the stillborn child, pretending that it was Francis who said the prayers and raised the cross, when in fact it was Teddy who did those things. Teddy remembers the village in question as sparkling and sunny; Grace recalls it as rainy and dull. Teddy is sure that the cross is long since gone; Grace that it must still be there. In the end, it is not even safe to assume that Teddy can be trusted as an objective professional witness, for it transpires that he has been secretly in love with Grace all along. This was something which Hardy, with his second sight, *knew;* and the healer may even have sought his own death so that Grace would be free to join herself to a man of compassion who could return her love.

Although a mere manager, Teddy shows a subtle awareness of the power of illusion, of the capacity of words and names to confer a sense of reality, and of the way in which this gift seemed to pass from Hardy to his clients in those successful moments of healing. So, in the Welsh village where all ten supplicants were cured, an old farmer could say: "Mr. Hardy, as long as men live in Glamorganshire, you'll be remembered here." "And whatever way he said Glamorganshire," recalls Teddy, "it sounded like the whole world."[25] Teddy knows, however, that that power to maintain a successful illusion is jeopardised by Hardy's self-analytical brain, his self-questioning, his mockery of himself as a mere "performer." Soon, Teddy sees, he will come to believe even more in his own mockery than in his own performance. He could have been a great artist but he had too many brains, analytical brains which allowed him to see that everybody else is a con-man and an illusionist too. Hardy's anger at the allegations made by Grace's father does not last, for "I had some envy of the man who could use the word 'chicanery' with such confidence."[26] Even the recognition that professional lawyers are also illusionists, employing the paraphernalia of gowns, wigs and a secret jargon, does not save the healer from himself. Hardy, the greatest liar in the play, is also the only honest man.

The healer keeps the inaccurate newspaper report of his feats not so much for reassurance as for self-identification: "it identified me, even though it got my name wrong."[27] The namer of things needs someone to name him; and the distorter of names and histories yearns for someone to distort his own. Like Grace, like Beckett's clowns, he too needs someone to give him the illusion that he exists. It is brutally appropriate that, in a drama which has made such play with true and false names, Hardy in the end should not even know the names of two of the men who come to kill him, thereby continuing the assault on his identity begun in the botched newspaper report. As the men advance menacingly on him, he begins to feel that they also are fictions, illusions without physical reality, and that each man present exists only in his need for others. He senses that they need the fiction of his death in order to satisfy their rage against a life which has so cruelly maimed their friend.

*Faith Healer* is an eloquent apology for the distortions of memory, for it argues that every man must be an artist and illusionist, that every man must recast his memories into a pattern that is gratifying enough to allow him to live with himself. As a consummate artist, Friel implicates himself in this process, for *that* is precisely what he has done in his play to the Deirdre legend—remoulded it subtly in accordance with his current artistic needs. There is a theory propounded by Harold Bloom in *The Anxiety of Influence* which suggests that every major artist is a kind of Francis Hardy. Bloom's strong artist creatively misreads a work of past art in order to clear a little imaginative space for himself.[28] Like Hardy, such an artist cannot afford to be a critic seeking the absolute truth, but must follow the accidents of impulse, creatively distorting an available myth in order to express something of himself—otherwise, he will be smothered by the influences of the past. The artist thus has a vested interest in misunderstanding and distorting a received text, for if he ever fully understands his model, then he will be overwhelmed by it and become a derivative writer, much as Arnold in *The Scholar-Gipsy* failed to do more than rewrite some of the better-known lines of Keats. The strong artist imperfectly assimilates past models and is therefore not overwhelmed, but saved, by his mistake. Like Blake, he goes wrong in order to go right. So Joyce in *Ulysses* can rewrite *The Odyssey*, but in the process remould it to his modern purposes, inflating the Telemachus father/son theme, while ignoring many other crucial elements, in a model of the original which is (in Bloom's immortal Dublin phrase) "the same, only different." As Joyce was later to show in *Finnegans Wake*, the same can somehow manage to be the new. Not for him the gloomy elegance of Beckett who opened a novel with the line: "The sun shone, having no alternative, upon the nothing new."[29] For Joyce, everything changes even as it remains itself and the differences give the repetitions point and meaning. Many of the deviations from *The Odyssey* are tragicomic in implication, as Hugh Kenner has pointed out—tragic when Stephen refuses to pray for his dying mother, unlike Telemachus who was tactful and considerate; comic when it dawns on the reader that Mrs. Bloom is something less than a faithful Penelope.[30] But most of the differences are finally crucial in allowing Joyce to redefine the nature of heroism for the modern world. There is a heroic honesty in Stephen's refusal to pray to a God in whom he does not believe, and a heroic wisdom in Bloom's refusal to take revenge on Boylan, unlike Odysseus who slaughtered those who tested the purity of his wife.

So it is in *Faith Healer* where Friel's heroic myth is creatively misinterpreted so that he can redefine heroism for the modern Gaelic world. In the ancient legend, Deirdre's name meant "troubler" or "alarmer" and she was remembered for the prophecy at her birth that many would die because of her beauty. Grace, the modern Deirdre, is heroic not so much for the suffering which she inflicts (though she has some of the cruelty of the ancient heroine) but rather for the pain which she must endure. Similarly, Teddy is not allowed the easy "heroic" option of instant death for the man and woman he worships, but is more realistically left behind at the end to pick up the pieces that remain, in a life of quiet desperation rather than heroic enterprise. The ultimate realism is to deny Deirdre the fake glamour of a romantic death such as she had in medieval versions, and instead to give her a lonely death in a bedsitter as a nervous wreck. In this respect, Friel returns to the oldest versions of the tale, which had Deirdre dash out her brain on a rock, the hopeless act of a woman crazed with grief, a year and a day after the execution of her lover. Perhaps most significant of all is Friel's decision to give Hardy the central role, just as Naoise was the pivotal figure in the oldest version from *The Book of Leinster*.

Underlying Joyce's depiction of Bloom as a modern Ulysses, Friel's of Hardy as a modern Naoise, is the conviction that primitive myths are *not* impositions of a culture but innate possessions of every single man, who professes to be a unique being but is in fact a copy, consciously or unconsciously emulating the lives of more original predecessors. Hence, the characteristic modern *malaise* of inauthenticity, which assails men sophisticated enough to sense the frustrations of a life lived in quotation marks. Hence, also, the supreme importance to Leopold Bloom and to us of those small differences with which history repeats itself, for they are our sole guarantee of individuality. And what applies to people is true also of authors. Friel retells an old story, borrowing characters, situations, even phrases from the tale—and to that extent, like Francis Hardy, he is a con-man. But, like Hardy's pretence that his wife was barren and could not bear a child, he also remoulds his tale and his people to some private standard of excellence of his own—and, to that extent, he is indeed an artist. It adds to the poignancy of Hardy's life that he is quite unaware that he has re-enacted the story of Deirdre and the Sons of Usna, just as it adds to the poignancy of Leopold Bloom's plight that he is never for a moment aware that in his wanderings through Dublin he reenacts the voyage of Odysseus. But that very unpretentiousness and unselfconsciousness adds not only to the poignancy but also to the final likeness. This may be Friel's and Joyce's underlying point—that heroism is more often unselfconscious of itself than not.

# NOTES

1. Brian Friel, *Faith Healer*. London: Faber (1980), p.16.

2. J. M. Synge, *Collected Plays 2*, ed. A. Saddlemyer. Oxford: Oxford University Press (1968), p.249.

3. *Ibid.*, p.247.

4. J. M. Synge, *Collected Works: Prose*, ed. Alan Price. Oxford: Oxford University Press (1966), p.216.

5. *Faith Healer*, p.11.

6. Seamus Heaney, *Wintering Out*. London: Faber (1972), p.48.

7. *Faith Healer*, p.27.

8. *Ibid.*, p.29.

9. *Ibid.*, p.11.

10. *Ibid.*, p.12.

11. Seamus Heaney, "Digging and Divining," talk on B.B.C. Radio 3, 1975.

12. Anthony Bailey, "A Gift for Being in Touch; Seamus Heaney Builds Houses of Truth," *Quest*, January/February 1978.

13. Seamus Heaney, "Digging and Divining"; see also "Feeling into Words," *Preoccupations: Selected Prose 1968-78*. London: Faber (1980), p.41-60.

14. *Faith Healer*, p.13.

15. Lawrence Graver and Raymond Federman, *Samuel Beckett: The Critical Heritage*. London: Routledge and Kegan Paul (1979), p.173.

16. *Faith Healer*, p.15.

17. *Ibid.*, p.15.

18. *Ibid.*, p.44.

19. *Ibid.*, p.22.

20. *Ibid.*, p.32.

21. *Ibid.*, p.20.

22. Brian Friel, *Philadelphia Here I Come*. London: Faber (1965), p.96.

23. *Faith Healer*, p.14.

24. *Ibid.*, p.30.

25. *Ibid.*, p.32.

26. *Ibid.*, p.41.

27. *Ibid.*, p.40.

28. Harold Bloom, *The Anxiety of Influence*. Oxford: Oxford University Press (1975).

29. Samuel Beckett, *Murphy*. London: Picador (1973), p.5.

30. Hugh Kenner, *Dublin's Joyce*. London: Faber (1956), p.212.

# NEGOTIATING HISTORY, NEGOTIATING MYTH: FRIEL AMONG HIS CONTEMPORARIES

## Claire Gleitman

In recent years, a crop of playwrights has emerged in Ireland whose work is so fresh, so politically incisive and so theatrically rich as to prompt more than a few commentators to speak of a second Irish renaissance in dramatic literature.[1] Among these Irish playwrights, clearly it is Brian Friel who has achieved the widest international acclaim. Yet Friel is hardly a solitary star in an otherwise vacant sky. Rather, he writes amidst a constellation of innovative dramatists whose output owes something to the luminaries of the first Irish renaissance, but even more, perhaps, to a tradition of postmodernism marked with a distinctly Irish personality. Postmodern literature, according to Linda Hutcheon, "is a critical revisiting, an ironic dialogue with the past."[2] This is an apt description of not only the theatrical mood in Ireland, but of a theoretical and cultural climate in which it is widely felt that everything Irish, "including our politics and our literature, has to be rewritten—i.e., re-read."[3] Friel and his contemporaries are deeply invested in rereading and reassessing Ireland's history; hence, they escape the charges of regressive solipsism that have been levelled at other examples of postmodern art and criticism.[4] Indeed, Ireland's recent drama assiduously engages political and economic realities even as it participates in the more general postmodern reflection on representation.

The present article shall consider Brian Friel alongside two of his most prominent playwriting compatriots: Tom Murphy, whose career, like Friel's, is long and varied; and Frank McGuinness, a younger but increasingly visible and prolific dramatist. All three authors' involvement in the rereading project is manifested by their shared manipulation of (even reinvention of) the genre of the history play. Together, these authors have concentrated their attention upon charged events in Irish history and crafted from them a skeptical, ambivalent and affecting drama that dissects the mythologies that the culture holds most dear: mythologies that accrue around cataclysmic national events and around the very notion of Irishness itself. Their plays simultaneously restage history and question its reliability, thus acknowledging the contingency of any act of historiography.

For instance, in three important history plays—Friel's *The Freedom of the City* (1973); Murphy's *Famine* (1968); and McGuinness's *Observe the Sons of Ulster Marching Towards the Somme* (1985)—the dramatists revisit events that have taken on great emotional and political weight in sectarian mythologies, both Nationalist and Unionist. The subject of *Freedom of the City* is Bloody Sunday, 1972, when British paratroopers shot and killed thirteen unarmed citizens of Derry during a banned civil rights march. Friel's fictionalized enactment of Bloody Sunday concerns three civil rights marchers who stumble into Derry's Guildhall while striving to escape the British army's CS gas. In *Freedom*, as in the later play *Making History* (1988), Friel interrogates the process by which ideology transforms "brute fact" into myth. *Freedom* juxtaposes the actual events of the day as experienced by the marchers with the extravagant distortions of those events conjured by various "witnesses." Thus we see history being altered by its interpreters even at its inception, as the marchers metamorphose for their Irish admirers into messianic heroes of the stature of Patrick Pearse, and for their British revilers into a gang of fifty armed gunmen with sedition on their minds. Meanwhile, the actual story of three anonymous and bewildered citizens randomly caught in the crossfire (and eventually assassinated) is erased by the day's chroniclers, who are thoroughly engrossed by their own, spectacular revisions.

It is worth noting that *Freedom of the City*, which ostensibly is a history play, dispenses with historical fact almost entirely. In the drama, Friel shifts his dramatic moment from 1972 to 1970, and creates a scenario that—though based upon actual events and particularly upon the Widgery Tribunal—is in essence fiction. [5] Friel's casual rearrangement of historical phenomena, a characteristic of *Translations* also, suggests the impossibility of accessing "actual" history except as it is filtered through subjective and often self-serving interpreters. The real occurrences are of little importance to those interpreters: what matters is the way in which the actual can be manipulated for the sake of the mythic. In this regard Friel seems to intimate what Glover and Kaplan assert in another context:

> Though searching for an objective truth about this past against which to measure present deformations is no longer a viable political or theoretical project, thinking politically and historically about the many versions of it now in circulation certainly is. [6]

Tom Murphy's *Famine*, in its way, is also concerned to demystify the mystificatory impulses behind the making of history. But Murphy enacts the demystification through his analysis of a man who is himself a victim of an outmoded mythology. The central character in *Famine*—John Connor, an impoverished descendent of a long line of kings and chieftains—is as economically and politically marginalized as Friel's marchers, but he fails to realize it. Instead, Connor remains wedded to those concepts of noblesse oblige and ancient tribalism that were foundational for his ancestors. Such concepts drive him to play the patriarch in his village although he is as far removed from the ancient tribe of Connors as Jack Durbeyfield is from the knightly d'Urbervilles. Connor attempts to apply tribal ideals and an archaic, abstract value system to a situation that is implacably material: that is, the devastating potato blight of the 1840s. In the first scene of the play, John insists that the guests attending his daughter's wake must be fed generously: "We can't send them off mean . . . She *was* regal . . . And—we—won't—send—them—off mean."[7] The fact that John's daughter died of starvation and that his other children are starving as well is not sufficient to deter him from acting the part of the chieftain, whose honor depends upon his gracious gentility.

Thus, on the shaky foundation of abstractions that sum up the tribe's ethos, John formulates "a resolution" to guide the village's actions during the crisis: they must wait, he insists, and do what is "right." Out of touch with the realities of his historical moment, John believes that salvation is possible through a collective commitment to home, hearth and the all-knowing divine will. Conflating tribal laws with Christian ones, he insists that the village must endure with stoicism, denouncing all suggestions of active resistance: "Help will come, because it's right. And what's right has to be believed in if we're to hope" (40-41). But John's passivity results not in salvation but in his family's collapse: in the end, he is driven to the murder of his wife and a young son.

Murphy offers no assurance that a more active approach would have saved Connor. On the contrary, it is clear that the other options available to him also entailed risks and compromises. Nor does the play underestimate the repugnant amorality of the powers-that-be, who sit smugly pondering Irish dirtiness as crowds clamor for food outside their office doors. The image of fully laden corn carts laboring under police protection past the emaciated frames of Irish peasants; the abysmally cold and calculated "business" sense that proposes either starvation or the "option" of emigration; the obtuseness of the House of Commons arguing in its London luxury while tens of thousands starve—all of this, so vividly portrayed within *Famine*'s expansive epic frame, conjures a picture of arrogance and indifference all the more horrifying given its basis in historical fact.

And yet there is something deeply vexing about the play's immobile "hero," whose ethical touchstones seem so woefully inadequate to the occasion. In fact, Murphy's history play interrogates one of modern Ireland's defining moments only to find failures all around. The British are what one expects, and the mythic Irish tribe proves unequipped to deal with the situation that confronts it. One conclusion invited by *Famine* is that disembodied notions of morality, no matter how heroic, are powerless to counteract the forces of economics and politics. But another, more troubling message is that Irish tribal culture may have abetted its own demise by virtue of its devotion to antiquated and, in the event, fatal concepts of tribal ideals. An abandonment of those ideals, for John, would necessitate a recognition of his family's devastating social and economic decline. Hence, he clings to them with ever more fervent desperation: "*All* that land was Connors' once! And I'll not go . . . I was born here, and I'll die here, and I'll rot here! . . . Cause I'm right" (81). In the end, John's unwavering view of "right" collapses beneath the weight of modern nation-state colonial politics.

Such a torturous passage is again staged in McGuinness's *Observe the Sons of Ulster Marching Towards the Somme*. Here, the audience witnesses the experiences of eight Protestant Irish soldiers, seven of whose lives ended at the Battle of the Somme. As is well known, many of the Irish Protestants in the 36th Ulster division chose to serve in the first World War in order to display their unwavering loyalty to the Crown at a time when threats of Home Rule loomed. When thousands of those enlisted men died at the Somme, they were extolled at home as martyrs to a sacred cause. As the *Belfast News-Letter* put it, "Ulster Protestants took their stand where their fathers stood . . .[in] costly self-sacrifice to our Empire."[8] Adding further sheen to the mythology, the Battle of the Somme began on July 1st, which is thought to be the anniversary of the Battle of the Boyne.[9] That battle, fought in 1690, ended in victory for the Protestant King William over the Catholic James; hence, it was viewed as a death-knell for Catholic Ireland and a great Protestant triumph. When the Battle of the Somme happened to fall on the same date, this seemed to add mystical confirmation to the Protestant wish to see the British war as a fight for home and country.

*Observe the Sons of Ulster* is cast in the form of a memory play in which one survivor, named Pyper, recalls events that preceded the battle. His memories revolve around the experiences of seven other soldiers, all working-class tradesmen, with whom he lived and fought. Although Pyper is an aristocrat, his homosexuality severed him from his family and class, and he feels an increasingly profound alliance with his disenfranchised fellow fighters. All eight of the soldiers enlisted in the British Army, they assure each other, for Ulster and "For the glory of his majesty the king and all his people." [10] But the men's declared mission of keeping Ireland safe from "Fenian rats" turns out to be a slogan veiling a far more complex array of motives (26). These marginalized characters shield themselves from despair by means of vehement sectarian pride. The consequence is a huge contribution to Unionist mythology, which McGuinness shows in the making.

As the play begins, the Elder Pyper complains about recurrent visitations from ghosts of that July day in 1916. Yet his mutterings reveal that he has become a kind of Ian Paisley figure extolling the nearly theological mission of Irish Protestantism:

> There would be, and there will be no surrender. The sons of Ulster
> will rise and lay their enemy low, as they did at the Boyne, as they
> did at the Somme, against any invader who will trespass on to their
> homeland. Fenians claim Cuchullian as their ancestor, but he is ours
> . . . Sinn Fein? . . . It is we, the Protestant people, who have always
> stood alone . . . and triumphed, for we are God's chosen. (10)

The hyperbole of the speech and its Unionist appropriation of Cuchullian, a central figure in Republican myth, display the nature of the mythic version of history which plagues Irish culture. Its dramatic irony is revealed through the remembered and reenacted scenes of July 1916. On the morning of the battle, the men turn to parody, performance and finally ritual in an effort to steel themselves for what awaits them. Their games are self-protective: they seek to avoid a recognition of their irrelevance in the theatre of war by showering contempt upon another group of marginalized people. First, a character named McIlwaine offers a burlesque version of the Easter Rising, which also took place in 1916. In McIlwaine's telling, the revolutionary figure of Patrick Pearse becomes a pathetic clown who "took over a post office because he was short of a few stamps"; he ends up being shot by his mother, who declares: "'That'll learn him, the cheeky pup. Going about robbing post offices" (64-65).

Thus the Easter Rising, which would find a central place in the opposing side's catalogue of mythic victories, is rewritten by the Unionist to rob it of valor.

Later, the men decide to "play" the Battle of the Boyne—or, more accurately, to play the Battle of Scarva, which is the annual reenactment of the Battle of the Boyne held on its anniversary. By restaging not the actual battle but its annual commemoration, McGuinness (like Friel) suggests that actual history can be accessed only through representation—and in this case representation has been co-opted by the ideological imperatives of Unionism. As the "director" of the piece remarks, "remember, . . . we know the result, you know the result, keep to the result" (70). While the battle is being performed, the director provides appropriate commentary, stressing the virtues of Protestant William versus the vices of the demonized Catholic James. His "script" loads the representation with the necessary ideological freight; thus he cloaks historical events under the propaganda of Unionist, Protestant myth.

But Pyper—who has acted as anarchic truth-teller throughout the memory-play—surprises the others by straying from the script. Though his role is to play the trusty steed for the victor, Pyper trips. His rider, King William, comes crashing to the ground, and James and his horse find themselves the startled victors. As one of the men declares woefully, this is "Not the best of signs" (71). Pyper's action is troubling because it destabilizes the ideologically cathected myth which had provided the thinnest veneer over the terrifying actuality they are facing. This deconstruction of the mythology might be considered a salutary act, except that it removes comforting delusions from men who are about to die. Pyper himself seems to regret depriving the men of their myths just when they most needed them, and he shows his contrition by quickly attempting to re-patch the mythology. After a ritualistic exchange of Orange sashes to confirm their confederacy, Pyper delivers an impassioned sermon in which he assures them that their fight has meaning; it is dedicated to Ulster: "Observe the sons of Ulster marching towards the Somme. I love my home. I love my Ulster" (80).

At the last moment, Pyper retreats from the abyss and clings to the mythology. Yet the play does not criticize him for doing so. Rather, McGuinnness suggests this paradoxical truth about mythologizing: it is arbitrary and artificial, yet it sustains as it deludes. The play provides no way out of the paradox; instead, it enacts the paradoxical formations and deformations of history-in-the-making. The process by which Pyper, the gadfly skeptic of 1916, becomes the righteous scourge of Unionism is a dramatic articulation of mytho-historiography: he participates in uncovering the hollow center of myth at the same moment that he helps to write another chapter of it.

McGuinness's play, then, reveals an insight into the ways that history is written: he recognizes that both sides of any historical impasse mythologize events, thereby distorting them into the shapes that their ideological imperatives require. In addition, his concentration on Unionist foot solders reflects his interest in history's silences, an interest that Friel and Murphy share. In all three plays that I have examined thus far, the dramatized episode is filtered through the perspective of figures typically relegated to the margins in historical narratives: that is, the weak, the powerless, the food for powder. In *Freedom*, in *Famine*, and in *Observe*, we see the event from a margin's-eye-view.

And Friel, Murphy and McGuinness manipulate other theatrical gestures in common within those margins. For instance, in the literal margin of no-man's-land, the forward trenches, McGuinness's soldiers await the order that will send them to their deaths, and endure the lull before zero-hour by enacting self-reflexive, performative gestures in an effort to persuade themselves that those deaths will have meaning. As I have discussed, the soldiers narrate burlesque versions of the Easter Rising; they "play" the Battle of Scarva; they cooperate in staging solemn and highly charged rituals.

This habit of performance is another tactic that the three playwrights share, and one to which I shall now turn. In a striking number of Ireland's recent dramas, performance serves as a strategy for coping with the experience of marginalization and loss.

To grasp the nature of the dispossession that prompts performance, it is necessary to consider the social and political backdrop against which these authors write. Friel and Murphy were born within six years of each other during the decade following Ireland's independence. Both grew up in a climate of deep economic malaise, when an Irish citizen's attachment to his or her homeland had to do battle with the knowledge that a decent life could not be had there by a large portion of its residents. McGuinness, born some two decades later, entered his young manhood during the painful resurrection of the "Troubles." These circumstances left their mark on the playwrights, whose works tend to be rooted in the economic and spiritual realities of mid- and late-twentieth century Ireland. [11] There are some generational differences to be noted, to be sure, and I shall have more to say about that later. Yet all three writers show a continuous interest in characters whose lives are circumscribed by material distress and social strife, and who respond by resorting to performance, ritual, story-telling or play.

In Friel's *Philadelphia, Here I Come!* (1964), for instance, the central character splits himself in two and performs endless duets with his alter ego. In the play's first episode alone Gar sings; he pantomimes conducting and then playing Mendelssohn's Violin Concerto; he dances; and he performs various scenes from his life with his alter ego as narrator, spectator, director, and co-star. In this manner, Gar seeks to distance himself from the miserable realities of his daily life and probable future, reconstructing them through energetic, nearly desperate play. Yet Gar is no Christy Mahon: imagination does not succeed in catapulting him toward mythic stature, nor does it allow him, as it allows Christy, to "talk [himself] into freedom."[12] Rather, Gar ends the play plagued by agonizing indecision, as the barrenness of *both* his options—that is, leaving Ireland or trying to make a life there—forces itself resoundingly to his attention.

Similarly, John Joe in Murphy's *A Crucial Week in the Life of a Grocer's Assistant* (1964) struggles to negotiate the conflicting promises of emigration and remaining at home. Incapable of acting decisively, he retreats into expressionistic fantasies or dream-plays that carry him away, briefly, from a sterile emotional and economic climate that seems intractable. Both Gar and John Joe mystify departure, imagining it in exotic terms akin to the escape fantasies so common in *Dubliners*. But, like Joyce, these playwrights are unflinching in their deflation of such fantasies: their characters are trapped not merely by economic distress but by an emotional poverty born out of the ravages of famine and colonization. Thus John Joe's mother clings to her son, assaults him with guilt, and ahistorically sings the praises of tribal loyalty, land and Mother Ireland: "We will stick to our own and the soot, as we did through the centuries."[13]

As these plays persistently indicate, it is this kind of self-defeating mythology that plagues the Irish consciousness. In a work evocatively titled *Carthaginians* (1988), McGuinness revisits Bloody Sunday to depict its aftermath in the lives of seven grieved survivors. While Friel concentrated upon a fictionalized version of the event itself, McGuinness suggestively sets his drama in 1988, sixteen years later. The choice is indicative of an attitude of impatience that abounds in McGuiness's drama, a sense that it is rather late in the day for rehearsing the same old pieties and grievances. In contrast to the focused analyses of Friel and Murphy, McGuinness's tendency is to examine Ireland against the backdrop of an international canvas that works not to diminish the island's problems but to contextualize them within the framework of broader geopolitical realities. Thus, *Observe the Sons* places Protestant Ulster in the shadow of the first World War; *Someone Who'll Watch over Me* (1992) takes Ireland and Britain's squabbles and chains them to a wall in Beirut; and *Carthaginians'* title serves to inflect Bloody Sunday through the broader paradigm of imperialist confrontation and extermination.

Moreover, for McGuinness, performance often serves the purpose of exuberant debunking. *Carthaginians* is set in a graveyard, where the seven characters have withdrawn from the world and live in hope of the rising of the dead. Their hard-won success in putting Bloody Sunday behind them is accomplished at last with the aid of a play-within-the-play which they collaborate in staging. The play, entitled "The Burning Balaclava," is written by *Carthaginians'* central character and chief anarchist, a homosexual known as Dido, Queen of Derry. Dido's play appropriates the discourses of popular sentiment, popular culture, and canonized literature in a joyful send-up of a host of Irish sacred cows, ranging from the Troubles to *Juno and the Paycock*. Dido's success as play-maker and healer seems to stem from his transgressive posture, from his ability to slip the confines of either/or oppositions that so structure and debilitate Northern Irish lives. His play cheerfully deflates the cherished mythologies of sectarianism and literary sentiment, and as a consequence it seems to clear the air of the cant and morbid obsession that an event like Bloody Sunday can accrue. After participating in the play, which is followed by a ritualistic recital of the names of the Bloody Sunday dead, the graveyard dwellers at last are able to sleep. Yet the playwright who scripted the burlesque concludes *Carthaginians* by announcing his intention to leave the troubled city, in a phrase that encapsulates not only Dido's own tortured ambivalence but also (mutatis mutandis) Gar's and John Joe's: "I believe it is time to leave Derry. Love it and leave it."[14] The actual, unpromising circumstances of life in Ireland assert themselves even on the heels of a triumphant act of play.

In this regard, the self-reflexive tendency in contemporary Irish drama is another reflection of the postmodernist spirit. Modernist self-reflexivity often assumes an ahistorical pose vis-à-vis its own production, focusing attention upon the work in an endless regress to an aestheticized consciousness. Postmodern self-reflexivity, however, installs historical horizons in the work's enunciatory moment.[15] Such gestures are part and parcel of the more general postmodern restaging of history. Characteristic of this restaging, as I have suggested, is a demystification of dominant mythologies—those associated both with particular historical events and with the notion of an essential Irish character as Yeats, for one, imagined it. It is with this latter brand of mythologizing that I shall conclude.

At first glance, two of Friel's most popular plays— *Translations* (1980) and *Dancing at Lughnasa* (1990)—seem prominently to feature the figure of the lovably drunken and eccentric Stage-Irishman (or woman).[16] In *Translations*, Hugh and Jimmy Jack Cassie bluster and strut and grow progressively drunker; and *Dancing at Lughnasa* contains an ensemble of comely maidens, each endowed with her own winning idiosyncrasies. Yet a corrosive undercurrent in both plays destabilizes the sentimentality, suggesting a rottenness at the heart of these apparent idylls of peasant harmony and good will. In *Translations*, as many readers have noted, Friel circumvents nostalgia by blending fondness with a trenchant critique. Rather than writing "a threnody on the death of the Irish language," which Friel early on maintained that he wished to avoid,[17] he provides in *Translations* a gradually emerging critique of what Leonard Pilkington calls the "quixoticism" in Gaelic culture "that contributes to economic decline."[18] The playwright implicitly attributes the act of imperial dispossession that *Translations* chronicles to an attitude of mind on the part of the peasantry that made the country ripe for colonizing. In addition, *Translations* establishes its context with reference to three general sources of instability operating concurrently with colonization: the economic hardships that pressured the young to abandon their country in increasing numbers; the incipient resistance movement that threatened community stability from within as did the imperialist presence from without; and the imminent blight of the potato, the staple of the community's diet.

Thus, in the Chekhovian spirit, Friel suggests that the struggle between old and new worlds is won by the new not only because of its efficient brutality, but because the old is exhausted and effete, and indulges in fantastic self-deception rather than finding practical methods to adapt to a changing world. The central characters in the play are defeated in part (like John Connor) by their dedication to an antique way of life. They are also a collection of cripples, mutes and drunks; they exhibit, Friel has remarked, "a physical maiming which is a public representation of their spiritual deprivation."[19] In short, the interplay between regret and irony in *Translations*, between its lament for a lost culture and its critique of that culture's malaise, allows the play to transcend simple nationalist sentiment in order to dissect a complex national condition.

Similarly, *Dancing at Lughnasa* invokes the Yeatsian mythology of a spiritually robust Ireland even as it deconstructs it. The god Lugh hovers over the play, whispering from the back hills of a vanishing culture in tune with its most lusty impulses. At centerstage is a family of women who have nearly lost touch with that ancient spirit and who seem to find their way back to it only through the magic of their sporadically reliable Marconi radio. As their sensibility and means of survival are under threat from religious, ideological and technological forces, the Mundy sisters are seduced despite themselves by the primal passions that the festival of Lughnasa once celebrated. These passions come to the fore halfway through *Lughnasa*'s first act, when the sisters suddenly give themselves over to a wild, passionate and almost frantic dance. One sister, whose fingers are covered with flour, "pulls her hands down her cheeks and patterns her face" with what looks like warpaint; another tosses a priest's surplice over her head in a gesture of religious burlesque, like a participant at a black Mass. Together, they dance as if they are possessed by alien spirits; their behavior, Friel writes, is both "out of character and at the same time ominous of some deep and true emotion."[20]

This scene, so quickly famous, is strikingly effective in its evocation of the repressed impulses that lie beneath the sisters' calm exteriors. "[T]here is a sense," the stage directions tell us, "of order being consciously subverted" (22), and this is as true formally as it is thematically and emotionally. For a brief moment, the play modulates from Friel's characteristic naturalism into an expressionistic interlude that reveals, with breathtaking compression, the subterranean lives of the characters. And what we see is only a hint of what there is to see. For the bulk of the play the sisters remain enigmas, who bury passionate longings and ferocious regret beneath impassive and amiable facades.

The release that the women experience through dance is akin to what their Uncle Jack describes when he tells of the Ugandan native ceremonies that he witnessed during his twenty-five years as a missionary there. During such ceremonies, he recalls, the entire village would light fires, drink palm wine and dance, "believe it or not, for days on end! It is the most wonderful sight you have ever seen" (48). By juxtaposing Jack's memories with the dying embers of the Lughnasa celebrations, the play suggests a link between the vitalism of Uganda's still-thriving customs and a lost Gaelic paganism—both of which are placed in opposition to the rigid decorum of Catholicism and a sterile, industrialized modernity. Yet, once again, a counterpointing irony subverts the apparent romanticism. In his innocent wonder at Ugandan rituals, Uncle Jack barely acknowledges the fact that the celebrants amongst whom he lived were the diseased inhabitants of a leper colony. Hence, his assumptions regarding their untarnished joy are questionable at best. Further, all of the action of the play excepting the narrator's monologues is the stuff of memory: everything that the audience witnesses has passed through a veil of years, of sentiment, of transfiguring wish. In his final monologue, the narrator confesses that the moment of the past which haunts him most evocatively is one that "owes nothing to fact": "In that memory atmosphere is more real than incident and everything is simultaneously actual and illusory" (71). The years that he recalls are tinged with disappointment, failure, and oppressive material demands. The Mundy sisters and their Uncle Jack find refuge from those demands through brief, ritualized forays into an age that they recreate and romanticize as surely as Michael romanticizes his childhood, wrapping it, as he says, in "a very soft, golden light" (70).

Like *Translations* and *Lughnasa*, Tom Murphy's play *Bailegangaire* (1985) considers the interplay between the past of Irish legend—the past of the rural Irish mythologized culture—and the present of economic and cultural deprivation. Though the drama is set in a "traditional three-roomed thatched house," this relic from the past is pierced by outside forces that are in marked contrast to the style of the cottage, and to the world that old Mommo summons in the story she tells her incessantly to her disaffected granddaughters.[21] A radio that broadcasts the news, the "putt-putt" of one granddaughter's motorcycle, the "rubber-backed lino" in the same woman's house, the computer plant bought out by the Japanese—all of these elements in the drama work to counterpoint Mommo's story of the past with the impoverished post-industrialism of the present. Meanwhile, there is little doubt that the past was any less limited than is the present. In *Bailegangaire*, the bucolic rural paradise of Irish legend is a fiction that has spawned an obsessive and crippling preoccupation with the past. Meanwhile, the present doles out destitution to a population that does not know how to make its way into the future except by limping along with the broken-down crutch of a partial mythology.

The centerpiece of *Bailegangaire* and the focal point of the interplay between past and present is Mommo's tale of a laughing contest, one that took place years ago in a town called Bochtán and renamed Bailegangaire, or "the town without laughter." Mommo's manner of telling her story is gleefully mock-epic: she makes use of stock epithets ("bold Costello"), grand foreshadowing gestures ("For there was to be many's the inquisition by c'roner, civic guard and civilian on all that transpired in John Mah'ny's that night" [55]), and boasting challenges ("'I'm a better laugher than your Costello'" (59). Mommo's tale summons the ancient Celtic and Norse traditions of flyting, of poetic contests, of Bardic rituals—while simultaneously and thunderously deflating them. This is, after all, no titanic battle between Conchubar and Cuchullian. It is a contest between peasants in a remote country pub to determine who is the finer laugher; and its combatants are a pair of peasants who are down on their luck. For all of its grand gestures, the laughing contest ends in a crescendo of pain, as the company speaks of the circumstances that engender frustrated lives: "the damnedable crop"; the rotted hay; and the children who refuse to stay alive:

> All of them present, their heads threwn back abandoned in festivities of guffaws: the wretched and neglected, dilapidated an' forlorn, the forgotten an' tormented, ragged an' dirty, impoverished, hungry, emaciated and unhealthy . . .—glintin' their defiance . . . an' rejection, inviting of what else might come or *care* to come!—driving bellows of refusal at the sky through the roof. Och hona ho gus hah-haa! . . . The nicest night ever. (75)

In vehement resistance to romantics who would have it otherwise, Murphy paints a portrait of a rural existence plagued by poverty, desperation and death, in which the only response available to the villagers is a defiant "bellow of refusal," a vehement challenge to an inscrutable God.

In fact, in its deflation of romantic mythologies and its depiction of a woman's paralysis within a fictionalized past, *Bailegangaire* can be read as a kind of political quasi-allegory. Mommo and her granddaughters are reflections of a people hobbled by a past that they cannot fully face, except through fragments of a mythologized narrative that sidesteps crucial elements. By the close of the play, the women at last succeed in bringing their story to its conclusion. Once they do so, they are brought to terms with the past in all of its hideous facticity. The result is that they are able to see the present clearly and to imagine a richer future—both for themselves, and for a baby yet to be born. The difficulty that Mommo and her granddaughters have in finishing their narrative of the past is emblematic of the problem of accessing Irish history in all of its troubled complexity. But the very fact that the story does, at last, get told, indicates Murphy's sense of the importance of the attempt. The Irish history play, as manipulated by all three of these playwrights, can be viewed as a process of stripping away, of uncovering the sedimented deformations of successive layers of history. The process does not jettison the past; it does not destroy it. But neither does it enshrine it.

In short, I have been arguing, the contemporary Irish drama is characterized by a vigorous and complex reanalysis of Ireland's history and character, an exercise, I have maintained, that animates many intellectual and artistic endeavors in Ireland today. Conceivably, this activity is prompted by the "sense of fatalistic exhaustion" that Eamonn Hughes has diagnosed in contemporary Ireland, an exhaustion generated by a fear that the country's geographic, religious and political divisions have become an intractable part of life.[22] Motivated perhaps by an urge to pierce beyond and through that sense of intractability, these playwrights restage history in such a way as to resist the kinds of totalizing narratives that inevitably seem to result in stalemate. Their work critiques the construction of nationalist mythologies and imperialist dogma at the same time as it stages the material pressures that render Ireland's situation so seemingly intransigent. Like other postmodernist fictions, these dramas "structurally both install and subvert the teleology, closure and causality of narrative, both historical and fictive."[23] That these playwrights engage the concerns of the post-modern while at the same time creating a drama of astonishing emotional texture and richness suggests something of the wonder of this theatrical moment in Ireland—a moment eminently deserving of the international respect and attention that it has begun to receive.

# NOTES

1. Michael Conveney, for instance, in a review for *The Financial Times*, referred to Frank McGuinness's *Observe the Sons of Ulster Marching Towards the Somme* as "one of the finest in the extraordinary playwriting renascence in Ireland" (28 July 1986).

2. Linda Hutcheon, *A Poetics of Postmodernism: History, Theory, Fiction* (New York: Routledge, 1988) 4. Further references are noted in the text.

3. Seamus Deane, "Heroic styles: the tradition of an idea," *Ireland's Field Day* (London: Hutchinson, 1985) 58.

4. See Steven Connor, "Postmodernism and Cultural Politics," *Postmodernist Culture: An Introduction to Theories of the Contemporary* (Oxford: Basil Blackwell, 1950) 224-248.

5. See Richard Pine, *Brian Friel and Ireland's Drama* (London: Routledge, 1990), 110ff., for a useful discussion of the Widgery Report and Friel's dramatic response to it.

6. David Glover and Cora Kaplan, "Guns in the House of Culture?: Crime Fiction and the Politics of the Popular," *Cultural Studies*, ed. Lawrence Grossberg, Cary Nelson and Paula A. Treichler (New York: Routledge, 1992) 216.

7. Tom Murphy, *Famine* (Dublin: Gallery Books, 1984) 19-20. Further references are noted in the text.

8. *Belfast News-Letter* (11 July 1916); quoted in Philip Orr, *The Road to the Somme: Men of the Ulster Division Tell Their Story* (Belfast: The Blackstaff Press, 1987) 197.

9. As Orr notes, "The battle [of the Boyne] was generally celebrated on 12 July but on the Julian Calendar, in use up to 1752, it had been on the first day of the month" (161).

10. Frank McGuinness, *Observe the Sons of Ulster Marching Towards the Somme* (London: Faber and Faber, 1986) 22. Further references are noted in the text.

11. Even many of the plays that are ostensibly about earlier centuries (such as *Making History, Translations, Famine*) or other geographical locales (such as *Someone Who'll Watch Over Me*), can be read as analyses of contemporary Irish politics and personalities. John Andrews, for instance, has argued that *Translations* is "a play about late twentieth-century Ireland" (Brian Friel, John Andrews and Kevin Barry, " *Translations* and *A Paper Landscape*: Between Fiction and History," *The Crane Bag* 7 no. 2 (1983) 120; and Fintan O'Toole remarks that *Famine* is "a play about the twentieth century, about the spiritual and emotional famine of Murphy's own times." See *The Politics of Magic: The Work and Times of Tom*

*Murphy* (Dublin: Raven Arts, 1987) 89.

12. Seamus Deane, *Celtic Revivals* (London: Faber and Faber, 1985) 58.

13. Tom Murphy, *A Whistle in the Dark and Other Plays* (London: Methuen, 1989) 104.

14. Frank McGuinness, *Carthaginians and Baglady* (London: Faber and Faber, 1988) 70.         •

15. See Hutcheon: "Modernism's 'nightmare of history' is precisely what postmodernism has chosen to face straight on" (88).

16. One might argue cynically that it is this, in part, that accounts for the plays' international success. It is worth noting that Friel's later play, *Wonderful Tennessee*, which contains no comely dancing maidens and no winning clowns, survived for less than a week on Broadway. American audiences, one might venture, have certain expectations for Irish playwrights, which *Wonderful Tennessee* failed to meet.

17. Brian Friel, "Extracts from a Sporadic Diary," Tim Pat Coogan, *Ireland and the Arts* (London: Quartet, n.d.) 58.

18. Leonard Pilkington, "Language and Politics in Brian Friel's *Translations*," *Irish University Review* 20 no. 2 (Autumn 1990) 291.

19. In Paddy Agnew, "Talking to ourselves: Brian Friel talks to Paddy Agnew," *Magill* (Dec. 180) 60.

20. Brian Friel, *Dancing at Lughnasa* (London: Faber and Faber, 1990) 22. Further references are noted in the text.

21. Tom Murphy, *After Tragedy: Three Plays by Tom Murphy* (London: Methuen, 1988) 43. Further references are noted in the text.

22. Eamonn Hughes, "'To Define Your Dissent': The Plays and Polemics of the Field Day Theatre Company," *Theatre Research International* 15 no. 1 (Spring 1990) 70.

23. Hutcheon, 63.

# SELECTED BIBLIOGRAPHY

## Primary Works

### I. PUBLISHED PLAYS

*American Welcome*, in *Best Short Plays* 1981, ed. Stanley Richards. Radnor, PA: Chilton Book Co., 1981: 112-14.

*Aristocrats*. Dublin: Gallery Press, 1980: London, Faber and Faber, 1983.

*The Communication Cord*. London: Faber and Faber, 1983.

*Crystal and Fox*. London: Faber and Faber, 1970. Also in *Two Plays*. New York: Farrar, Straus and Giroux, 1970.

*Dancing at Lughnasa*. London: Faber and Faber, 1990.

*The Enemy Within*. Newark, Delaware: Proscenium Press, 1975; Dublin: Gallery Press, 1979.

*Faith Healer*. London: Faber and Faber, 1980; New York: Samuel French, 1980.

*Fathers and Sons*. London: Faber and Faber, 1988.

*The Freedom of the City*. London: Faber and Faber, 1974; New York: Samuel French, 1974.

*The Gentle Island*. London: Davis-Poynter, 1973.

*Living Quarters*. London: Faber and Faber, 1978.

*The London Vertigo*. Dublin: Gallery Press, 1990.

*Lovers*. New York: Farrar, Straus and Giroux, 1968; London: Faber and Faber, 1969.

*The Loves of Cass McGuire*. London: Samuel French, 1966; London: Faber and Faber, 1967; New York: Farrar, Straus and Giroux, 1970.

*Making History*. London: Faber and Faber, 1988.

*Molly Sweeney*. Dublin: Gallery Books, 1994.

*A Month in the Country*. Dublin: Gallery Press, 1992.

*The Mundy Scheme*. London: Samuel French, 1970. Also in *Two Plays*. New York: Farrar, Straus and Giroux, 1970.

*Philadelphia, Here I Come!* London: Faber and Faber, 1965.

*Selected Plays*, ed. Seamus Deane. London: Faber and Faber, 1984; Washington, D.C.: Catholic University of America Press, 1986.

*The Three Sisters*. Dublin: Gallery Press, 1980.

*Translations*. Faber and Faber, 1981; New York: Samuel French, 1981.

*Volunteers*. London: Faber and Faber, 1979.

*Wonderful Tennessee*. Dublin: Gallery Press, 1993.


## II. OTHER DRAMATIC WORKS

*Aristocrats* (radio adaptation), BBC Radio 3, 1989.

*The Blind Mice* (radio adaptation), BBC Northern Ireland Home Service, 1963.

*The Blind Mice* (stage play), produced by Eblana Theatre, Dublin, 1963.

*A Doubtful Paradise* ( *The Francophile*) (radio adaptation), BBC Northern Ireland Home Service, 1962.

*The Enemy Within* (radio adaptation), BBC Third Programme, 1963.

*The Enemy Within* (television adaptation), BBC, 1965.

*Faith Healer* (radio adaptation), BBC Radio 3, 1980.

*Farewell to Ardstraw* (screenplay, with David Hammond), BBC Northern Ireland TV, 1976.

*The Founder Members*, (radio play), BBC Light Programme, 1964.

*The Francophile* (stage play), produced by Group Theatre, Belfast, 1960.

*The Loves of Cass McGuire* (radio play), BBC Third Programme, 1961.

*Making History* (radio adaptation), BBC Radio 3, 1989.

*The Next Parish* (screenplay), BBC Northern Ireland TV, 1976.

*Philadelphia, Here I Come!* (film adaptation), 1970.

*Philadelphia, Here I Come!* (radio adaptation), BBC Third Programme, 1965.

*A Sort of Freedom* (radio play), BBC Northern Ireland Home Service, 1958.

*Three Fathers, Three Sons* (screenplay), RTE TV, 1964.

*To This Hard House* (radio play), BBC Northern Ireland Home Service, 1958.

*Translations* (radio adaptation), BBC Radio 3, 1989.

*Winners* (radio adaptation), BBC Third Programme, 1968.

## III. FICTION

*The Diviner*. Dublin: The O'Brien Press; London: Allison and Busby, 1983.
*The Gold in the Sea*. New York: Doubleday; London: Victor Gollancz, 1966.
*The Saucer of Larks*. New York: Doubleday; London: Victor Gollancz, 1962.
*The Saucer of Larks: Stories of Ireland*. London: Arrow Books, 1969.
*Selected Stories*. Dublin: Gallery Press, 1979.

## IV. NON-FICTION

"A Challenge to *Acorn*," *Acorn* 14 (Autumn 1970): 4.
"Extracts from a Sporadic Diary," in Carpenter, A. and Fallon, P. (ed.), *The Writers: A Sense of Ireland*. Dublin: O'Brien Press; New York: George Braziller, 1980: 39-43; and in Coogan, T.P. (ed.), *Ireland and the Arts*. London: Quartet: 56-61.
"For Export Only," *Commonweal* (15 Feb. 1957): 509-10.
"The Future of Irish Drama: A Discussion between F. Linehan, H. Leonard, J.B. Keane and B. Friel," *The Irish Times* (12 Feb. 1970).
"Important Places," an introduction to Charles McGlinchey, *The Last of the Name*. Belfast: Blackstaff Press, 1986.
"Plays Peasant and Unpeasant," *The Times Literary Supplement* (17 March 1972): 305-6.
"Self-Portrait," *Aquarius* 3 (1972), 17-22.
"The Theatre of Hope and Despair," *Everyman* 1 (1968): 17-22.
"*Translations* and *A Paper Landscape*: Between Fiction and History." With John Andrews and Kevin Barry. *The Crane Bag* no. 7 (1983): 118-124
Untitled essay, in *Enter Certain Players: Edwards-MacLiammoir and The Gate 1928-1978*, ed. Peter Luke. Dublin: Dolmen Press, 1978: 21-22.

## V. INTERVIEWS

"Epiphany's Threshold" (with Matt Wolf), *American Theatre* 11.4 (April 1994): 12-18.
"The Man from God Knows Where: An Interview with Brian Friel (with Fintan O'Toole), *In Dublin* (28 Oct. 1982): 20-23.
"The Saturday Interview: Brian Friel" (with Elgy Gillespie), *The Irish Times* (5 Sept. 1981).
"An Ulster Writer: Brian Friel" (with Graham Morrison), *Acorn* 8 (spring, 1965): 4-15.

# Major Criticism

I. BOOKS

Andrews, Elmer. *The Art of Brian Friel: Neither Reality Nor Dreams*. London: Macmillan, 1995; New York: St. Martin's, 1995. A dialectical study that argues Friel moves between postmodernism and liberal humanism, ultimately aligning him with the latter. Andrews finds faith and hope in Friel's resistance to determinism. He also provides superb analysis of Friel's fiction and a bibliography that includes citations of reviews.

Dantanus, Ulf. *Brian Friel: The Growth of an Irish Dramatist*. Gothenburg Studies in English. Gothenburg: Acta Universitatis Gothoburgensis, 1985; Atlantic Heights, New Jersey: Humanities Press, 1986. Revised and updated as *Brian Friel: A Study*, London: Faber and Faber, 1988. Emphasizes two contexts of place: an Irish tradition of separating Dublin life from the rest of the country (an East-West split) and another tradition that focuses on Nationalist debates (a North-South split). The book richly covers the early works, and has a good bibliography.

Maxwell, D.E.S. *Brian Friel*. Lewisburg, Penn: Bucknell University Press, 1973. An early study of Friel's work (up to *The Freedom of the City*) which shows a sharp awareness of Friel's ability to record cultural anxieties.

O'Brien, George. *Brian Friel*. Twayne English Authors Series. Boston: Twayne Publishers, 1990. A highly readable introduction to Friel's life and works, incorporating biography and criticism in a play-by-play format, and including an annotated bibliography.

————. *Brian Friel: A Reference Guide 1962-1992*. New York: G.K. Hall and Co., 1995; London: Prentice Hall International, 1995. A thorough bibliographical guide, arranged chronologically. The book extensively covers writings about Friel's life, as well as both reviews and scholarly criticism of his work (excluded are Friel's journalism and his radio plays). O'Brien's understanding of both popular and academic responses to Friel comes across in his introduction, a survey of the playwright's reception over thirty years.

Peacock, Alan, ed. *The Achievement of Brian Friel*. Ulster Editions and Monographs: 4. Gerrards Cross: Colin Smythe, 1993. The first critical anthology on Friel, containing seventeen pieces by Irish and English authors.

Pine, Richard. *Brian Friel and Ireland's Drama*. London: Routledge, 1990. A challenging study that is in itself a poetic work. Pine's associative style and philosophical digressions do not serve a reader looking for a quick take on a given topic, but they prove worth the effort they demand. This far-reaching survey includes chapters on "Plays of Love," "Plays of Freedom," "Plays of Language," and "A Field Day."

## II. ARTICLES AND PARTS OF BOOKS

Coakley, James. "Chekhov in Ireland: Brief Notes on Friel's *Philadelphia.*" *Comparative Drama* 7, no. 3 (Fall 1973): 191-97. A discussion of Friel's use of the idea of departure, and an introduction to the oft-noted parallels between Friel and the great Russian playwright.

Deane, Seamus. "Brian Friel." In *Celtic Revivals*. London: Faber and Faber, 1986. A major critic's thoughts on Friel, emphasizing the playwright's rich meditations on art's public role.

————. "Introduction." *Selected Plays*, by Brian Friel. London: Faber and Faber, 1984: 11-22. This brief essay has become one of the most cited readings of Friel's plays, as it gracefully describes the playwright's growth from *Philadelphia, Here I Come!* to *Translations*.

Foster, John Wilson. *Forces and Themes in Ulster Fiction*. Dublin: Gill and Macmillan, 1973. A useful study of fiction, it provides a broad context for reading Friel's stories, which have too often been viewed as merely apprentice work.

Heaney, Seamus. "Digging Deeper." Review of *Volunteers*. *Times Literary Supplement*, 21 March, 1975: 306. Reprinted in *Preoccupations: Selected Prose 1968-1978*. London: Faber and Faber, 1980: 214-216. A rejoinder to widespread criticism of Friel's play.

Hickey, Des, and Gus Smith. *A Paler Shade of Green*. London: Leslie Frewin, 1972. U.S. edition, *Flight from Celtic Twilight*. Indianapolis: Bobbs, Merill,

1973. This volume of portraits includes a brief but eloquent biographical sketch.

Johnston, Denis. "Brian Friel and Modern Irish Drama." *Hibernia*, 7 March 1975. The elder playwright describes his younger colleague. Interesting in its generational mix.

Kiberd, Declan. "Friel Translating." In *Inventing Ireland*. London: Random House, 1995; Cambridge, Mass: Harvard University Press, 1996: 614-23. A late chapter in an ambitious literary history of Ireland. Kiberd reads *Translations* as a balancing of Friel's place in two traditions: he is the "Abbey revivalist and the Shavian socialist."

Kilroy, Thomas. "Friel's Plays." Introduction to *The Enemy Within*, by Brian Friel. Dublin: Gallery Press, 1979. A brief, elegant appraisal of Friel's work.

King, Kimball. *Ten Modern Irish Playwrights*. New York: Garland, 1979. Puts Friel in the context of other Irish playwrights after the Irish Renaissance, from Brendan Behan to Friel and his contemporaries.

Leary, Daniel. "The Romanticism of Brian Friel." In *Contemporary Irish Writing*. Ed. James D. Brophy and Raymond J. Park. Boston: Iona College Press, 1983: 127-41. Uses Friel's fiction—which Leary reads as primarily romantic—as a foil to the anti-romantic voices in the drama, especially *Faith Healer*. The combination of a continued "vision of home" and a distancing cynicism creates Friel's "bitter romanticism."

McGrath, F.C. "Language, Myth, and History in the Later Plays of Brian Friel." *Contemporary Literature* XXX. 4 (Winter 1989): 534-45. Discusses Friel's involvement in the Field Day project of demythologizing, and his increasing attention to the public nature of language.

Murray, Christopher. "Friel and After: Trends in Theater and Drama." In *New Irish Writing: Essays in Memory of Raymond J. Porter*. Ed. James D. Brophy and Eamon Grennan. Boston: Iona College Press, 1989: 13-34. A survey of Irish drama since 1960, focusing on how different playwrights have approached local cultural tensions.

Niel, Ruth. "Digging into History: A Reading of Brian Friel's *Volunteers* and Seamus Heaney's 'Viking Dublin: Trial Pieces.'" *Irish University Review* 16, no.1 (Spring 1986): 35-47. Explores how two major works use ideas of Viking remains.

Roche, Anthony. *Contemporary Irish Drama from Beckett to McGuinness*. Dublin: Gill and Macmillan, 1994. A chapter on Friel emphasizes his concern with exile and return. *Philadelphia, Here I Come!* and *Faith Healer* are central.

*Theatre Ireland*. A journal published by the Dublin Arts Council from 1984-1993. It is a wonderful source of local reviews and articles about Irish theatre and culture.

Throne, Marilyn. "The Disintegration of Authority: A Study of the Fathers in Five Plays of Brian Friel." *Colby Library Quarterly*, Vol. 24, no. 3 (September 1988): 162-72. Discusses *Living Quarters, Aristocrats, Philadelphia, Here I Come!, Faith Healer,* and *Translations*. Throne sees Friel's fathers as a "crippling" force, providing no aid across generational lines.

Winkler, Elizabeth Hale. "Brian Friel's *The Freedom of the City*: Historical Actuality and Dramatic Imagination." *Canadian Journal of Irish Studies*, Vol. 7, no. 1 (June 1981): 12-31. A source study that sheds light on Friel's history play.

# CONTRIBUTORS

**PATRICK BURKE** is a professor at St. Patrick's College, Dublin City University. He has published a variety of articles on Irish drama.

**KATHLEEN FERRIS** teaches at Lincoln Memorial University in Tennessee, and has recently published *James Joyce and the Burden of Disease*.

**CLAIRE GLEITMAN** teaches dramatic literature at Ithaca College. She has published articles on drama in *Comparative Drama* and *The Canadian Journal of Irish Studies*, and she is currently at work on a book-length study of the contemporary Irish drama.

**CLAUDIA W. HARRIS**, a professor at Brigham Young University, is currently completing a study of Charabanc Theatre Company. She has published several articles about contemporary Irish drama and culture.

**RICHARD KEARNEY**, a professor of philosophy at University College, Dublin, has written many books on philosophy and literature. He recently published his first novel, *Sam's Fall*.

**WILLIAM KERWIN** has recently completed a dissertation on Early Modern English drama and social medicine, and teaches at Florida International University.

**DECLAN KIBERD**, a lecturer at University College, Dublin, has written many books on modern literature. His most recent work is *Inventing Ireland*, a history of twentieth-century Irish literature and culture.

**GARLAND KIMMER** is completing a dissertation at the University of North Carolina at Chapel Hill on twentieth-century Irish poetry.

**F.C. MCGRATH** teaches at the University of Southern Maine. He has written articles on a wide range of subjects, including Walter Pater, William Butler Yeats, James Joyce, Brian Friel, T.S. Eliot and George Herbert.

**CHRISTOPHER MURRAY** is a Senior Lecturer in English at University College, Dublin. He was Director of the Drama Center from 1990 to 1995, is editor of *Irish University* Review, and is completing *Mirror Up to Nation: Irish Drama in the Twentieth Century.*

**GEORGE O'BRIEN**, creative writer and academic, teaches at Georgetown University. He has written three volumes describing life in Ireland, and two discussing the life and work of Brian Friel.

**LAUREN ONKEY** teaches at Ball State University, has published essays on Roddy Doyle and Molly Keane, and is completing a book entitled *Embodying the Nation: Post-Colonial Irish Women's Fiction.*

**W.B. WORTHEN** is professor of English and Theatre at Northwestern University, where he heads the Interdisciplinary Ph.D. in Theatre and Drama. He is the author of *The Idea of the Actor* and *Modern Drama and the Rhetoric of Theatre*, has edited anthologies of drama and drama criticism, and is now writing *Shakespeare, Authority, and Performance*.

# INDEX